Palgrave Studies in the History of Finance

The study of the history of financial institutions, markets, instruments and concepts is vital if we are to understand the role played by finance today. At the same time, the methodologies developed by finance academics can provide a new perspective for historical studies. Palgrave Studies in the History of Finance is a multi-disciplinary effort to emphasise the role played by finance in the past, and what lessons historical experiences have for us. It presents original research, in both authored monographs and edited collections, from historians, finance academics and economists, as well as financial practitioners.

More information about this series at
http://www.palgrave.com/gp/series/14583

André A. Villela

The Political Economy of Money and Banking in Imperial Brazil, 1850–1889

palgrave
macmillan

André A. Villela
Escola Brasileira de Economia e Finanças
Fundação Getulio Vargas
Rio de Janeiro, Rio de Janeiro, Brazil

ISSN 2662-5164 ISSN 2662-5172 (electronic)
Palgrave Studies in the History of Finance
ISBN 978-3-030-32773-6 ISBN 978-3-030-32774-3 (eBook)
https://doi.org/10.1007/978-3-030-32774-3

This Palgrave Macmillan imprint is published by the registered company Springer Nature Switzerland AG.
The registered company address is: Gewerbestrasse 11, 6330 Cham, Switzerland

For my parents, Annibal and Heloisa

Preface

This book owes its existence, in some measure, to chance. In May 2018, I received an email from Ruth Noble, assistant editor in the Finance division at Palgrave Macmillan, asking me if I could evaluate a book proposal that had just been submitted to them. The topic of the proposed book was banking houses in nineteenth-century Brazil, the very same *casas bancárias* that I had encountered over twenty years ago while doing research for my PhD thesis on monetary and banking policy in imperial Brazil. As the topic itself interested me and, additionally, little is known as yet about the activities of these banking houses—although contemporaries and historians alike are in no doubt as to their importance to the Brazilian economy at the time—I did not hesitate in accepting the invitation to write a brief evaluation of the manuscript.

Shortly after sending back my report, Ruth Noble popped the question: 'Would you be interested in writing a book for our Palgrave Studies in the History of Finance series?' My gut reaction at the time was to reply "no". Indeed, for the past few months I had been working on a short piece to be included in a larger volume co-organized with colleagues, but nothing remotely resembling a manuscript for a full-sized book. It then occurred to me that, actually, I did have some old material that could potentially be transformed into a book—my PhD thesis, presented in 1999 to the Department of Economic History of the London School of Economics and titled "The Political Economy of Money and Banking in Imperial Brazil, 1850–1870". Parts of the thesis had come out as articles in academic journals in Brazil, but the opportunity to publish a revised version of the complete manuscript through such a prestigious house as Palgrave Macmillan was an altogether different (and exciting) proposition.

After explaining to Ruth how my own doctoral research on commercial banks and monetary policy in mid-nineteenth-century Brazil differed from (and dovetailed into) the proposal that I had just finished evaluating for Palgrave Macmillan, I submitted a formal outline of the manuscript to the editors. In the following weeks, I received inputs from three anonymous scholars invited by Palgrave to look into my book proposal. It would be fair to say that, on average, their assessment was positive. Still, they (rightly) insisted on an adaptation of the original academic text to the new medium (a book) and, in one case, suggested that I extend the original time frame of my research from 1850–70 to the end on the imperial period, that is, to 1889.

The first suggestion was straightforward and inescapable, but the second one gave me second thoughts about the whole endeavor. After all, at that point in time I did not see myself going back to the archives and libraries in the time left over after completing my tasks as lecturer in and Head of the undergraduate program in Economics at FGV/EPGE (Fundação Getulio Vargas/Escola Brasileira de Economia e Finanças). Further consideration and a desire to close a chapter in my intellectual and professional life prodded me on, however. I therefore accepted the challenge and submitted a revised proposal, to which Palgrave Macmillan gave the go-ahead.

Informing my decision to embark on a project that I knew would occupy my free time for the next six months (in the end, due to delays of my own making, it was more like nine) was the conviction that the book would be an excellent opportunity to revisit my first major academic achievement after two decades of reading, teaching, and doing research on topics linked to the macroeconomic history of Brazil. In a sense, it would be a different, more seasoned, author covering the same topic that had attracted me at a younger age.

Furthermore, it dawned on me that the "new" period that an extension of the original time frame entailed (i.e., 1870–89) had already been covered by several talented scholars. I could (and did), therefore, rely on a fairly large body of secondary literature consisting of high-level academic output, including PhD dissertations, and complemented it with material gleaned from a host of primary sources that are currently (but, lamentably, not twenty years ago) available online. The latter includes, to name but the most important, the entire collection of the priceless annual reports presented by Ministers of Finance to Parliament (*Relatorio do Ministerio da Fazenda*), the annals of the debates held in both the Chamber of Deputies and the imperial Senate, the reports on two of the major commercial crises to hit Brazil in the nineteenth century (in 1857 and 1864), and a number of classic books and contemporary newspapers.

The final product is the book you have in your hands. It is an abridged, extended, and revised version of my doctoral dissertation. This apparent oxymoron is easily explainable. The book's length is approximately one-quarter shorter than my thesis, in part due to the editor's limits on the number of words (80,000, as opposed to the 100,000 words—I think—the University of London imposed on its PhD candidates). The historical period covered by the manuscript, as already indicated, extends to the fall of the monarchy, in 1889. The process of covering more historical ground over a smaller number of pages forced me to revise thoroughly the original text. Along the way, I was led to prune several parts that seemed less vital to my main arguments or were, plainly, obscure to me twenty years after they had been originally written. Other passages that now appeared somewhat rough-edged were dully polished, rendering the prose (I hope) clearer to the reader. Finally, I included new material, not only in Chap. 4 (which covers the 1870–89 years), but also elsewhere, having benefited, as noted, from academic contributions made over the past two decades.

As for the content of the book, its title is self-explanatory. The pages that follow both present and analyze the conduct of monetary and banking policy during part of the Brazilian Second Reign, in the second half of the nineteenth century. Lest an anachronistic use of the term be conveyed to the reader, monetary policy is employed throughout the book as a shorthand for the mounting legislative corpus and policy measures undertaken at the time and which dealt with different aspects related to the issue of currency (not only notes and metallic coins, but also other forms of script), including the chartering and operation of issuing banks.

For students of Brazilian history specifically, the book's "selling points" are manifold. Economists and economic historians will find, I hope, detailed material on a crucial dimension in the formation and functioning of a market economy—monetary policy. I am well aware of previous monetary histories of Brazil and have made use of this literature throughout the book. What sets the present monograph apart, I believe, is the richer detail provided here, combining monetary and political history, as well as an attempt to identify possible rationales behind the recurrent policy shifts in the monetary and banking realms throughout the period.

In discussing the constraints, domestic and external, under which contemporary policymakers operated and which involved issues of not only a more materialistic nature but also ideology, it is hoped the book will be of interest to a public that goes beyond the community of experts on the economic history of Brazil. Students of macroeconomic history—especially those working on the development experiences of export-oriented economies gradually integrating into the evolving classical globalization of the time—should find here material worthy of comparative exercises with other countries' experiences. Likewise, questions relating to the constitution of private banks entrusted with "proto central bank" functions, as discussed in the book in connection with the early experience of the third Bank of Brazil, are bound to attract scholars working on the early history of monetary authorities and state building more generally. Finally, those whose interests lie in exchange-rate history and the relative merits of a fixed-exchange-rate regime (including the gold standard) versus a floating one may gain new insights when looking at Brazil's rich experience in the period under study here.

Rio de Janeiro, Brazil André A. Villela

Usage

The Brazilian currency throughout the imperial period was the *milréis*, expressed as 1$000. One thousand milréis made up a *conto de réis* (or *conto*, for short), expressed as 1:000$. At the official 1846 parity of 27d/1$000, one pound sterling amounted to 8$890, or 8.89 milréis. As the rate of exchange floated throughout the period under study here (except for the later months of 1889), the quotation of sterling varied accordingly.

Between 1833 and 1887, the financial (or fiscal) year in Brazil for statistical purposes ran from 1 July to 30 June. Data for 1888 comprise three semesters; thereafter, the financial year coincided with the calendar year.

Acknowledgments

As this book is to some extent an outgrowth of my doctoral dissertation, it is only proper that I begin by thanking the many individuals and institutions who helped me back in the mid-late 1990s, when I was doing my PhD in London.

I must begin by expressing my deepest gratitude to Colin Lewis, who gracefully welcomed me into his office at the London School of Economics (LSE) in August 1995 and has been a friend ever since. His unflagging encouragement and guidance throughout the years when he supervised my doctoral research and beyond are part of the reason why the present book is coming to light.

My application to the PhD program in Economic History at the LSE owes a great deal to Profs. Marcelo de Paiva Abreu and Luiz A. Correa do Lago. I had the privilege to sit through their economic history courses while studying for a master's degree in Economics at PUC-Rio in the early 1990s. We have become friends ever since and, hopefully, will be co-authors soon.

Wilson Suzigan, an old family friend and my late father's co-author in a classic account of economic policymaking in Brazil in the early republican period, provided detailed comments on preliminary chapters of my doctoral dissertation. Fabio Giambiagi, Mauricio Moreira and the late Prof. Werner Baer also offered their time to read material dealing with a topic that in all likelihood seemed arcane to them.

It has been claimed (rather implausibly) that Nobel laureate Nadine Gordimer once said that her writing was better than her thinking. I believe there is a grain of truth in this maxim. Indeed, the final version of a published text, including academic work, tends to be written in much better prose than the first scribbling that comes out of our minds, through our hands, and onto a piece of paper or computer screen. Successive revisions to a text tend to render it much more reader-friendly than the original version. This was certainly the case with my doctoral dissertation and I thank my sister Monica and brother-in-law Andrew for this.

When defending my thesis at the University of London (the "viva", as it is known in England), I was fortunate to have as members of the examining committee Profs. Forrest Capie and Leslie Bethell, both of whom are renowned authorities on financial and Brazilian history, respectively. The thoughtful questions and comments I received on the occasion forced me to rethink many aspects of my original argument, which were subsequently incorporated in the book.

While studying in London I benefited from a full scholarship (which included tuition and a monthly stipend) from the Brazilian National Research Council—CNPq. In other words, the Brazilian taxpayer footed the bill. Coming from a country (in)famously marked by income inequality, I can only feel indebted to society at large for that opportunity. By helping to form economists at a high-level program such as Fundação Getulio Vargas (FGV) for the past twenty years, I hope to be partially paying back to Brazilian society the funds invested in my own education.

In the process of editing the manuscript for the book, I counted on the careful proofreading courtesy of Carlos Accioly. Although not trained as an economist or a historian, Carlos knows the English language better than most native speakers, helping me improve grammar and style as I submitted renewed versions of the text to him. Luiz Aranha C. do Lago once more came to my rescue, this time around by providing meticulous reading of Chaps. 4 and 5 of the book. In the process of discussing his detailed comments on style and content in, literally, every single page of those chapters, I got free lessons on Brazilian numismatic history, for which I am very grateful as well.

Being an avowed technologically challenged individual, I was fortunate to be able to draw on the endless goodwill of Wanderson Carvalho, who, during his lunch break, would always find the time to help me solve glitches that appeared in the editing of the final manuscript or when drawing up a figure or table.

I have enjoyed long conversations with Carlos Gabriel Guimarães on sundry topics relating to our common passion—Brazilian history. Gabriel has an encyclopedic knowledge of the literature on the economic history of Brazil and he seems to know everyone working on different fields in the area. As was the case when I was doing research for my thesis, he once more was generous with his time in discussing specific points in my work and helped me by indicating material for the book.

My greatest debt of gratitude is owed to my parents, Annibal and Heloisa. I was lucky to be raised, surrounded by books, by two extremely cultivated, well-traveled, and polyglot parents who inoculated me and my many siblings with boundless curiosity and a love of History. I dedicate this book to them.

Contents

Abbreviations

ACD	*Annaes da Câmara dos Deputados*
ACE	*Atas do Conselho de Estado*
ASI	*Annaes do Senado do Império do Brasil*
EPGE	*Escola Brasileira de Economia e Finanças*
FGV	*Fundação Getulio Vargas*
RCJC	*Retrospecto Commercial do Jornal do Commercio*
RMF	*Relatorio do Ministerio da Fazenda*
SAJ	*The Brazil and River Plate Mail and South American Journal*
SFCE	*Imperiaes Resoluções do Conselho de Estado na Seção de Fazenda*

List of Figures

List of Tables

CHAPTER 1

Introduction

In 1850, Pedro II was in the tenth year of his rule over the Brazilian Empire, a rule that would extend up to November 1889, comprising the Second Reign (1840–89).[1] In a way, 1850 marked the beginning of a golden age in the political and economic history of the Empire. On the political front, the last of the major provincial revolts (the Praieira) had been quelled and centralization of power at the hands of the monarch in Rio was firmly established. As for the economy, 1850 saw the promulgation of three pieces of legislation that sought to regulate the markets for the major inputs in the production process. As a result, trade in capital (with the Commercial Code), labor (via the Euzébio de Queiróz Law, marking Brazil's definitive acceptance of an end to the importation of slaves from Africa), and land (by means of the Land Law) would be henceforth regulated by the state. In a sense, this could be considered Brazil's first experiment in building an institutional framework adapted to the capitalist system starting to take root in many parts of the globe at the time, even though the Empire itself remained firmly committed to (and dependent on) a non-capitalist form of labor—slavery.[2]

In order to grease the wheels of an economy that, after years of lethargy, had begun to move forward on the back of ever-increasing coffee exports, Brazil counted on a monetary circulation in 1850 consisting of legal tender Treasury notes, metallic coins, and short-term promissory notes (the so-called *vales*) issued by a handful of commercial banks. As this book will document in detail, the nature of money over the rest of the

A. A. Villela, *The Political Economy of Money and Banking in Imperial Brazil, 1850–1889*, Palgrave Studies in the History of Finance, https://doi.org/10.1007/978-3-030-32774-3_1

imperial period (i.e., from 1850 to 1889) would change significantly, with the government and the private sector swapping places as the main providers of currency to the economy. Likewise, the banking sector would not be confined to the few *vale*-issuing banks that were in place in 1850. As time went on, other banks would eventually be allowed to issue their own notes, and, for part of the period, a semi-official Bank of Brazil would be entrusted with responsibilities typically associated with central bank-type institutions. Still, there is no disputing that Brazil's commercial banking sector would remain underdeveloped to the very end of the imperial period, as indicated both by the high average spread that existed between private banks' interest rates and the return on bonds issued by the central government (*apólices*), and by the high degree of market concentration in the industry.[3]

This financial underdevelopment immediately brings to mind a perennial question asked by scholars working on the economic history of Brazil, namely, why did the country fail to match the performance of the American economy in the nineteenth century? More specifically, in connection with the topic of the book, could an underdeveloped banking system be *part* of the reason why Brazil fell behind?

There do not exist as yet reliable estimates of the size and rates of growth of the Brazilian economy in the imperial period. Yet, researchers tend to agree that at the time of Independence, in 1822, output per capita was lower than the one observed in the United States. As the century unfolded, differences in rates of growth in the two continental economies ensured that by the end of the imperial period, in 1889, Brazil had unequivocally lost significant ground relative to America.[4] However, not only are the magnitudes involved far from clear in the case of Brazil, but the explanations for this laggard performance are not consensual.

One interpretation that has gained increasing (and belated) traction with academics working on the subject is due to Nathaniel Leff's pioneering research, in the cliometric tradition, into the roots of Brazilian economic underdevelopment. Writing in the 1960s and 1970s, Leff published a host of academic articles, later brought together in book form. On his account, supply factors linked to the overwhelming predominance of low-productivity family agriculture in the Empire combined with the under-provision of transport infrastructure and other public goods to forestall the division of labor and gains from trade in Brazil for most of the nineteenth century.[5]

Although financial underdevelopment was not part of Leff's explanation for Brazil's laggard performance, it is probably one of the factors that compounded the effects of the other barriers to growth highlighted by his research. After all, an underdeveloped banking sector tended to credit-constrain economic agents, with a negative impact on consumption and investment possibilities. Furthermore, market formation and development—and, hence, the room for Smithian (efficiency) gains—would also tend to be checked if banks were limited in their capacity to provide means of payment (either deposits or fiat money, in the case of banks of issue) to the economy.

The book will not try to engage in a counterfactual exercise of the type "what would have been the aggregate rate of growth of the imperial economy if Brazil's banking sector had not been so constrained?" Rather, it will attempt to offer a plausible explanation for contemporaries', predominantly, conservative approach toward the expansion of the banking sector. In other words, it will discuss the reasons why for most of the period the Brazilian government held back monetary growth and bank formation.

This objective will be accomplished by highlighting how this stance was linked to a broader—and equally conservative—view of monetary matters entertained by most individuals involved in policy and debate at the time.

In this respect, the book will seek to answer two larger questions, subsequently broken into four specific ones. The larger questions are as follows:

1. What form did monetary and banking policy take in Brazil between 1850 and 1889?
2. What were the drivers of the frequent policy shifts in this area?[6]

As for the more specific questions to be raised by the detailed discussion of monetary and banking policy in the period, they are the following:

1. Did the Bank of Brazil perform "proto-central bank" functions from its inception, in 1853, until the mid-1860s? If so, how?
2. What was the nature of the three major financial crises to hit the Empire in 1857, 1864, and 1875? How similar were they? Did the government react in the same fashion on the three occasions?
3. Was the 1864 (Souto) crisis a direct consequence of government policy taken years earlier (in particular, the 1860 banking law)?

4. Did monetary and exchange-rate policy at the time usually meet the interests of the coffee sector, as might be expected, given the latter's undisputed political clout?

The aim of the book, in short, is to study the evolution of monetary and banking policy in Brazil from 1850 to 1889. Yet, this is not a traditional monetary history of the period, in the sense that its main concern is *not* to discuss the major trends in monetary aggregates over the period, relating them to the broader economic history of Brazil.[7] Rather, the focus will be on the evolving institutionality in the monetary sphere, identifying the rationale behind the policies set by the government, and, eventually, implemented. This will involve giving pride of place to the political dimension of the policymaking process, thus allowing for an examination of the effective constraints under which nineteenth-century Brazilian policymakers were operating.

One of the issues the book will address (see question 4) may be summarized as follows. If monetary and banking policies at the time were characteristically orthodox—taking the form, among other things, of government-imposed restrictions on the banking system, the pursuit of convertibility, and a bias toward an appreciated rate of exchange—what does this suggest about the underlying polity? More specifically, how do these facts square with the perceived hegemony of the planter class (*fazendeiros*) during the imperial period, given that for them "soft money", and a depreciating milréis, would have been desirable?

A set of stylized facts will highlight some of the issues to be addressed in the book and the major interpretations available in the literature. Since the mid-1840s, the Brazilian government flirted with the idea of instituting convertibility of the circulating medium. Concurrently, it sometimes sought to set up a monopoly in the issue of banknotes in an effort to prevent uncontrolled money creation. As the money supply was equated by most contemporaries with the volume of notes and metallic coins in circulation (i.e., bank deposits were not considered part of the money supply) and, additionally, money thus defined was seen as the main determinant of the rate of exchange, authorities were bent on exercising strict control over banks of issue. As a result, banking activity was firmly regulated during most of the imperial period, leading to the underdeveloped banking sector mentioned above and, potentially, to a brake on overall economic growth.

Contemporary official accounts of events in the monetary and banking sphere are testimony to the prevalence of orthodox views on the topic. They attach great weight to monetary restraint and emphasize the benefits arising from the adoption of a fixed exchange rate, the latter resulting from convertibility of the milréis into gold.[8] Although this view did not go unchallenged (as will be seen in the book), it was widely held during the period.

The treatment that Brazilian monetary history has received from the literature has varied over time. Early-twentieth-century works and those that appeared after the Second World War have reflected concerns uppermost at the time when its authors were writing. Thus, books published in the late nineteenth and early twentieth centuries—when Brazil formally joined the gold standard system—would tend to praise the orthodoxy associated with monetary restraint and currency convertibility.[9] Scholars writing after the Second World War, on the other hand, tended to approach the whole question of money and banking in the Empire through "developmental" lenses, reflecting the then-current debates surrounding Brazil's experience of fast industrialization. Consequently, their main concern was with the perceived failure of the banking system to aid economic development during the nineteenth century.

In this respect, two complementary views stand out. The first one starts with Furtado's landmark book. His analysis of monetary and banking policy in both the Empire and First Republic inspired most of later research on the subject. According to Furtado, monetary restraint and the pursuit of convertibility over much of the imperial period (1822–89) and the First Republic (1889–1930) were detrimental to economic development and should be attributed to mimicry, that is, an uncritical importation of financial orthodoxy from Europe.[10]

Later writers echoed Furtado's interpretation of the existence of a persistent orthodox bias[11] in imperial monetary and banking policy, which, coinciding with the arrival of the first British banks in the 1860s, allegedly furthered the interests of foreign bankers, rather than those of the country.[12] Although inspired by Furtado's work, other contributions attempt to set monetary orthodoxy (especially as regards the centralization of issuing powers) within a broader context of disputes between urban and agrarian interests, or as part of the hegemonic aspirations of the Rio-based planter class (the so-called *saquaremas*).[13]

The book will address the main questions raised by authors sympathetic to the orthodox view, as well as those put forward by critics in the "developmental" tradition. In the process, the research will clarify some crucial points of historical fact. It does so by adopting a slightly different approach to politics than has been the case in most of the monetary historiography. Levy and Andrade, for example, posit a direct correspondence between events in the banking and political spheres. According to them, the move toward a monopoly of note issue in the early 1850s was the economic counterpart of the political process of centralization achieved in the previous decade.[14] Likewise, plurality of note issue, instituted at the end of the *Conciliação* period, in 1857–8, would have reflected conciliation between different positions concerning the right to note issue. Finally, Levy and Andrade suggest, perhaps inadvertently, that when promoting hard money policies, the imperial government managed to impose its will on the land-owning class, thus displaying a degree of autonomy from the economic elite (Levy and Andrade 1985, pp. 35–6).

Schulz, on the contrary, sees the financial policies of the Empire as being largely sympathetic to agrarian interests.[15] Financial orthodoxy, in his view, was not as pervasive as imagined by authors such as Furtado. Similarly, Guimarães claims that financial policy was controlled, at least in the early 1850s, by economic interests based in Rio. This group included businessmen in the export and import trade, and, crucially, provincial planters (Guimarães 1998, pp. 41–2).[16] Additionally, and again in parallel with political events, it is claimed that Liberals tended to be in favor of the expansion of the banking system (and, presumably, soft money), while Conservatives were associated with the centralization of issuing rights and financial orthodoxy (ibid., pp. 58–9). Finally, Granziera has asserted that adherence to the gold standard and, implicitly, to a stable and appreciated currency was pursued by the imperial government in the interest of English firms (Granziera 1979, p. 75).

Suggesting different underlying models of the polity, the above interpretations of the political motivation for financial policy in imperial Brazil are clearly at odds with each other. Some subscribe to the traditional view of policy as being set by the economic elite, which sometimes included foreign interests. Others appear to admit to a degree of autonomy on the part of the imperial State. Yet, none of the above contributions—or, for that matter, other works on money and banking in the Empire—set out their underlying political model explicitly. This has major implications for the consistency of their analyses and conclusions.

Economic policymaking does not take place in a void. Rather, it is a result of the political process.[17] In placing monetary and banking history within an institutional context, the book will attempt to capture the political dimension of the policymaking process. It is hoped its main findings will contribute to the debate about the relative autonomy (or otherwise) of the imperial State, hitherto analyzed in respect to policy areas such as taxation, slavery, land policy, and railways.[18] More specifically, the book will assess the degree to which the ruling class of politicians and bureaucrats was independent of the dominant class, that is, landowners.

During the period discussed here—and, especially, between 1850 and 1866—monetary and banking policy was one of the main arenas of inter-elite conflict. The starting point for this was the institutional and political breakthrough brought about by the abolition of the trans-Atlantic slave trade and the subsequent search for new investment opportunities, as capital invested in this activity sought alternative destinations (which the Commercial Code would now define more clearly).

In this context, provision of cheap credit became a central demand of the productive classes. The coffee sector, which had been expanding since the 1830s, was still unhindered by labor shortages and declining productivity. Nevertheless, planters complained about the cost of credit and what they saw as its main cause—the lack of currency in circulation. Given a choice of monetary policy and exchange-rate regime that best suited their interests, *fazendeiros* opted for an abundant supply of—and, hence, depreciated—milréis. In other words, for soft money.

The government, on the other hand, had a different set of preferences. Even though its foreign exchange commitments remained within a safe margin until the mid-1860s, the Treasury (as other debtors in sterling) would be required to increase its milréis-equivalent service payments whenever the value of the currency slipped. Moreover, not only an appreciated but also a stable rate of exchange was deemed necessary by the authorities, for it sent the proper signals to foreign creditors as to their commitment to sound monetary policies. Finally, the macroeconomic stability that an exchange rate under control indicated allowed the government to raise domestic credit more easily.

In short, exchange-rate politics was a decisive factor when setting monetary and banking policy at the time, considering that contemporaries saw monetary growth, by the hands of either the Treasury or private banks of issue, as the main determinant of the value of the milréis against sterling.

The argument of the book is presented over five chapters, including this Introduction. Chapter 2 documents in detail the first decade of Brazilian monetary and banking history following the institutional changes brought about by the three pieces of legislation enacted in 1850 (the Commercial Code, Euzébio de Queiróz Law, and the Land Law). It starts by describing the activities of the few joint-stock banks, mostly centered in Rio de Janeiro, that were allowed to operate with discounts and deposits and which also engaged in the issuing of *vales*. This period also witnessed the creation of the (third) Bank of Brazil, a semi-public corporation with the right to issue notes that were accepted for payment of taxes and that were convertible on demand into gold or Treasury paper. The Bank will be seen to play a pivotal role in the official reaction to the 1857 crisis, the first instance of Brazil's exposure to the aftershocks of financial panics originated abroad. As this crisis coincided with the extension of issuing rights to other joint-stock banks by the government, contemporaries saw a connection between the two events and pressed for stricter limits on the activities of note-issuing banks. The ensuing corporate and banking law of 1860 would be the culmination of the orthodox backlash against earlier flirtation with plurality of issues, and marks the endpoint of the chapter.

The 1860–1866 years are covered in Chap. 3, which starts by analyzing the effects of the new banking legislation on the operation of the issuing banks created in the 1850s. It also draws attention to a less visible—though far from unimportant—part of the banking system consisting of private banking houses (*casas bancárias*). This unregulated segment of the industry played a vital role in providing services to depositors, big and small, discounting bills and issuing their own *vales*. Their operation far from authorities' radar would ultimately contribute to the eruption and dissemination of the worst commercial crisis of the imperial period, the 1864 Souto crisis, named after the largest of those houses and its most notorious casualty. The chapter concludes in 1866, two years into the Paraguayan War, with the revision to the contract signed in 1853 between the government and the Bank of Brazil. With war finance uppermost among the government's concerns, monetary orthodoxy would have to be sacrificed on the altar to national security; accordingly, note-issuing rights were once again placed exclusively in the hands of the Treasury, which would proceed to put the printing presses to work.

Government monopoly of note issue would persist until the final year of the imperial period (1889). Over more than two decades, monetary and banking issues would be relegated to a secondary position in contemporary debates. In their place—and in the wake of the final victory over Paraguay, in 1870—demands for reform of the electoral legislation and political system, to which was added republican and abolitionist propaganda, led to the first cracks in the monarchical edifice to appear. Amid a measure of economic growth and gradual modernization brought about by Brazil's integration into a globalizing economy, the government maintained a steady hand in the conduct of monetary policy.

New note issues on the part of the Treasury would be rare, and responded to pressing needs associated with the human tragedy caused by severe spells of drought in the Northeast, or in response to demands from banks for assistance with liquidity on two occasions. Chapter 4, which covers the 1866–89 period, discusses this history, documenting the insistence with which the government throughout strived to restore the exchange rate to the 1846 parity of 27 pence to the milréis. Even during the long spells when this objective appeared ever more elusive, as in the decade between the mid-1870s and mid-1880s, officials would not relent on their goal of bringing back the rate of exchange to this notional level, after which, it was hoped, convertibility in gold could be finally declared.

As it turned out, a peculiar set of circumstances combined to bring the milréis to parity a few months before the Ouro Preto cabinet came to office in June 1889. As part of the Prime Minister's strategy to win over coffee planters' support in the aftermath of abolition without compensation, as decided by Parliament in May 1888, a generous injection of gold-backed notes issued by private banks was promoted. This latest shift in the orientation of monetary and banking policy during the imperial period would turn out to be the last, as the monarchy ended up toppled by a military coup in November, ushering in the republic.

Chapter 5 looks back at monetary and banking history in Brazil over the whole 1850–89 period, as analyzed in detail in the previous chapters. But it does so from a different—higher, as it were—vantage point as a means to discern more clearly longer-term trends in monetary policy during these four decades. This endeavor, inevitably, required a discussion of the accuracy of the data that seek to measure "money" at the time. Moreover, the chapter examines possible motivations behind the frequent shifts in monetary and banking policy during the period under study here. Materialistic considerations arising from the gains and losses that exchange rate variations promote are emphasized, as are decisions arising from particular world views entertained by the major actors involved in policymaking and in the monetary debates of the time. Needless to say, money (material gains) mattered when deciding on policy. Yet, as the book will show, ideas mattered a great deal, too.

Notes

1. The First Reign, under his father, Pedro I, lasted from Independence, in 1822, until his abdication in 1831. In between the two Reigns was the Regency period (1831–40).
2. Bethell and Carvalho (1989).
3. Average spread between the two rates was 580 basis points between 1835 and 1889. Concentration in the Rio banking sector did decline over time, but the Bank of Brazil's primacy throughout conferred to that institution a marked degree of market power; see Summerhill (2015, pp. 194–200).
4. Haber, ed. (1997). On trends in the rate of growth of the Brazilian economy during the imperial period, Abreu and Lago (2014).
5. See Leff (1982) and Leff (1997).
6. As will become clear along the book, those drivers include elements of both a material and non-material nature, the latter meaning to encompass *ideas*. For this reason, the book will reproduce quite a few quotes drawn from contemporary debates and official reports. My intention in resorting to these quotes is to capture a glimpse of the mindset of influential actors in the monetary debates and policymaking at the time. It is hoped that by doing so the reader will gain a better impression of the diverse views, theories, and priors informing those very debates and policies.
7. For this type of approach, see Peláez and Suzigan (1976), in the spirit of Friedman and Schwartz (1963).
8. For a flavor of the dominant (orthodox) views on monetary matters, see most of the annual reports of the Ministry of Finance of the period, the *Jornal do Commercio* (Rio's main financial paper), and, especially, *Relatorio da Commissão de Inquerito de 1859* (undated) and *Relatorio da Commissão de Inquerito de 1864* (1865).
9. Prominent among these are Wileman (1896), Calógeras (1910), Ortigão (1914), Andrada (1923), and Souza (1924).
10. Furtado (1970). It should be noted that Furtado's objective was not the writing of a monetary history of Brazil, although the discussion of monetary and banking matters is central to his arguments in chapter 27.
11. See, for example, Levy (1977), Levy and Andrade (1985, 1993), Andrade (1987), Teixeira (1991), and Guimarães (1998).
12. Granziera (1979).
13. For the latter approach, see Gambi (2013).
14. This argument is further elaborated by Gambi (2013).
15. Schulz (1996, chapter 1).
16. This is also the opinion held by Mello, for whom the banking reform proposed by Itaboraí in 1853 aimed at "privileging big business in the Rio market and the related coffee interests of the Paraíba Valley". Cf. Mello (1984, p. 98).
17. For a reaffirmation of this point, see Dixit (1996).
18. For a discussion, see Carvalho (1988).

References

Abreu, Marcelo de P., and Luiz A.C. do Lago. 2014. A Economia Brasileira no Império, 1822–1889. In *A Ordem do Progresso: dois séculos de política econômica no Brasil*, ed. Marcelo de P. Abreu, 1–28. Rio de Janeiro: Campus/Elsevier.

Bethell, Lelie, and José M. de Carvalho. 1989. 1822–50. In *Brazil: Empire and Republic, 1822–1930*, ed. Leslie Bethell, 41–112. Cambridge: Cambridge University Press.

Calógeras, João P. 1910. *La Politique Monetaire du Brésil*. Rio de Janeiro: Imprensa Nacional.

de Andrada, Antonio Carlos R. 1923. *Bancos de Emissão no Brasil*. Edições Leite Ribeiro: Rio de Janeiro.

de Andrade, Ana Maria R. 1987. 1864: conflito entre metalistas e pluralistas. MSc. dissertation, Universidade Federal do Rio de Janeiro.

de Carvalho, José M. 1988. *Teatro de Sombras: a política imperial*. Vértice/IUPERJ: Rio de Janeiro.

de Mello, Evaldo C. 1984. *O Norte Agrário e o Império, 1871–1889*. Rio de Janeiro: Nova Fronteira.

de Souza, Carlos I. 1924. *A Anarquia Monetária e Suas Conseqüências*. São Paulo: Monteiro Lobato.

Dixit, Avinash K. 1996. *The Making of Economic Policy: A Transaction Cost Politics Perspective*. Cambridge: MIT Press.

Friedman, Milton, and Anna Schwartz. 1963. *A Monetary History of the United States, 1867–1960*. Princeton: Princeton University Press.

Furtado, Celso. 1970. *Formação Econômica do Brasil*. 10th ed. São Paulo: Companhia Editora Nacional.

Gambi, Thiago F.R. 2013. *O Banco da Ordem: política e finanças no Império brasileiro (1853–1866)*. São Paulo: Alameda.

Granziera, Rui G. 1979. *A Guerra do Paraguai e o Capitalismo no Brasil: moeda e vida urbana na economia brasileira*. São Paulo: Hucitec/Unicamp.

Guimarães, Carlos G. 1998. *Bancos, Economia e Poder no Segundo Reinado: o caso da Sociedade Bancária Mauá, MacGregor & Companhia (1854–1866)*. Ph.D. dissertation, Universidade de São Paulo.

Haber, Stephen, ed. 1997. *How Latin America Fell Behind: Essays on the Economic Histories of Brazil and Mexico, 1800–1914*. Stanford: Stanford University Press.

Leff, Nathaniel. 1982. *Underdevelopment and Development in Brazil*. Vol. 2. London: Allen and Unwin.

———. 1997. Economic Development in Brazil, 1822–1913. In *How Latin America Fell Behind: Essays on the Economic Histories of Brazil and Mexico, 1800–1914*, ed. Stephen Haber, 34–64. Stanford: Stanford University Press.

Levy, Maria Barbara. 1977. *História da Bolsa de Valores do Rio de Janeiro*. Rio de Janeiro: IBMEC.

Levy, Maria Barbara, and Ana Maria R. de Andrade. 1985. Fundamentos do Sistema Bancário no Brasil: 1834–1860. *Estudos Economicos* 15 (Special Issue): 17–48.

———. 1993. El Sector Financiero y El Desarollo Bancario en Río de Janeiro (1850–1888). In *La Economia Financiera y la Formación de la Banca Central en España y Latinoamerica*, ed. Carlos Marichal and Pedro Tedde, 209–254. Madrid: Banco de España.

Ortigão, Ramalho. 1914. *A Moeda Circulante no Brazil.* Rio de Janeiro: Typographia do Jornal do Commercio.

Peláez, Carlos M., and Wilson Suzigan. 1976. *História Monetária do Brasil.* 2nd ed. Brasília: Editora da Universidade de Brasília.

Relatorio da Commissão de Inquerito Nomeada por Aviso do Ministério da Fazenda, de 10 de Outubro de 1859. (undated).

Schulz, John. 1996. *A Crise Financeira da Abolição.* 1st ed. São Paulo: Edusp/ Instituto Fernand Braudel.

Summerhill, William R. 2015. *Inglorious Revolution: Political Institutions, Sovereign Debt, and Financial Underdevelopment in Imperial Brazil.* New Haven: Yale University Press.

Teixeira, Arilda M. C. 1991. *Determinantes e Armadilhas da Política Monetária Brasileira no II Império.* MSc. dissertation, Universidade Federal Fluminense.

Wileman, Joseph P. 1896. *Brazilian Exchange: The Study of an Inconvertible Currency.* Buenos Aires: Gali Brothers.

CHAPTER 2

From Plurality of Issue to Monopoly and Back: 1850–60

2.1 The *Vale*-Issuing Banks

In 1850, two forces were being felt on Brazil's capital markets. On the supply side, capital hitherto employed in the trans-Atlantic slave trade was suddenly made idle by Brazil's final acceptance of British demands to end this commerce.[1] Simultaneously, pressure was exercised on the demand side by planters eager for cheap credit, as the coffee economy began to expand westward, in the direction of the fertile plateaux of São Paulo.

To cope with the new demands that arose from the coffee sector, as well as commercial activities in general, the Empire counted on a financial system consisting of just three joint-stock banks: the Banco Commercial da Bahia, the Banco Commercial do Rio de Janeiro, and the Banco Commercial do Maranhão. All of them issued *vales*,[2] as well as accepting deposits and offering loans. Apart from these banking corporations, commercial houses, discount houses, and private (partnership) banks—the so-called *casas bancárias*—operated in the major commercial centers.

Every year, at harvest time, part of the circulating medium in Rio—consisting of Treasury notes and coins—was exported to the provinces, where it helped ease the shortage of money. This, in turn, led to the emergence of proposals in 1850 for the creation of a national bank. This establishment would be entrusted with the withdrawal of the Treasury notes in circulation and would be responsible for the money supply, ensuring the necessary liquidity in an expanding market. At the time, total note issues

A. A. Villela, *The Political Economy of Money and Banking in Imperial Brazil, 1850–1889*, Palgrave Studies in the History of Finance, https://doi.org/10.1007/978-3-030-32774-3_2

in the Empire amounted to 48,000 *contos*, the bulk of which consisted of Treasury notes (Brasil, IBGE 1990, p. 498).[3]

In his 1850 report to the Assembly, the then Minister of Finance Joaquim José Rodrigues Torres (from 1854 onward, Visconde de Itaboraí[4]) displayed sympathy for the idea of an enlargement of the banking system (*Relatorio do Ministerio da Fazenda*[5] 1850, pp. 34–6). The aim was to create deposit and discount banks in the provinces, a move that, it was hoped, would 'fertilize industry and enrich the country' (*RMF* 1849, p. 36). However, Itaboraí was quick to point out that he did not see 'any usefulness in banks of *issue*' (emphasis added) (ibid.). He doubted whether the creation of such banks was compatible with what would be the main objective of the government in the coming years: to regulate the money supply.[6]

Two pieces of legislation passed at the time suggest that the government was treading carefully in this matter: Decree 575, of 10 January 1849, and Law 552, of 31 May 1850. Articles 9 and 10 of the former established that no joint-stock bank would be allowed to operate before one-fourth of its capital had been subscribed. The decree also gave the government powers of inspection and the right to close banks that failed to comply with legislation. Article 3 of Law 552, in turn, stated that in 'no circumstance, and under no pretence whatsoever, shall the amount of circulating paper in the Empire increase, even if temporarily' (Cavalcanti 1893, vol. 2, p. 165). This provision was never observed, but it illustrates vividly the intentions of policymakers at the time. Instead of increasing the volume of Treasury notes in circulation or granting to a private establishment the right to issue legal tender notes, the government appeared to be approaching very cautiously the whole question of issuing rights.

In the beginning of the 1850 legislative year, a bill was presented to the Senate by Holanda Cavalcanti, a former Minister of Finance, proposing the creation of provincial issuing (or circulating) banks. This was an attempt to meet a growing regional demand for credit and to reduce the movement of currency from Rio to the interior at harvest time. Under the bill, each of the main provinces (and the city of Rio de Janeiro) would have a bank with permission to issue notes up to the amount of its capital fund, and backed by its shares. These notes would circulate only in the provinces where they had been issued and would be accepted in payment of taxes and debts. In all, Cavalcanti's plan provided for a potential note issue in the order of 20.7 thousand *contos*, an amount equal to about half the money stock at the time.[7] His bill was endorsed by the Finance

Committee of the Senate and approved in the first round of discussion on the floor. After a long delay, subsequent debate of the bill would resume only at the start of the 1853 legislative year, when it met an alternative proposal originating in the Executive. The latter called for a monopoly of note issue to be granted to a semi-official institution based in Rio. Faced with this new proposal, which appeared to sabotage his own initiative, Cavalcanti withdrew his bill from discussion.

The author of the new bill, Itaboraí, had returned to the Ministry of Finance after a brief interlude and gone on to become Prime Minister in May 1852. His bill for the creation of a 'solidly constituted bank, to help in the expansion of the operations of commerce and industry' was included in that year's Speech from the Throne, delivered by the Emperor at the opening of the legislative year on 3 May 1853 (*Fallas do Throno* 1872, p. 448). Although clearly emanating from the Executive, the Itaboraí proposal was originally meant as an amendment to the Holanda Cavalcanti bill. With the withdrawal of the latter, Itaboraí's bill ended up being endorsed by five senators. Thus, it became *de jure* a bill of the upper House of the Legislative, where it began to be discussed in the session of 13 May.[8] The bill consisted of six articles, its main points being: the social capital of the Bank was set at 30,000 *contos* (Art. 1); its notes would be redeemable in either specie or Treasury notes and would be accepted in payment of taxes (Art. 2); the Emperor would appoint its President (Art. 4); and it would be required to withdraw from circulation Treasury notes at a rate of 2000 *contos* annually, the first 10,000 *contos* of which would constitute an interest-free loan to the government for the duration of its charter (Art. 5). The bill also set a ceiling to the Bank's issue at twice the amount in its reserve fund, subject to an extension if the government saw it fit (*RMF* 1852, p. 15).

On 17 May 1852, the first criticisms were directed at Article 2 of the bill; in particular, the provision concerning the redemption of the notes of the Bank for either gold or paper money.[9] Itaboraí's defense came two days later when he stressed the sheer impossibility of demanding redemption exclusively in gold, given the costs this would involve for the acquisition of metallic reserves on such a scale. Additionally, Itaboraí maintained that permission to redeem Bank notes into Treasury paper stemmed precisely from the existence of the latter. In the absence of Treasury notes in circulation, redemption would have been done solely into gold.[10] After a few more sessions of debate, the bill was finally approved in the Senate without any modification, on 6 June 1853.

In the Chamber of Deputies, where the bill arrived on 17 June, Itaboraí was charged with changing his mind too quickly on the need for banks of issue. After all, as noted, he had already publicly proclaimed his reservations concerning this type of establishment (*RMF* 1849, p. 35). His about-face had been explained earlier to the Assembly:

> The public wealth and, with it, the sum of transactions, has increased (since 1850); the industrial spirit has begun to develop in a pronounced way; and, finally, the insufficiency of paper money is shown by the presence of 16 to 20 thousand *contos* in coins, with which the mass of the circulating medium has been augmented. (*RMF* 1852, p. 14)

Circumstances had in fact changed between 1850 and 1853, but not in the direction that Itaboraí would have thought ideal. On the positive side, there had indeed been a marked improvement in the accounts of the imperial government, which displayed a surplus of 4700 *contos* in the 1852–3 financial year.[11] This contrasted with a deficit of nearly 7000 *contos* in the previous year. Still, on the monetary front, there had been no reduction in the amount of Treasury notes in circulation, a necessary step, as stated by Itaboraí in his 1850 report, before the private issue of banknotes could be considered (Cavalcanti 1893, vol. 2, p. 173). Meanwhile, the existing *vale*-issuing banks operating in the Empire increased their combined circulation sharply (Table 2.1).

Despite this increase in *vale* circulation, all was not well in the Rio market. Contemporary sources indicate that the main commercial center of the Empire experienced a "monetary pressure" in the first half of 1853.[12] According to the testimony given by one of the many merchants heard by the committee set up to investigate the causes of a crisis that would erupt years later, the origins of the pressure in 1853 could be ascribed to a

Table 2.1 *Vale*-issuing banks and their main accounts, 1850–3. (in *contos*)

Year	*No. of banks*	*Capital*	*Issues*	*Deposits*	*Loans*
1850	3	4870	1147	9448	14,079
1851	4	9390	1290	14,631	19,139
1852	5	12,337	4526	24,998	16,392
1853	5	16,524	5310	19,954	35,043

Source: Table A2 in the Statistical Appendix

Note: Figures do not include the Banco Commercial do Pará, for which no data were available

number of factors (*Relatorio da Commissão de Inquerito de 1859*, undated, Annex A, pp. 102–3). Firstly, capital released by the cessation of the trans-Atlantic slave trade had been "recycled" by many banks, who lent liberally (and irresponsibly, according to some) for periods of up to one year, exposing their portfolios to considerable strain. Second, the fact that *vales* were not accepted in public offices made their redemption for Treasury notes and specie necessary for the payment of taxes and debts to the government. Additionally, currency (Treasury notes and coins) had to be shipped to the provinces, where they were accepted, as payment for slaves and other goods.[13] Finally, in the early 1850s, the exchange rate in Recife and Salvador—the main commercial centers of the North—was often higher (more appreciated) than in Rio, rendering it profitable to ship Treasury notes and gold to those markets for the purchase of bills of exchange.[14]

There are clear indications that contemporaries did experience a shortage of money in the Rio market in the first half of 1853. This was evidenced by the rise in discount rates,[15] in spite of the expansionist activities of the two *vale*-issuing banks based in the capital city.

The first of these, the Banco Commercial do Rio de Janeiro (BCRJ), started its operations in 1838, although its statutes would only be officially approved in June 1842. On that occasion, the government expressly denied the BCRJ the possibility of ever becoming an issuer of notes, as proposed in Article 2 of its statutes. In its first decade in operation, the BCRJ annually discounted an average of 4800 *contos* in commercial bills, while its outstanding issue of *vales* averaged slightly over 200 *contos*.

In the early 1850s, as the coffee economy around Rio de Janeiro expanded, Irineu Evangelista de Sousa (from 1854 onward, Barão de Mauá) opened the doors of the "second" Bank of Brazil.[16] This was the first bank to be created under the new rules laid down by the 1850 Commercial Code. Organized as a limited company, its statutes were approved by the imperial government on 2 July 1851, with one major modification: instead of being able to issue five-day *vales* in an amount equivalent to one-half the bank's liquid holdings, that limit was reduced to one-third.[17]

The figures in Table 2.2 show that prior to the arrival of the second Bank of Brazil on the scene, the BCRJ relied to a very modest extent on the use of its own *vales* in discounting commercial paper. The main source of profits for the bank derived from receiving funds on interest-paying deposits (*dinheiro a prêmio*) of 4%–4.5% p.a. and relending them at much

Table 2.2 Issuing banks in Rio de Janeiro: *vales* outstanding and bills discounted, 1840–54. (in *contos*)

	Average 1840–49	*1850*	*1851*	*1852*	*1853*	*1854*
BCRJ						
outstanding issue of *vales*	213	5	2	257	1574	n.a.
bills discounted	4801	6657	8417	10,997	10,629	n.a.
Bank of Brazil (Mauá)						
outstanding issue of *vales*	–	–	98	1594	1937	1880
bills discounted	–	–	3903	6926	9033	9364

Source: Compiled from data in Cavalcanti (1893, Vol. 2, pp. 151–60)

Notes: Figures are as of 31 December. Mauá's Bank of Brazil began operations in 1851
n.a. = data not available

higher rates. Nevertheless, from 1852 onward, there appears to have been a shift in strategy. The Banco Commercial increased both its issues of *vales* and the volume of discounts, in competition with the new entrant in the Rio market, Mauá's Bank of Brazil. In the space of just two years, the combined volume of discounted bills increased by approximately 80%, while *vales* issued by the two banks jumped from just 100 *contos* to more than 3500 *contos*. Competition between the Commercial and the Bank of Brazil led them both to overlook the quality of the paper being discounted, and to lower rates of discount to an unprecedented level of 4% in late 1851 (Barman 1981, pp. 245–6).[18]

As both banks increased their loans, their issue of *vales* also expanded. However, as Treasury notes were being exported to the northern provinces, bearers of *vales* found it increasingly difficult to redeem them at their respective issuers, who reacted by raising their rates of discount.[19] At the height of this monetary pressure, in July 1853, the government was prompted to offer credit of up to 4000 *contos* in interest-bearing Treasury bills (*letras*) to the two Rio banks. Furthermore, it considered giving their *vales cours forcé* in Rio (*ACD* 1853, Tome II, pp. 182–4). In the end, only Mauá's Bank of Brazil would take the offer of credit, and only to a modest extent (Ribeiro and Guimarães 1967, p. 76). In light of this episode, the government saw the need to take definitive steps toward solving the underlying problem of providing adequate liquidity to a growing economy, while maintaining a stable monetary circulation. An institution that it could monitor closely seemed the best option. Thus the "third" Bank of Brazil was born.

2.2 Monopoly Achieved: The "Third" Bank of Brazil

The circumstances surrounding the creation of the third Bank of Brazil reveal the interplay of opposing forces in the monetary controversies that would erupt in mid-century Brazil. In 1850—and amid a declining supply of Treasury notes in the economy,[20]—lawmakers in favor of plurality of note issues backed the Holanda Cavalcanti proposal calling for the creation of several provincial banks of issue. In a sense, this was the economic version of the political (and military) disputes which beset the Empire from its inception in 1822, and which pitted centrifugal forces in the provinces against the powers of centralization.[21] The latter, victorious at last after the defeat of the Praieira revolt in 1850, would again triumph in the new "battlefield" of banking policy.[22]

Although favorable to the creation of a national bank operating with discounts, deposits, and note issue, Itaboraí staunchly opposed the setting up of a state-run institution, lest it run counter to (the government's) position as an 'impartial protector of all interests in society' (*RMF* 1852, p. 14). His "counter-bill" to the Holanda Cavalcanti initiative, while shunning the creation of a state-run bank, nevertheless ensured a considerable degree of government control over the operation of a Rio-based establishment. Thus, to political centralization would be added monetary centralization, in the hands of a bank bestowed with many privileges, and where the Emperor would appoint both the president and the vice-president.

After a third round of discussions in the Chamber of Deputies, the Itaboraí bill, outlined above, was finally approved without any modification. On 5 July, Law 683 was sanctioned by the Emperor, 'authorizing the Government to grant the incorporation and approve the statutes of a bank of deposits, discounts and issue, based in the city of Rio de Janeiro' (*Legislação Sobre Papel-Moeda* 1923, pp. 35–7).[23]

The new Bank of Brazil was created with a capital of 30,000 *contos* (£3.5 million), divided into 150,000 shares of 200 milréis each. It came into being as the result of the amalgamation of the existing Bank of Brazil—which had evolved into the country's main bank—and the BCRJ. As the major partners in the merger, shareholders of the second Bank of Brazil were entitled to 50,000 shares of the new bank, while those of the Banco Commercial kept 30,000 shares. The remaining 70,000 shares were reserved for the bank's provincial branches (40,000) and for subscription by the public in Rio de Janeiro (30,000 shares).

Under these circumstances, it was only natural for Mauá and his group to expect to control the Bank and, therefore, to be able to set policy. To their disappointment, however, the Emperor appointed João Duarte Lisboa Serra, a member of the Chamber of Deputies, president of the Bank. Mauá, along with six other shareholders of the former Bank of Brazil, did manage to secure seats in the 15-member board of the new bank (Guimarães 1998, pp. 128 ff.). Yet, the majority of seats were in the hands of representatives from the former Banco Commercial, which had the royal family as clients. Feeling defeated and realizing he would be unable to control the new bank, Mauá went on to found a new (*vale*-issuing) bank—the Mauá, MacGregor (Barman 1981, pp. 246–7).[24]

The statutes of the Bank of Brazil were approved by Decree 1223 (of 31 August 1853) and comprised 79 articles. The main provisions of the Itaboraí bill were retained, thus entitling the institution to carry out all operations pertaining to a commercial bank, such as bill discounting, buying and selling of precious metals, opening sight and interest-bearing deposit accounts, and lending (Art. 11). Additionally, the Bank of Brazil was granted the right to issue notes payable to bearer on demand (Art. 11, paragraph 11), with total issues limited to twice the amount in its reserve fund, consisting of both Treasury paper and gold (Art. 16, paragraph 1). Both its president and vice-president were to be appointed by the Emperor (Art. 39)[25] and, as anticipated in the Senate bill, it would be required to withdraw from circulation 2000 *contos* per year in Treasury paper, the first 10,000 *contos* of which would comprise an interest-free loan to the government (Art. 56).

In addition to the regular operations associated with a deposit and discount bank, the Bank of Brazil was granted the right to issue notes redeemable in "currency", which at the time comprised specie and Treasury notes.[26] Notes issued by the new Bank of Brazil, unlike *vales*, were accepted in payment of taxes and debts owed to the government. Yet, their circulation was restricted to the region where they had been issued. That is, in and around the city of Rio de Janeiro, in the case of notes from the head office, and in the respective provinces where its branches were allowed to be set up and issue notes.

Clearly, the privileges accorded to the Bank were manifold, leading to repeated accusations of favoritism. To begin with, not only were its notes accepted in the public offices of the provinces where the Bank operated but also Article 16, paragraph 1, of its statutes allowed it to redeem them for either currency or gold, at its own discretion. Noteholders were unable, thus, to demand redemption in gold.[27] The idea was that, given a rate of exchange at (or very near) the par value of 27d to the milréis, gold and Treasury notes were equivalent. Yet, in practice, the Bank would seldom give gold in exchange for notes, regardless of the rate of exchange. In addition, whenever there was pressure on its reserve fund (*fundo disponível*), the Bank could seek permission from the government to suspend convertibility. Finally, the very fact of having a monopoly of note issue was an additional privilege for the Bank.

Article 16, paragraph 1, of the Bank of Brazil's statutes also established a maximum ratio of 2:1 between note issue and the reserve fund. This limit could only be relaxed after obtaining government approval (pending deliberation of the Council of State). Should the Bank feel that its operations were being compromised by the amount of gold or Treasury notes in its fund, it could seek the government's guarantee to obtain foreign loans (up to an amount equivalent to the Treasury notes withdrawn from circulation) to reinforce it.

The monopoly of note issue awarded to the new bank would come with strings attached, however. As already noted, Itaboraí, formerly an opponent of any sort of bank of issue, admitted that circumstances had changed of late. His change of mind, however, was only partial. First, just a single bank would be given government authorization to issue notes and, even then, under strict rules which, in many instances, were to the advantage of the government itself. For instance, among the Bank's main duties was the yearly withdrawal of 2000 *contos*' worth of Treasury notes from circulation. The first 10,000 *contos* would act as an interest-free loan to the government while the Bank's charter lasted (in principle, for thirty years). The Bank would be reimbursed (with interest) for the remaining Treasury notes withdrawn from circulation, which, it was hoped, would ultimately lead to a full, gold-backed, circulating medium consisting exclusively of Bank of Brazil notes. Lastly, Article 56 of the Bank's statutes suggests that the government expected it to act as a regulator of the currency, although this point was far from clear-cut. For some, Article 2 of the 1846 Law (which introduced the new 27d gold parity) actually entrusted the *government* with the task of maintaining monetary stability.[28]

Either way, there was no disputing the semi-official nature of the Bank, which granted the Executive branch considerable influence over its activities. Government control was made explicit, of course, by the fact that both its president and vice-president were to be appointed by the Emperor personally. Official discretion over the affairs of the Bank was further ensured by the provisions of Article 50, regarding the powers of the president of the institution. Among the latter's responsibilities, according to paragraph 3 of the said article, was to 'preside over and serve the decisions of the board of directors and the general assembly of shareholders'. However, he could 'suspend decisions judged to be contrary to the statutes, and refer the issue on to the government, which would ultimately decide if (these) should be carried out'.[29] The final say over Bank decisions, therefore, remained with the government, even though it was not a shareholder. This was simply the corollary of its appointing the two top officials in the institution.

As noted earlier, the road taken by Mauá after his bank was merged into the new Bank of Brazil was the creation, in July 1854, of the Mauá, MacGregor Bank.[30] This bank had a capital of 20,000 *contos* (two-thirds of that of the new Bank of Brazil), which was subscribed by former shareholders of the defunct bank and foreign merchants. Given that a traditional partnership would have demanded unlimited financial liability from each of the partners and, hence, hinder his efforts in raising large sums of capital, Mauá opted instead to organize his new venture as a limited partnership (*sociedade em comandita*). Taking advantage of a lacuna in the Commercial Code, he divided the firm's capital into freely transferable shares. This gave the appearance of a corporation but, crucially, evaded the governmental intrusion that such a form of organization would have entailed (Barman 1981, pp. 251–7).

Mauá's scheme found huge opposition both in Parliament and in the Executive, which contested the legality of his arrangements for the bank.[31] A decree issued in December 1854 forbade the division of the capital of *sociedades em comandita* into shares, and ordered the Commercial Court to cancel the registration of the partnership deeds of firms with such a share capital.

No sooner had Mauá clashed with the government, he found himself again in the midst of another dispute. This time the matter involved the issue of *vales* by the Mauá Bank in the Rio market. In the 1854 *Relatorio da Fazenda*, Minister Honório Hermeto Carneiro Leão (Marquês de Paraná from December 1854) pointed out the dangers arising from the Mauá, MacGregor Bank issuing *vales* to the bearer with five- to ten-day maturities. In practice, *vales* circulated as if they were notes, in breach of the monopoly enjoyed by the Bank of Brazil.

Clearly, the government was not willing to tolerate unauthorized issues of money. The Rural & Hypothecario, for instance, was limited to issue *vales* of no less than thirty days, payable to a particular individual and only transferable through endorsement. The government (rightly) considered *vales* issued by the Mauá, MacGregor as close substitutes to money and, as such, illegal, given that this was not among the operations stated in that bank's statutes (*RMF* 1854, pp. 9–10). The *vales* were promptly withdrawn from circulation by the Mauá Bank.

Meanwhile, the peculiar status of the Bank of Brazil, that is, its semi-official nature, began to cause tension between its public facet and the interests of its many private shareholders. The withdrawal of Treasury notes from circulation—and, as some considered to be among its duties, the maintenance of a stable (and preferably appreciating) rate of exchange—would be judged against the desire to increase its discounting activities and, hence, note issues. Thus, in September 1854, barely four months after the start of its operations, the Bank of Brazil sent the first of a number of memoranda to the government seeking alterations to its statutes. The most important of those concerned the relaxation of the limits on the types of paper it was allowed to discount. It requested permission to discount not only commercial bills and bills of exchange with two known signatures (Art. 11, paragraph 1), but also paper from other banks and firms of renowned financial soundness (Cavalcanti 1893, Vol. 2, p. 206). After hearing the Finance Standing Committee of the Council of State, the government refused to grant permission to the Bank to lend against shares of joint-stock banks or other firms. The Committee agreed that at the time there were many such firms operating with very little surveillance, which increased the risk of them "contaminating" the Bank's portfolio.[32]

Six months later, on 26 March 1855, the Bank again turned to the government. This time it sought permission to increase the leverage of its reserve fund, allowing it to raise its note issue from a ratio of 2:1 to 3:1 (*RMF* 1855, p. 10).[33] The seasonal drain of both coins and paper money to the Northern provinces for the purchase of crops and in the Center-South in payment for the importation of slaves by planters was still causing difficulties for the money market in Rio (Banco do Brasil, *Relatorio dos Fiscaes* 1857, p. 8).[34] To try to remedy this problem, the Bank pressed ahead with its program of setting-up provincial branches (*caixas filiais*), with their own locally circulating notes.[35]

Sensitive to the Bank's arguments concerning the need to expand its issues but, at the same time, conscious of the potentially dangerous precedent it was setting, in April the government sanctioned an increase in the leverage to up to three times the amount of the reserve fund, but for one year only.[36] The government's apprehensions turned out to be well founded, for two months before the authorization to increase its note issue expired, the Bank applied for, and obtained, the right to maintain the 3:1 ratio, which was also extended to its seven offices in the provinces through Decree 1721, of February 1856.

Still, this measure was not enough to stave off the monetary pressure that was being felt in the capital of the Empire in 1856 and the resulting loss of reserves. In a sense, Itaboraí, president of the Bank of Brazil since April 1855, had already anticipated this result. In the annual report to shareholders, he remarked that the installation of the *caixas filiais* would not solve the problem of the drain of currency from Rio, while there remained a deficit in transactions with the North (Banco do Brasil, *Relatorio* 1856, p. 4).[37]

The dilemma in which the Bank found itself—that is, the need to balance its private interests with the stabilizing role it was expected to provide to the economy as a whole—was perceived by its shareholders. It was thus expressed in the annual report for 1856:

> The drain on the reserve fund entails either a restriction of discounts, or sacrifices that the establishment makes by importing precious metals. The Board of Directors, unwilling to accept the first remedy, which would cause great harm to the country, prefers the second, which brings some loss to shareholders, reducing the dividends to which they are entitled [...], convinced that they understand that the purpose of the Bank of Brazil is not solely to afford advantages to its shareholders, but also to serve to a great extent the general interests of commerce and industry. (Banco do Brasil, *Relatorio dos Fiscaes* 1856, p. 8)[38]

In that same year, the Bank of Brazil would start the process of withdrawing government paper money from circulation at a rate of 2000 *contos* p.a. In May 1857, Minister of Finance João Maurício Wanderley (Barão de Cotegipe) remarked on the delicate position under which the Bank had been operating:

> It is a fact that is present in the balance sheets of the Bank of Brazil that since June 1855, and up until late last March, this establishment has been importing approximately 20 thousand *contos* in gold and that, nevertheless [...], its reserve fund has increased since then by just 4,000:000$; from which it can be seen that there has been, and still is, a permanent export of coins from this to other markets in the Empire, and perhaps overseas. (*RMF* 1856, p. 17)

Even so, instead of pushing for an expansion of the Bank's issuing activities or, even, the creation of other institutions that could alleviate the shortage of money, Cotegipe opted for leaving things as they stood:

> It is clear that the country's circumstances do not yet allow the Bank to increase its operations, as a bank of issue, up to the amount of capital already paid-in. Thus, creation of other Establishments of the same nature, either in this Court, or in the places where the Bank already has an office, would bring no advantage to the public, even if they were submitted to the same conditions imposed on the Bank of Brazil, and were directed with the same circumspection as repeatedly demonstrated by the administration of that establishment. (Ibid.)

Not everyone was impressed by the Bank's circumspection, though. A commission appointed by its own board of directors to investigate the state of the Bank's *fundo disponível* concluded that 'having encountered facility in the use of its issues (the Bank) lent its credit beyond what was suitable to the maintenance of its reserve fund'.[39] In light of this, the commission recommended that the Bank of Brazil gradually increase its rate of discount and, at the same time, start accepting interest-bearing deposits as a source of loanable funds.[40]

Less than three months after Cotegipe's declaration of faith in prudence in monetary and banking matters, government policy took a dramatic turn. The Executive approved incorporation of the first of six new banks of issue. Plurality of note issue was thus officially instituted, bringing to an end the brief monopoly enjoyed by the Bank of Brazil since it started its operations in 1854.[41]

2.3 Plurality by Executive Decree: The New Banks of Issue and the 1857 Crisis

To some extent, the roots of the changes in the banking regime were political. In the previous years, Liberals had been voicing their disgruntlement over the current electoral system, which allowed few chances of representation in the Chamber of Deputies for the party in opposition. The situation was made worse by the vote rigging carried out by whoever happened to be in power. This state of affairs prompted calls for reforms in the electoral process, a cause that was embraced by the Marquês de Paraná, an old-time Conservative valued for his moderation. Since

September 1853, Paraná led a cabinet composed for the most part of moderate Conservatives, too young to have taken part in the political conflicts of the previous decades. This new arrangement, which eschewed earlier confrontation, would herald the period that came to be known as the *Conciliação* and which would extend into the late 1850s.[42]

Paraná was directly responsible for the electoral law of 1855, which introduced the so-called one-deputy electoral circles. The new system bypassed the previous influence of regional political chiefs in the voting process, thus bringing the National Assembly in direct contact with the local bosses. As a result, the gates were open for a measure of opposition representation in the Chamber of Deputies. Accordingly, in the first elections to be held under this new system, the Liberals were able to take 17% of the seats in the lower House, thus reversing the previous 100% Conservative-dominated "unanimous Chamber".

Upon the death of Paraná, in September 1856, the Emperor appointed Brazil's chief military commander, Luís Alves Lima e Silva (Caxias), to preside over the cabinet. An arch-Conservative, Caxias felt that the results of the parliamentary elections, by ushering in a small, but vocal, Liberal minority, represented a risk to his leadership. Accordingly, he resigned, making way for the moderate Conservative, Pedro de Araújo Lima (Marquês de Olinda), to come to office, in May 1857. The thirteenth cabinet of the Empire, it would maintain the conciliatory note of the Paraná government and, in acknowledgement of the recent electoral results, include two Liberals in the six-member cabinet. At the helm in the Ministry of Finance was Bernardo de Souza Franco, a Liberal senator from the northern province of Pará.[43]

In mid-1857, as the coffee sector started to experience a shortage of labor, wages also increased, leading to demands for an expansion of the money supply (*RMF* 1857, p. 4). The accompanying requests for authorization to incorporate new banks of issue were met with sympathetic ears by Minister of Finance Souza Franco. From late August, he gave permission for the establishment of six new banks of issue (out of 50 requests), thus breaking the monopoly hitherto held by the Bank of Brazil (Soares 1865, p. 50).[44] The rules governing the issue of notes were similar for all six banks, and broadly in line with those that applied to the Bank of Brazil. They could issue notes to the bearer, redeemable on sight in gold or Treasury notes, to an amount equal to their respective paid-in capital. Notes were to be backed by consolidated government debt (*apólices*), and shares of railways and other companies benefiting from government dividend guarantees.

Crucially, creation of the new banks of issue was not done by means of a law, as had been the case in 1853 with the third Bank of Brazil. Instead, it was an act of the Executive, taken during the parliamentary recess. In doing so, Souza Franco was moving into a legal gray area. In fact, banking legislation fell into the broader rules governing incorporation, as laid down in the 1850 Commercial Code.[45] Article 295 of the said legislation determined that corporations could only start operations after obtaining authorization from the government and, when these operations entailed a special privilege, pending legislative approval. Clearly, the issue of banknotes was a privilege and recognized as such when the third Bank of Brazil was incorporated.

Still, none of this deterred Souza Franco from his objective of meeting, even if only partially, the demands for an expansion of the volume of money and, it was hoped, credit to the economy. In the section on "Banks and the Circulating Medium" in the 1857 *Relatorio da Fazenda*, the Minister justified the decision to allow the incorporation of the new banks on the following grounds:

> In general, and especially in the places where the Bank of Brazil or its branches operated, the new establishments were aimed at bringing the advantages of credit to industry, or to the classes of society to which the other (banks) could not extend their discounts, because of the special nature of their organization, and at supplying funds to Commerce, and circulating medium to the market. (*RMF* 1857, p. 6)

This passage from Souza Franco's report is most illuminating, in that he advocates the establishment of new banks of issue precisely in the towns where the Bank of Brazil was already operating. Implicitly, he is suggesting that the Bank was not fulfilling its role of providing adequate liquidity and credit to the market.[46] Unsurprisingly, the Bank attacked Souza Franco's decision to allow the creation of new banks. It considered this unfair competition, and a violation of the (implicit) monopoly granted when it was set up four years earlier (Banco do Brasil, *Relatorio dos Fiscaes* 1858, p. 2).

Nevertheless, misfortune had it that the bold policy shift promoted by Souza Franco coincided with a major crisis at the international level. It was triggered by the dramatic drop in some commodity prices, following bumper cereal and wool production in the United States and Eastern Europe, after the end of the Crimean War. The failure of the Ohio Life Insurance and Trust Company, in August 1857, led to a panic in the American market, requiring the shipment of gold from Britain. In order to stem the drain on its reserves and ensure the functioning of the gold standard, the Bank of England increased its discount rate to 10%, causing a rediversion of capital to London and the spread of panic to continental markets.[47]

News of the crisis in the United States reached Rio on 13 November, followed by packet boats from Europe bringing accounts of interest rate rises in London. This came barely three months after the first of the governmental decrees was promulgated but before any of the new banks started issuing notes.[48] Foreign trade was badly hurt in Rio and across the major ports in the provinces, as creditors demanded immediate settlement of commercial debts.[49] At the same time, the practice of purchasing goods on consignment was suspended, as orders placed in Europe were required to be accompanied by the corresponding payments in hard currency.[50] Business in Rio came to a virtual standstill.

At first, the Bank of Brazil suffered a run for redemption of its notes in gold. The Bank obliged, in an attempt to calm the market. Yet, it was aware of the limits to its efforts. The difficult balancing act that it was forced to perform was clearly perceived by its directors. At the same time that the Bank had an interest in (and felt a duty to) meeting demands from the market, on the other, it had to maintain the level of its reserves. As tension mounted, businesses brought an increasing amount of bills to be discounted at the Bank.[51] From an average of 42,000 *contos* in September–November, the Bank's portfolio increased to just under 52,000 *contos* in December (Table 2.3).[52]

In his 1858 report, the president of the Bank of Brazil indicated that in late December 1857 to early January 1858, the Bank was following what would later become known as "Bagehot's rule" in the case of financial distress. This meant lending liberally—and dearly—to banks deemed solvent. Its (inter-bank) rates of discount were increased from 8% to 10% on 15 December, and to 11% on the 23rd.[53] For other businesses, the rates, when discounts were available, were as high as 15%.

As the drain on its reserve fund continued, the Bank felt that its potential note issues—and, hence, the volume of discounts it was able to carry out—was being compromised. As a result, on 27 November, it unilaterally decided to suspend convertibility of its notes into gold.[54] Shortly afterward, the government let it be known that it was willing to help the Bank reinforce its reserve fund by means of a guarantee on a loan in the amount of 3000 *contos* (£340,000) to be arranged in London.[55]

Table 2.3 Bank of Brazil, Head Office: selected indicators, June 1857–June 1858 (in *contos*)

Month/Year	*Reserve fund*	*Notes in circulation*	*Value of portfolio*
June 1857	13,125.7	32,804.9	40,193.7
July	13,049.8	33,366.8	38,895.4
August	13,467.1	32,983.5	38,404.6
September	12,872.1	29,312.9	39,009.9
October	12,848.2	30,208.4	41,426.4
November	11,322.7	30,522.3	46,424.5
December	10,859.3	33,175.0	51,836.6
January 1858	11,105.8	31,084.8	49,538.5
February	10,994.1	28,858.1	47,668.3
March	9978.8	27,131.6	46,210.5
April	8877.3	24,545.9	43,843.4
May	8829.6	23,418.4	42,965.2
June	8753.0	25,607.0	45,780.0

Source: Banco do Brasil, *Relatorio Apresentado á Assembléa Geral dos Accionistas* 1858

On 1 December, the first in a series of memoranda was exchanged between Bank and government. The Bank indicated that 3000 *contos* were insufficient to restore calm to the market and that until it could gauge the actual extent of its needs for bills of exchange some £600,000 would be necessary.[56] The second Bank memorandum, in turn, called attention to the extent of the drain in its reserve fund and the effect this was having on its ability to pursue regular discounting activities. The Bank then asked the government to be allowed to increase the limit of its note issue from three to four times the reserve. Three days later, the government replied in the affirmative to these requests, although the wording of its two memoranda was vague. Briefly, the government stated that it was conscious of the need to maintain both internal (i.e., discounts) and external (i.e., exchange rate) stability and would do its utmost to help the Bank. Nevertheless, Souza Franco did not commit himself to a specific amount for the guarantees.[57] Soon afterward, an operation to prop up the rate of exchange began.

The strategy consisted of selling drafts on London (guaranteed by the Treasury) at a relatively appreciated rate of exchange. The first draft, totaling £100,000, was made on the Union Bank of London, on account of a credit which that bank had offered to the Bank of Brazil earlier in the year. One month into the operation, the exchange rate continued to fall (depreciate). Since the arrival of news of the panic overseas, the milréis had dropped by about 15%, being quoted at 23½d and 24d on 31 December. On 9 January, Souza Franco sent a new memorandum to José Pedro Dias de Carvalho, acting president of the Bank, inquiring about his plans to sustain the rate of exchange. On the same day, Dias de Carvalho replied that the Bank was willing to continue selling drafts on London, so long as the government would furnish it with the necessary Treasury notes to compensate for the loss of gold from its reserve fund. The government obliged, putting 1000 *contos* at the disposal of the Bank, which went on to sell £200,000 worth of drafts in the market at the rate of 25d. With this operation, the government sought to force the rate of exchange up by increasing the supply of sterling.

By late January 1858, when the packets brought news of a worsening of the crisis in Europe, the Bank experienced difficulty in procuring bills of exchange locally for purchase. This ultimately forced it to dip into its own reserves, leading to further losses of gold. In light of this—and in an effort to safeguard its fund—the Bank once again took unilateral action. This time, by deciding to shift its efforts from defense of the rate of exchange to concentrating on providing discount facilities to the domestic market.[58] In a reversal of the previous trend, its discount rate for the best private paper was lowered from 11% to 10% on 27 January and then to 9% on 10 February (see Table 2.4).

This "washing of hands" of what many considered the Bank's duty to defend the rate of exchange was later justified by its directors on the grounds that it was a commitment impossible of being honored from the moment that the new banks of issue were allowed to operate:

Table 2.4 Bank of Brazil: rates of discount charged, 1856–62 (in %)

Date	*Rate of discount*	*Date*	*Rate of discount*
June 1856	8	15 December 1857	10
27 November 1856	9	23 December 1857	11
12 January 1857	8	27 January 1858	10
6 May 1857	9	10 February 1858	9
13 August 1857	8	8 January 1862	10

Sources: Banco do Brasil, *Relatorio Apresentado á Assembléa Geral dos Accionistas*, various issues; and *Relatorio da Commissão de Inquerito de 1864* (1865)

Note: Rates correspond to bills with two known signatures and, therefore, should be regarded as a minimum (prime) rate

> The removal of the means to satisfy an obligation contracted at a time when those very means were made available should liberate the obligee. The Bank of Brazil, unable, thus, to comply with the mission to which it was committed when it was the sole (bank) with issuing powers, should have the right to demand exemption from its duties, confining itself to being a mere bank of deposit and discount with the faculty to issue (notes) in competition with the other (banks), only to make profits that will reward its shareholders' capital.[59]

In practice, the directors were saying that even if the Bank of Brazil had attempted to take a different path and reduce its note issue (and, hence, money supply) in an effort to prop up the rate of exchange, it would never be certain of the end result, given the actions of the other banks of issue:

> The only ostensible result, thus, of the efforts undertaken by the Board of Directors of the Bank of Brazil to re-establish the value of the circulating medium, and therefore meet the most important commitment that it had undertaken with the State, is the reduction in the profits of its shareholders, while helping to bolster those of the other issuing banks. (Banco do Brasil, *Relatorio dos Fiscaes* 1858, p. 2)

The "free rider" problem that the Bank of Brazil feared did indeed manifest itself in the second half of 1858. While the issues of its head office contracted substantially and those of the *caixas filiais* remained at the level of 20,000 *contos*, other banks increased their own note circulation. From April, the Banco Commercial & Agrícola started its issuing operations, partially compensating the reduction in the note circulation of the head office of the Bank of Brazil. The banks in the provinces of Pernambuco and Bahia, with issues of more than 1000 *contos* each, also helped dampen the effects of the contraction in the amount of Bank of Brazil notes in circulation throughout 1858. Clearly, any attempt by the Bank of Brazil to support the exchange by reducing the volume of its own issues voluntarily would have been thwarted by the actions of its competitors (Table 2.5).

If, as regards the reduction of its issues in Rio being offset by competition from the Commercial & Agrícola, the directors of the Bank of Brazil were partly right, their complaints in relation to diminishing profits were not warranted. Instead, they appear to have been directed at pressuring the government into reconsidering the question of plurality of issue altogether. In the financial year ending in June 1858, the Bank displayed record profits as discounting operations expanded, despite competition

Table 2.5 Total notes outstanding, by issuing bank: January–December 1858. (in *contos*)

	B. of Brazil (head office) (a)	*B. of Brazil* (caixas) *(b)*	*Total BB (a) + (b)*	*Banco Com. & Agrícola*	*Novo Banco de Pernam-buco*	*Banco do Ma-ranhão*	*Banco da Bahia*	*Total*
Jan 1858	31,084.8	21,201.6	52,286.4	–	–	–	–	52,286.4
Feb	28,858.1	21,346.7	50,204.8	–	–	–	–	50,204.8
Mar	27,131.6	21,621.8	48,753.4	–	–	–	–	48,753.4
Apr	24,545.9	21,354.2	45,900.1	1850.0	–	–	–	47,750.1
May	23,418.4	20,975.3	44,393.7	3574.3	248.3	90.0	–	48,306.3
Jun	25,607.0	20,332.0	45,929.0	4324.1	484.9	145.0	–	50,883.0
Jul	23,620.0	20,436.3	44,056.3	4850.0	484.9	240.0	–	49,631.2
Aug	20,874.0	20,281.6	41,155.6	4850.0	484.9	240.0	–	49,631.2
Sep	18,848.7	19,373.2	38,221.9	5437.0	984.9	360.0	–	45,003.8
Oct	19,349.2	18,971.9	38,321.1	5350.0	1000.0	360.0	–	45,031.1
Nov	19,661.9	19,146.7	38,808.6	5390.2	1125.0	360.0	825.0	46,508.8
Dec	22,125.5	19,811.3	41,936.8	5390.2	1460.0	430.0	1287.5	50,504.5

Source: *Relatorio da Commissão de Inquerito de 1859* (undated)

Note: Figures for the Commercial & Agrícola refer to the head office only

Table 2.6 Bank of Brazil: selected indicators, 1854–8 (in *contos*)

Financial year	*Bills discounted (a)*	*Payments (b)*	*Portfolio balances (a)–(b)*	*Interest earned on bills discounted*	*Net profits*
1854–5	99,258.6	75,138.5	24,120.1	1567.2	1332.8
1855–6	120,442.9	91,007.5	29,435.4	2054.8	1868.8
1856–7	128,453.0	117,694.7	40,193,7	2330.2	2285.4
1857–8	208,250.6	162,470.6	45,780.0	3506.4	3852.3

Sources: Banco do Brasil, *Relatorio Apresentado á Assembléa Geral dos Accionistas*, various issues; and *Relatorio da Commissão de Inquerito de 1859* (undated)

Notes: Figures refer to head office only, except interest earnings and profits, which include the *caixas filiais*. "Bills discounted" include portfolio balances from previous financial year

from other banks. While the amount of bills discounted doubled between 1854–5 and 1857–8, net profits increased three-fold, in part as a result of higher rates of interest charged toward the end of the period (Table 2.6).

However serious the free rider problem might have been, the initial handling of the crisis by the Bank of Brazil was heavily criticized by the Finance Standing Committee of the Council of State (Seção de Fazenda do Conselho de Estado). The Committee met at the request of the Emperor on 26 March 1858 to examine the 'causes for the fall in the rate of exchange and the measures that the government should take to remedy this situation' (*SFCE*, vol. IV, pp. 258–264).

The decision to lower the discount rate in the early months of 1858 was seen by the Committee as a mistake, which simply added to the Bank's woes concerning the reduction of its reserve fund. The Committee took the view that the Bank failed to react to the first news of the crisis in the United States and Europe with the necessary speed and commitment.[60] In particular, Committee members argued that discount rates should have been raised even earlier in 1857 in order to stem the drain on the reserve fund.[61] In other words, had the Bank kept discount rates at a high level, there would be less demand for redemption of its notes—consequently, less pressure on the reserve fund, and no need to abandon convertibility. Furthermore, in their opinion, the Bank's early decision to suspend convertibility was to blame for the subsequent devaluation of the currency (*SFCE*, vol. IV, p. 261). Overall, they reasoned, the exchange rate could have been kept near par.[62] Finally, the Committee attacked ongoing efforts at raising the rate of exchange through operations on London, which it deemed as having only 'ephemeral results' (ibid.).

In a way, this hardly veiled indictment of both government and Bank of Brazil policies during the crisis can be imputed to Itaboraí's personal antipathy for Souza Franco's liberal ideas on monetary and banking matters. Itaboraí had resigned the post of president of the Bank of Brazil in June 1857 in protest over Souza Franco's plans (subsequently approved by Parliament) to transfer to the Bank the surplus deposits in the provincial treasuries and the Caixa de Amortização (Amortization Office).[63] In this case, Itaboraí's conservative views on money dominated any possible consideration of the obvious benefits such a move would bring to the Bank, by allowing it to re-loan these funds at a much higher rate.[64] Following his stepping down from the presidency of the Bank, Itaboraí would go on to exercise opposition in the imperial Senate to Souza Franco's liberal policies. That is, until he returned to the command of the Bank, in December 1858.

Meanwhile, the decline in the value of the milréis would persist—the exchange rate reached 22¾ on 4 March 1858. On 10 March, as the deadline for the handing-in of the semi-annual instalment of 1000 *contos* in Treasury notes to the Caixa de Amortização drew near, the directors of the Bank decided to bring 700 *contos* from the offices in Bahia and Pernambuco to reinforce the reserve fund at the head office (Pacheco 1979, vol. II, p. 224). Two days later, the Bank again turned to the government, calling its attention to the problems caused by the export of the silver coins still in circulation. The Bank believed this could only be stopped if additional efforts were employed to force up the rate of exchange. It would be willing to draw on London at the rate of 25d if the Treasury gave the usual guarantees and exempted the Bank from any obligation concerning a timetable for the shipment of bills to London. In its own words, it was requesting permission to '[…] draw freely on the next packet-boat, so as to satisfy any reasonable need […] and at such a rate of exchange as to meet the objectives of the Law of 11 September 1846, and in harmony with the interests of the Bank and the market' (*RMF* 1857, Annex, p. 12).

Souza Franco's reply came on the same day, 12 March. He made it clear that he found the Bank's proposal too vague, for no specific figure was attached to the amount of guarantees sought from the government. Moreover, and as a sign that he was losing patience with what he perceived as foot-dragging on the part of the Bank, Souza Franco affirmed that the government had decided to undertake the defense of the rate of exchange directly through the Treasury, without the Bank's help. In other words, the capacity of the Bank of Brazil to act as a lender of last resort and overseer of the good functioning of the monetary market was put in doubt by the government.[65] Nevertheless, Souza Franco kept the door open. He was willing to extend the same guarantees as before should the Bank publicly announce that it would be drawing up to £400,000 at a rate not lower than 25½ by the March packet and up to £200,000 (at a rate of at least 26d) by the April packet. The Minister demanded a prompt reply from the Bank to what turned out to be his last offer (*RMF* 1857, Annex, p. 12).

At this point, versions differ greatly. The 1857 *Relatorio da Fazenda* simply states that the Bank of Brazil refused this last offer from the government dated 12 March. As a result, the Minister of Finance immediately turned elsewhere for help (ibid., p. 9). By contrast, the Bank's version of the events, as presented in its 1858 report, is as follows. Upon receiving Souza Franco's memorandum (No. 11) dated 12 March, the president summoned an extraordinary meeting of the Board of Directors, to convene at 12 noon of that same day. Failing to obtain the necessary quorum to deliberate on the issue, the Bank immediately sent notice of that mishap to the Minister (memo No. 13), to which Souza Franco promptly replied, urging Dias de Carvalho to call a meeting of the directors for the following day (memo No. 14). The report goes on to add that in the meantime and shortly after the messenger had been sent over to the Ministry of Finance, a few more directors turned up at the Bank and agreed to a reply to Souza Franco's offer, which restated the Bank's initial position. Namely, the Bank was willing to help the government but, unfortunately, it was unable to offer drafts for sale by the next packet, for fear of seeing a further loss of gold from its reserve fund in a few months' time. However, should the government bear the responsibility of providing the funds (in bills of exchange or gold) to honor these drafts, the Bank would be ready to act (memo No. 12). In the Bank's account of the episode, 'the correspondence between the government and the Bank of Brazil on this subject came to an end with this memorandum, because the government did not deign to reply whether or not it accepted the services put at its disposal by the Board of Directors'. The copies of the memoranda exchanged between the Minister of Finance and the Bank of Brazil in those crucial months, which are reproduced in the 1858 annual reports of both institutions, do not lend support to the Bank's version of the events of 12 March.[66]

According to one author, at 2:00 p.m., soon after the messenger arrived at Souza Franco's office with news of the Bank's position, the Minister had Mauá summoned (Caldeira 1995, p. 338).[67] On the very same day, the Barão, through the Mauá, MacGregor Bank, announced he would be selling ninety-day bills of exchange at the rate of 25½d on the packet boat about to depart, a rate that was followed by other institutions. The total planned amount put at the service of his scheme to shore up the exchange rate would be as follows: £400,000 in March, £200,000 in April, £150,000 in May, and, finally, £60,000 in June. This declining scale of drafts attests to Mauá's confidence in the success of his efforts to re-establish the value of the milréis.

In practice, Mauá would sell bills of exchange from the Brazilian office of his bank, drawn on its London branch and guaranteed (up to £750,000) by the Treasury's reserves in that city. After being negotiated in Rio, the bills still had to be shipped to London, to be presented in ninety days. The bills would then be paid for in London with the Treasury's money and then sent back to Brazil, where the final settlement between the Mauá Bank and the Treasury would occur. In all, the process would take some 150 days (Caldeira 1995, p. 346).[68]

Fundamentally, the Barão was placing a bet against the market, by selling large amounts of the commodity perceived as most valuable at the time (sterling) in exchange for the discredited domestic currency. His reasoning for embarking on such an operation was as follows. The extent of the devaluation of the milréis since the outbreak of the commercial crisis, he estimated, was not warranted by any indicator of the "fundamentals" of the Brazilian economy, to use a modern term. The balance of payments was temporarily in deficit, he reckoned, largely because of a drop in the international demand for commodities exported by Brazil, especially coffee, the price of which, however, was hardly affected. Mauá thought he knew by what amount the balance of payments was in the red and what the supply of bills of exchange would be in the near future. If his estimates were right, there was room for (in this case stabilizing) speculation on his part. Also, given the existence of a mass of other speculators ready to bet against him (and ultimately the domestic currency), the opportunity to make a fortune—and prove them wrong in the process—was all too real.

At first sight, the odds were heavily against Mauá. The market was desperately trying to get hold of sterling at a time when the supply of bills of exchange was at a seasonal low, and, therefore, the direction of the rate of exchange was unequivocally downward. Nevertheless, as noted, Mauá reckoned that this was strictly a transitional phenomenon caused by the sudden retraction in the international market for Brazilian goods, and the exceptional drying-up of commercial credit that followed the panic in Europe. As soon as the next crops came to the market and Brazilian exports recovered their trend (which, at the time, was definitely upward), he thought, the increased supply of sterling would lead the milréis to recover the ground lost in recent months.[69]

In June 1858, as the time to settle accounts with the Treasury drew near, the players would finally have to show their hands. Winners and losers would soon be known. In England, business had returned to normal, and interest rates were lowered to 2.5%. In the meantime, the Brazilian market was about to become awash with sterling, as the government had just secured a loan in London of approximately £1.4 million, directed toward the nationalization and extension of the D. Pedro II railway. When news of this deal reached Rio, in June, the rate of exchange—which had been quoted at 25½ since the beginning of Mauá's rescue operation in mid-March—rose to 27d (18 June), only to fall back to 25½d five days later.[70] The pressure for appreciation of the currency, however, had made itself felt. In early July, the government withdrew its guarantees on the drafts on London. Meanwhile, holders of bills of exchange became increasingly nervous at the prospect of having to sell sterling at a lower price than they had paid earlier in order to meet pressing expenses in local currency. As August approached, so did the peak period in coffee shipments from the interior to Rio.[71] Accordingly, demand for the hitherto shunned milréis increased, adding pressure for the appreciation of the exchange rate, and allowing Mauá to settle his debts with the Treasury, with considerable gain for his bank.

In mid-August, judging that the worst was over, the government demanded that the Bank of Brazil resume the exchange of its notes for gold, on demand. On 25 August, convertibility was restored at the Bank of Brazil and the rate of exchange reached near par, at 26 5/8d. The crisis was officially over, but it would leave a lasting legacy on both policy and debate on monetary matters in Brazil. There were ninety bankruptcies across the country and in Rio alone losses amounted to an estimated 20,000–30,000 *contos* (£1.7–£ 2.5 million).

2.4 The Orthodox Backlash

Even before the denouement, the conduct of the whole affair by the government was met with a barrage of criticism in the Chamber of Deputies. Soon after the opening of the new legislative year, on 17 May 1858, a deputy from the province of Rio de Janeiro, Jerônimo José Teixeira Junior (the future Visconde de Cruzeiro), accused Souza Franco of sending mixed signals to the market throughout the crisis. According to Teixeira Jr., this had paved the way for wanton speculation, in the form of requests for the setting-up of new banks (*ACD* 1858, Tome I, pp. 32–6).[72] Alleging that official criteria for the chartering of new banks were contradictory, he filed a requisition for the government to provide the Assembly with the necessary clarifications, including copies of the records of meetings of the Finance Standing Committee of the Council of State, convened to examine the matter (*ACD* 1858, Tome I, pp. 32–6). This requisition would occupy most of the discussions in the following two months of debates in the Chamber of Deputies.

The sessions that followed were marked by accusations of favoritism toward the Mauá, MacGregor Bank and endless (and often empty) discussions about Teixeira Jr.'s requisition.[73] Events began to take a turn for the worst for the government in late June when Francisco Sales Torres Homem (the future Visconde de Inhomirim) and Itaboraí directed their assaults on the liberal banking policies of the Olinda administration, from the Chamber of Deputies and Senate, respectively. Torres Homem targeted Souza Franco as the man who personified bad economic thinking and reckless policy. His speeches were long, acrimonious, and usually contradictory, but that did not stop Torres Homem from establishing himself as an undisputed authority in financial matters, on a par with the likes of Souza Franco and Itaboraí (Caldeira 1995, pp. 353–5).[74]

Part of the attacks on Souza Franco on these occasions derived from the conviction that by creating new banks of issue by decree the government was acting in an area that was a preserve of the Legislative. The other fundamental criticism of the banks established by decree referred to their professed over issue of notes,[75] thus worsening the effects of a crisis that, everyone agreed, had been "imported". This other strand of criticism originated with advocates of a monopoly of note issue and, as expected, counted with the sympathy of the Bank of Brazil (Banco do Brasil, *Relatorio dos Fiscaes* 1858, Annex, 2).[76]

In the end, the campaign waged by Torres Homem and Itaboraí against Souza Franco and his policies bore fruit. Following the charge that the Minister of Finance had failed to hear the Chamber on the crucial subject of the new banks of issue, the Emperor put pressure on the Olinda cabinet, which finally resigned on 12 December 1858. The *Conciliação* era had come to an end.

According to a noted Brazilian historian, the Emperor himself was a firm believer in the virtues of orthodox monetary and banking principles and, in this sense, Torres Homem's assault on Souza Franco was, if not at the behest of His Majesty, at least directed toward currying favor with him.[77] If so, the strategy paid off nicely. Torres Homem was appointed to the Finance portfolio in the new Conservative cabinet headed by the Visconde de Abaeté, the monarch's third choice, after both Euzébio de Queirós and Paulino José Soares de Sousa declined the offer to form a new government. Soon after becoming Minister of Finance, Torres Homem invited Itaboraí back to the presidency of the Bank of Brazil.

One of the first measures implemented by Abaeté was to revoke, on 30 April, the permission granted to the Bank of Brazil to issue notes up to three times its reserve fund. After all, it was argued, since February 1856 the Bank had been making use of a relaxation of the original 2:1 ratio, granted in order to compensate for the drain of specie and Treasury notes from its vaults. Abuse of this facility, in the eyes of the government, left it with little choice but to curtail the amount of notes in circulation, including those of the Bank.[78] Paradoxically, while attempting to exercise control over the money supply by reining in the issue of Bank of Brazil notes, the government was pursuing a parallel strategy by which liquidity in the economy might increase. By means of Decrees 2383 and 2400, of 2 April 1859, Torres Homem gave permission for the establishment of 17 new deposit and discount banks, with a total capital of 400,000 *contos*, although in the end none of them would actually be incorporated (Carreira 1980, Vol. II, pp. 756–7).[79]

Two months after authorizing the incorporation of the new banks and in a drive to impose a complete U-turn on the previous liberal banking policy, Torres Homem presented a bill in the Chamber of Deputies. If approved, it would introduce severe limits on the issuing rights of the existing banks. His bill, dated 15 June 1859, consisted of a single, eight-clause article (Cavalcanti 1893, Vol. 2, p. 235).[80] Its main provisions were the requirement that the Bank of Brazil and those banks created by government decree in 1857 and 1858 be required to redeem their notes exclusively in gold, on demand, within three years of publication of the new legislation (paragraph 1); until that happened, issues of the said banks were capped at the maximum outstanding amounts in the early months of 1859 (paragraph 2). The bill also included the appointment of a government inspector to each bank, charged with overseeing its compliance with the new legislation (paragraph 4); exempted the Bank of Brazil from the requirement to withdraw Treasury notes from circulation as long as its own issues remained within the limits set out previously; and conferred on Parliament the authority to authorize the incorporation of new banks of issue or the extension of the operations of the existing ones (paragraph 7).

In essence, the Torres Homem bill was a slightly modified version of another bill that the Emperor had earlier forwarded to the Council of State, where it was met with a mixed reception.[81] Most of the participants in the twelve-member Council who actually made their votes clear stood against it. There were those, like Olinda, who adopted a legalistic approach to the question and remarked that the removal of a right (in this case, the possibility that the Bank redeem its notes in Treasury paper) from a party could not be done without its consent. Others opposed the bill on technical grounds.[82]

Although in a minority, backers of the bill crucially included the "Saquarema trinity", the very core of the old-time Conservatives, Itaboraí, Paulino José Soares de Sousa (Visconde de Uruguai), and Euzébio de Queirós. Uruguai's positioning in this case is particularly revealing. Himself a lawyer and *fazendeiro* from the province of Rio de Janeiro, in defense of the bill he highlighted the growing difficulties of the agricultural sector, particularly an ageing slave population. Nevertheless, he pondered that 'if to the hardships that result from such a situation is added a great mass of depreciated paper money, the circumstances will get even worse'.[83] In the end, the Emperor decided to go ahead with the proposal, in spite of considerable opposition in the Council, further suggesting the monarch's sympathies toward hard money.

Upon arriving in the Legislative, the Torres Homem bill was first examined by the relevant commission. After deliberation, the joint commission of Justice, Finance and Commerce of the Chamber of Deputies issued a report on 22 June. The report emphasized the following aspects to be observed in the proposal: its objective, its instruments, and its legality (Cavalcanti 1893, Vol. 2, pp. 236–8). For the authors of the report, it was clear that the aim of the Torres Homem bill was to 'fortify the value of the currency', thus preventing shifts in income distribution brought about by exchange-rate oscillations and inflation.[84] The means to achieve this objective was the institution of convertibility. Legality would depend on how Parliament decided on the future of banks of issue.

This effectively amounted to a reinterpretation of Article 1, paragraph 6, of Law 683 of 5 July 1853, which allowed the Bank of Brazil to redeem its notes in "currency" (i.e., specie or Treasury paper). The authors of the report recognized the need 'to impose on the banks the obligation to redeem their notes in gold on demand as the most efficacious means to preserve the value of the currency' (ibid., p. 237). However, they disagreed with paragraph 2 of the said Law, and, instead, proposed that issues of the Bank of Brazil be limited to twice its *fundo disponível* (as determined by its statutes), but with the proviso that the authority to grant permission to the Bank to alter this limit be transferred from the Executive to the Legislative power. Finally, as to the legality of the bill—and in an attempt to clear up the confusion which surrounded this crucial question—they were of the opinion that it required a clear statement of the Legislative's ascendancy on matters related to money and banking (ibid.).

Some deputies did not share the opinions of the majority of the members of the joint commission. Two of them, Manoel de Souza Dantas and Francisco de Paula Santos, published a minority report, in which they expressed their disagreement with both the original Torres Homem proposal and the views of the rest of the commission. Their main point concerned the legality of the bill that, in their view, represented a clear violation of the rights of shareholders of the banks concerned (the Bank of Brazil and those created by decree in 1857–8). For these deputies, any fundamental change in the contracts signed between the government and those institutions required consent from the latter and, therefore, could not come about unilaterally at the initiative of the government. The authors disagreed particularly with proposed limits on rights of issue and the convertibility requirements (paragraphs 1 and 2). To them, not only was this a unilateral change in the rules of the game but also a contradictory imposition. Indeed, at the same time that the government required that the institutions concerned ensure the redemption of their notes into gold, they were forced to accept inconvertible Treasury notes in payment of their loans.

To the Minister's great surprise, his bill was attacked from other quarters as well.[85] Journalists and businessmen alike condemned what they saw as too radical a change of course, which, it was argued, would bring not only the closure of the banks created by decree but also great hardship for the economy in general.[86] In the end, the Torres Homem bill passed in the Chamber by a very small margin, in spite of the considerable Conservative majority in that House.[87] Having presented the whole issue as a matter of confidence in the 1858 cabinet, Abaeté sought to convince the Emperor to dissolve the Assembly.[88] Instead, Pedro II dismissed the cabinet.

2.4.1 *The Inquiry into the 1857 Crisis*

The new Prime Minister, Ferraz, who also held the Finance portfolio, began his term by determining that all banking establishments and corporations in the Empire be required to present every month to the government an account of their operations. A second decree, dated 30 September 1859, further extended the supervision exercised by the Executive over businesses. Finally, on 10 November Ferraz commissioned an investigation into the 1857 crisis, to be headed by three distinguished civil servants.

The final report of the commission set up by Ferraz remains the single most important source of both statistical and anecdotal evidence about banking and monetary affairs in the period. In the five months that the inquiry lasted, the authors interviewed 28 businessmen and experts on trade and finance. On 30 April 1860, the report was published, offering a general abstract of all testimonies, excerpts from each of the interviews, as well as an impressive set of statistical data.

The ten questions that were asked of the interviewees, and a summary of replies, are given below:

1. Q: How are operations in foreign exchange conducted in the Rio market?
   A: The operations in foreign exchange are made by means of bills drawn for their most part against products that are exported. Those transactions in the exchange market with objectives distinct from the above, given their small share of the total, have exerted little influence on the rate of exchange.
2. Q: What determines, in general, the rate of exchange in this market?
   A: Two elements act on the rate of exchange: the relative monetary value of the currencies being exchanged and the comparative amount of money that must be shipped between the countries concerned.
3. Q: What are the causes behind the depreciation of the rate of exchange, especially in 1857 and 1858?
   A: In the years between the failure of the first Bank of Brazil and 1857, the large and frequent depreciations were mostly the result of issues of money in excess of the volume of transactions in the economy, as well as the poor state of government finances.
4. Q: What was the nature of the Crisis of 1857? What were its effects?
   A: The immediate impacts of the international crisis were far less important than those that resulted from purely internal factors,

the product of speculation and abuse in commercial activity. Preliminary estimates put the losses directly imputable to the international crisis at between 1500 and 3000 *contos*, and the number of import/export businesses that failed at between four and twelve. Total losses, however, are estimated at between twenty thousand and thirty thousand *contos* in Rio de Janeiro alone. The effects of the crisis were hardly felt in Bahia and Pernambuco.

5. Q: Can the depreciation of the exchange rate be attributed to an oversupply of banknotes?
   A: Most of the depreciation of the exchange rate must be blamed on the excessive issue of banknotes, which remains to this day. This depreciation in fact occurred with the aid of other causes that acted upon the economic circumstances of the time, given the direct and indirect effects of the 1857 crisis [...].
6. Q: Can competition between banks lead to over issue?
   A: Yes. Competition between banks of issue can raise the amount of notes beyond what the markets demand. In addition, the circulation of any one bank, instead of replacing that of another, actually increases the overall supply of fiduciary notes, harming its regularity and guarantees [...].
7. Q: Can the notes of the Bank of Brazil be considered as real paper money, on a par with government notes?
   A: No, they are different. Contrary to Bank of Brazil notes, government paper is not redeemable on demand.
8. Q: Have the *vales* issued by the Banco Commercial and others [...] behaved as banknotes before and after their maturity?
   A: Yes. Although the circuit in which *vales* are accepted is narrow, [...] it must be concluded that short-term *vales* and bills are equivalent in their effects to notes payable to bearer redeemable on demand, having the power in certain circumstances to replace coins and paper money.
9. Q: Are there any associations that operate as banks without government approval?
   A: In the province of Bahia alone the Commission identified in October 1859 eleven institutions (*caixas econômicas, caixas comerciais* etc.) operating without government authorization.[89] Many others in similar circumstances were operating in Rio.

10. Q: Who issues bills payable to bearer with maturities of less than ten days?
    A: The Commission unearthed countless cases of private individuals and companies that issued *vales* and other paper to bearer and redeemable on demand. For example, the Nictheroy & Inhomirim, Omnibus and Gondolas Co. issued its own private coins, given to passengers as small change. In addition, a Mr. Manoel Pereira de Souza Barros had *vales* printed in denominations of 50 to 10$000 to give in payment to his slaves for the produce from their plots.

Despite the diverse opinions presented at the inquiry, a general monetarist note characterized the findings of the Commission. It concluded that the origins of the crisis lay in Europe and the United States, but that the extent of its consequences in Brazil was due to the end of the monopoly of note issue enjoyed by the Bank of Brazil, and the excessive monetary expansion that (allegedly) ensued. Furthermore, and crucial in the authors' view, the abandonment of convertibility of the notes of the Bank further compounded the problems.

In concluding their report on this note, the commissioners were echoing the current credo, which equated sound monetary policy with convertibility. To the Minister who had commissioned the report, the Emperor himself, and many contemporaries, these findings sounded like the vindication of everything *metalistas*[90] had always stood for.

Yet, not everyone heard by the commission shared this view. Actually, several of the persons interviewed expressed opinions that, if not diametrically opposed to the conclusions, at least diverged to such an extent as to merit inclusion in the commissioners' final considerations. For example, Comendador José Ferreira Pinto, testifying on 31 December 1859, highlighted the indirect effects of monetary growth on the exchange rate, operating through an expansion in economic activity and the accompanying increase in the value of imports (*Relatorio da Commissão de Inquerito de 1859* undated, Annex A, p. 11). The imbalance between imports and exports, he insisted, was the main 'engine' of the rate of exchange, the latter being influenced by remittances of interest and amortization of the foreign debt.[91]

Balance-of-payments influences upon the exchange rate were also stressed by the next interviewee, Visconde de Ipanema, for whom 'as a rule the fall of the exchange rate in our market is caused by crop shortages.

(This was) especially (true) in 1857 and 1858 with coffee, as well as the extraordinary remittances which importing houses had to make to Europe' (ibid., p. 12). An unidentified foreign businessman based in Rio, in turn, remarked:

> The compared movement of imports and exports is what regulates, in general, the course of the exchange. The rate of discount, the nature and value of the circulating medium are two causes that also act irresistibly on the course of the exchange. From this point of view, the operations of the Bank of Brazil exercise a positive influence; and in many different countries in Europe, the decisive influence of the banks of issue on the course of the exchange has been proven. (Ibid., p. 44)

In the end, it was Mauá who provided the most eloquent defense of monetary heterodoxy. In one of the longest and most detailed testimonies offered to the Commission, he began by stating that 'as a principle, (he would) never deny the disastrous consequences that inconvertible paper money could have on the rate of exchange, for that would run counter to common sense' (ibid., p. 95). Yet, he was quick to point out that in order to assert that the decline of the exchange rate, which began in late 1857, was due to an over issue of notes and to the circulation of inconvertible paper money in excess of the needs of transactions, two things would have to be proven. First, that convertibility of notes into gold had been carried out before the onset of the crisis and, second, that the money supply in the Empire at the time exceeded the needs of the market. The answer to both points, Mauá insisted, was clearly "no". In fact, as already noted, the Bank of Brazil seldom gave gold in exchange for its notes before it officially announced it would confine convertibility to Treasury paper. In practice, therefore, the economy was technically under a peculiar type of monetary regime, where "gold-backed" Bank of Brazil notes were mostly redeemed in inconvertible government paper. As to the alleged overabundance of notes in circulation, Mauá pointed to the high interest rates in 1857 as an indication that the market was demanding more money than was on offer, not the reverse (ibid., pp. 95–6).[92] In that respect and, again, running counter to general opinion, he directed his criticisms at the gradual retirement of Treasury notes.

As noted, few of these less mainstream views were taken into account by the commissioners, who opted instead for a strictly monetarist interpretation of the events leading up to the 1857 crisis. In possession of their conclusions, Minister Ferraz felt confident to ventilate in the 1859 *Relatorio da Fazenda* the policies that he envisioned in order to restore the money supply to a "healthy" state (*RMF* 1859, pp. 65–82). His long exposition began with a digression about the recent events in the monetary market and the policies pursued by both the government and the Bank of Brazil. He then went on to stress the excessive liberty enjoyed by banks and corporations in the Empire. This involved, among other things, the issue of private bills by individuals or businesses, as well as the existence of banks operating exclusively under provincial authorization in open breach of legislation. More generally, he inveighed against the lack of official scrutiny of the conduct of many businesses, where unscrupulous individuals would often take advantage of uninformed investors. These considerations laid the ground for the subsequent submission of the infamous "Law of Impediments" (*Lei dos Entraves*),[93] which would regulate banking and corporate activity in the coming years. The Law's main points and consequences are discussed next.

Notes

1. According to a businessman testifying before the commission set up to investigate the causes of the 1857 commercial crisis, approximately 15 to 20 thousand *contos* (£1.8–2.4 million) were freed from the slave trade in 1851 and 1852. *Relatorio da Commissão de Inquerito de 1859* (undated, p. 104).
2. *Vales* were short-term promissory notes that circulated locally, performing a similar role to banknotes.
3. The estimates of the monetary aggregates used in the book were originally published in Peláez and Suzigan (1976). Their nature and limits will be discussed in more detail in Chap. 5.
4. A native of the province of Rio de Janeiro, Itaboraí was one of the three leading Conservative representatives of that province in Parliament. He formed, alongside Euzébio de Queirós and Paulino José Soares de Sousa (Visconde de Uruguai), the "Saquarema trinity", which would exercise considerable political influence in the Empire between 1840 and 1870. Itaboraí was a Mathematics graduate from the University of Coimbra, and held the Navy and Finance portfolios on many occasions. It was in the latter capacity that he gained his reputation for austerity and technical expertise, making him, arguably, the most respected authority in financial matters during the period. It was said that whenever cabinet re-shuffles occurred, the first thing financiers in London would ask was if Itaboraí had

been appointed Prime Minister or Minister of Finance, given his reputation as a firm conductor of economic policy de Lyra (1978, pp. 287–8).

5. Hereafter, *RMF*.
6. Ibid. 'What would be the use of withdrawing from circulation, at the cost of great sacrifice, five or six thousand *contos* in paper if the vacuum thus created were to be filled by an equal amount of banknotes, which also represent paper money?' (ibid., p. 37). Itaboraí was referring to Law 401 (of 11 September 1846), which established the new gold parity between the milréis and sterling at 27d (Art. 1). Article 2 authorized the government to withdraw from circulation whatever amount of paper money was necessary to keep the rate of exchange at that level.
7. Ibid., pp. 167–73.
8. This confirms the opposition's claims that the Senate bill was no more than 'a government bill in disguise'. See session of 17 June, in *Annaes da Camara dos Deputados* 1853 (hereafter, *ACD*), Tome II, p. 232.
9. See the summary of the parliamentary debates in Franco and Pacheco (1979, pp. 334–48).
10. Debate held in the Chamber of Deputies on 7 July, in *ACD* 1859, Tome III, p. 54.
11. See Table A6 in the Statistical Appendix. From 1830 to 1886, the financial year in Brazil ran from 1 July to 30 June. From 1888 onward, it would coincide with the calendar year.
12. PRO, Foreign Office, 13/303, Jerningham to the Earl of Clarendon, Rio de Janeiro, No. 34, 11 June 1853.
13. *Vales*, in turn, only circulated locally.
14. *Relatorio da Commissão de Inquerito de 1859* (undated, p. 104).
15. See Table A4 in the Statistical Appendix.
16. Mauá's Bank of Brazil was the third institution to bear that name, after the original 1808 bank, which closed its doors in 1829, and a failed attempt to incorporate a national establishment in 1833. Yet, it was the second bank actually to operate under that name.
17. Barman (1981).
18. Dividends paid out to shareholders of the Commercial fell from a high of 13.6% in 1850 to an average of less than 9% in the following three years. Cavalcanti (1893, Vol. 2, p. 152). Figures for Mauá's Bank of Brazil are incomplete and do not allow a comparison to be made.
19. 'The discount rate rose from 4–5% to 10–11% and, worse yet, both banks were so over-committed that they ceased to discount even the best paper. As their liquid assets shrank, so by their statutes the banks were forced to withdraw their credit notes from circulation, thus further shrinking the money supply' (Barman 1981, p. 245).

20. The amount of Treasury notes in circulation decreased by almost 10% between 1845 and 1850, from 50.4 thousand *contos* to 46.9 thousand *contos*. The increase in the issues of *vales* in the same period (from 600 to 1,100 *contos*) did not make up for the reduction in government legal tender in the economy. See Peláez and Suzigan (1976, Table IV.2, p. 79). Specie in circulation (estimated at 10–20 thousand *contos*) complemented the monetary base in the early 1850s.
21. Carvalho (1980, 1988).
22. For an elaboration, Gambi (2013, 2017).
23. Shortly before the act that created the third Bank of Brazil was passed, the government approved the statutes of a new bank in the city of Rio de Janeiro, the Banco Rural & Hypothecario. With a capital of 8000 *contos*, divided into 20,000 shares of 400$000 each, it had its application to engage in the issue of *vales* denied by the Council of State. The latter was a college of experienced politicians, who exercised substantial influence in the political arena. The Emperor, at the suggestion of the Prime Minister, appointed its 24 members (12 regular and 12 alternate) for life. This comprised the full Council—*Conselho Pleno*. Council members advised the monarch on the exercise of his Moderating Power, thus having a say in a host of important issues. Reports on submissions to the four standing committees (Seções) into which the Council of State was divided (Empire, Justice and Foreign Affairs, War and Navy, and Finance) often served as the basis for executive decrees. See Rodrigues, ed. (1978) (hereafter, *ACE*).
24. The activities of the Mauá, Macgregor Bank are discussed in Guimarães (2012). On the tribulations of the Barão in his relations with the imperial government throughout his long business career, see Caldeira (1995).
25. The dangers potentially arising from this provision, news of which had already been circulating before the Bank was established, did not go unnoticed by the British *Chargé d'Affaires* to the Court of Brazil. 'The Imperial Government will have the national bank more or less under their control; and if at some future period any Brazilian Minister find it convenient to abuse this power, and use it for their own ends and purposes, to the detriment of the community in general, I fear some danger may be apprehended not only for the commercial prosperity, but even perhaps for the peace and universal welfare of this Empire' (PRO, Foreign Office, 13/303, Jerningham to the Earl of Clarendon, Rio de Janeiro, No. 52, 8 July 1853).
26. As already noted, the reason for this awkward disposition stemmed from the sheer scarcity of gold in the country, which precluded the adoption of a fully gold-backed issue.
27. Tellingly, notes issued by the third Bank of Brazil bore the inscription "At the Bank of Brazil the bearer of this (note) shall be paid the amount…"

(*No Banco do Brasil se Pagará ao Portador Desta a Quantia de*, in the original). No explicit mention, therefore, of the possibility of redemption of the note into gold. See Maldonado and Antunes (2018).

28. According to the said article, 'The Government is authorized to retire from circulation the amount of paper money deemed necessary to raise and keep it at the value provided for in the preceding Article (that is, 27 pence to the milréis)'; 'for this purpose it will be allowed to undertake the necessary credit operations'. Law 401, of 11 September 1846. Brasil, Leis e Decretos, *Coleção de Leis e Decretos.*
29. Law 1223 of 31 August 1853.
30. On 1 October, the Mauá Bank started operations in Rio.
31. The newly created Bank of Brazil was also unpleased by the idea of limited partnership banks 'compet(ing) in circulation, without the burden that the Law placed on corporations in general, and on this Bank in particular'. Banco do Brasil, "Actas das Reuniões da Directoria", session No. 80, 22 August 1854, AD 001/11-A. These minutes of the meetings of the board of directors of the Bank of Brazil will henceforth be referred to as Banco do Brasil, "Actas".
32. See Resolution No. 375, 16 December 1854, in *Imperiaes Resoluções do Conselho de Estado na Seção de Fazenda* (hereafter, *SFCE*), Vol. III, pp. 352–55. It is worth noting that among the three councillors to sign the resolution was Itaboraí, the architect of the third Bank of Brazil who, from the outset, showed clear independence of opinion regarding the operations of his brainchild. For a survey of the Finance Standing Committee's deliberations on monetary matters, see Villela (2000).
33. See also Banco do Brasil, *Relatorio Apresentado á Assembléa Geral dos Accionistas do Banco do Brasil pelo Presidente do Banco* 1855, p. 4. Hereafter, Banco do Brasil, *Relatorio.*
34. By then, according to the internally appointed Bank inspectors, virtually all Treasury notes in Rio either had been exported to the interior or had found their way into the Bank's vaults (ibid., p. 7).
35. Partly due to the sheer difficulties of communication at the time, the *caixas* enjoyed considerable autonomy from the head office. Not only did they issue notes in their respective regions but they also had their own statutes and board of directors appointed by the head office. The provincial offices of the Bank of Brazil were created by Decree 1490, of 20 December 1854 (in Ouro Preto), and Decree 1580, of 21 March 1855 (in Salvador, Recife, São Luís, Belém, Porto Alegre and São Paulo). The latter decree transformed the earlier banks established in those provincial capitals into *caixas filiais* of the Bank of Brazil. The São Paulo and Porto Alegre offices of the Bank were formerly branches of the "second" (Mauá) Bank of Brazil. Given the delay in procuring notes for the *caixas*—which ended up being

imported from Britain, and still had to be signed by the respective directors—they would not start their operations until the early months of 1856. See Franco and Pacheco (1979, p. 404).

36. Decree 1581, of 2 April 1855.
37. 'It seems beyond doubt that as long as we (in Rio) cannot pay with our products those [...] which we consume from the North, or as long as the discount rate is lower in this market than in those of the said Provinces, the migration of precious metals and Government paper will go on unabated to those points in the Empire' (ibid.).
38. Early in that year the government assented to a request to allow the substitution of Bank of Brazil notes of 50$000 denomination for those of the Treasury deposited in provincial offices (*tesourarias provinciais*) and the Amortization Office (Caixa de Amortização). Banco do Brasil, "Actas", session No. 209, 7 January 1856, AD 002/11-A.
39. "Parecer da Commissão Nomeada pela Directoria do Banco do Brasil em Sessão de 22 de Abril de 1857 para Propor os Meios Mais Adequados para a Conservação do Fundo Disponível". Museu Imperial de Petrópolis, Arquivo da Casa Imperial, bundle 124, document 6202.
40. Ibid. The Bank implemented both recommendations soon afterward. The discount rate was raised from 8% to 9% on 5 May, and the rate of interest on *dinheiro a prêmio* set at 7% on 9 June.
41. Meanwhile, *vales* issued by private banks (but not joint-stock banks), businesses, and individuals would still be circulating, with major implications, as will be seen later in the book.
42. Symptomatically, the hallmark of his administration, he explained, would be conciliation, imprinting that 'spirit of moderation that is synonymous with conservative opinions'. Paraná concurrently held the Finance portfolio during the better part of the first *Conciliação* cabinet, and through a strict fiscal policy, managed to achieve a substantial budget surplus in the 1856–7 financial year. See Table A6 in the Statistical Appendix.
43. According to Nabuco, in appointing Souza Franco to head the Finance portfolio in 1857, Olinda was choosing a colleague, albeit of a different party. Most important from the point of view of subsequent events, the choice, still according to Nabuco, had been a conscious one. Olinda, who earlier had strongly criticized Paraná's *Conciliação* initiative, opted for appointing a known Liberal to a key post in the cabinet, something that his predecessor had not attempted. Surely, Souza Franco's heterodox views on banking policy could not have been lost on the old Conservative chief when he chose him for the post. For details on the whole *Conciliação* period, see Iglésias (1972) and Nabuco (1997, Vol. I, pp. 163–74). The other portfolio occupied by the Liberals was the Ministry of War, headed by Jerônimo Francisco Coelho.

44. The six new banks eventually given the go-ahead, and the dates of the decrees approving their statutes and authorizing their incorporation, are as follows: Banco Commercial & Agrícola (in the Court, on 31 August 1857); Banco Commercial do Rio Grande do Sul (based in Porto Alegre, on 24 October 1857); the Novo Banco de Pernambuco (in Recife, on 11 November 1857); Banco do Maranhão (in São Luís, on 25 November 1857); Banco da Bahia (in Salvador, on 3 April 1858); and the Banco Rural & Hypotechario (which was founded in 1853 in Rio, and to which the right to issue notes was now being granted) on 27 February 1858.
45. Law 556, of 25 July 1850.
46. Two years later, Minister of Finance Ferraz would still be referring to the problems caused by the shortage of currency in activities such as the cattle trade in the province of São Pedro do Sul, where the Bank of Brazil maintained one of its *caixas filiaes*. Still, the fact that notes from other provinces could not circulate locally did not deter *gaúcho* traders from making use of them at discounts of 3% to 4% of their face value. *RMF* 1859, p. 69.
47. On the 1857 global financial crisis, see Foreman-Peck (1983) and Kindleberger (1996).
48. Quotations in the Rio stock exchange show a stable milréis, hovering around par, until mid-December. Arrival of the steamer *Medway* in Rio on 12 December, bringing news of the increase in Bank rate to 10% in London, led to the subsequent fall in the exchange rate from 26 1/4 d to 23d. *RMF* 1857, p. 7. Exchange-rate quotations are in Arquivo Nacional, Junta de Corretores, Livro de Registro Official, various issues, P8 13, p. 203.
49. The hide trade in Rio Grande do Sul, for instance, was severely hit upon receiving news of the crisis overseas. See Parliamentary Papers 1861, LXIII, *Report by the Hon. H. P. Vereker, British Consul at Rio Grande do Sul, on the Trade of that Port during the year 1858*, p. 5.
50. Levy and Andrade (1993) and Prado (1991).
51. The Bank's directors were well aware of the challenge that lay before the institution. 'If the board of Directors of the Bank, on the one hand, was under the rigorous obligation to protect its reserve fund, on the other it was most willing to help out commerce, which [...] is wrestling with great difficulty as a result of the sudden withdrawal of the capital which used to aid it, and of the complete stagnation of exports. However, these two terms are so inter-linked when it comes to a bank of issue that the Board of Directors should see to both simultaneously and, therefore, raise the discount rate, satisfy the needs of foreign trade, and serve domestic trade liberally'. Cf. Banco do Brasil, *Relatorio* 1858, p. 6.
52. This increase should not be considered a seasonal phenomenon, as in previous years there had been little change in the Bank's portfolio at the end of the year.

53. One of the major sources of demands for loans from the Bank of Brazil at the time was the house of A. J. Alves Souto & Co., which suffered a run during the whole month of December, but managed to survive. As will be seen in the next chapter, the house of Souto would find itself at the epicenter of a major panic in 1864.
54. Session No. 332, extraordinary meeting of the Board of Directors. A similar proposal put forward by the Discount Commission of the Bank for the appreciation of the Board of Directors, on 11 November, had been rejected. See Banco do Brasil, "Actas", 1857–8, AD 003/11-A. This fact was overlooked by Cavalcanti, who maintained that suspension took place on the 11th, in which he was followed by Peláez and Suzigan; see Cavalcanti (1893, Vol. 2, p. 213) and Peláez and Suzigan (1976, p. 88).
55. These 3000 *contos* represented the amount of Treasury notes that the Bank had already withdrawn from circulation, and which, according to Article 60 of its statutes, served as a ceiling to the guarantees that the government could provide on such occasions.
56. For the full texts of the memoranda exchanged between the Bank of Brazil and the Minister of Finance, and between the latter and the Mauá, MacGregor Bank, see the Annex in *RMF* 1857, pp. 1–13.
57. See "Reserved Memorandum" from Souza Franco to José Pedro Dias de Carvalho (acting president of the Bank of Brazil), 4 December 1857, ibid., p. 6.
58. As noted by a contemporary, it was generally in the weeks between 15 June and 15 July, and 15 December and 15 January that the money market was at its tightest, because of the resources needed by the government to pay interest on its bonds (*apólices*), and by banks and other corporations, for payment of dividends. Testimony offered by an unnamed foreign businessman, in *Relatorio da Commissão de Inquerito de 1859* (undated, Annex A, p. 38).
59. Banco do Brasil, "Actas", session No. 446, 30 March 1859, AD 004/11-A.
60. The Committee was formed by Itaboraí, the Marquês de Abrantes, and the Visconde de Abaeté. Itaboraí would retain his seat in the Council of State (and its Seção de Fazenda) almost uninterruptedly from 1853 until his death in January 1872. From this position, as well as in the Senate, the Bank of Brazil, and the Ministry of Finance (which he would head again from July 1868 to September 1870), he was able to establish himself as Brazil's leading financial expert of the time, helping to shape both policy and debate on monetary and banking matters.
61. Itaboraí would repeat these arguments in a speech in the Senate on 17 April 1858. See *Annaes do Senado do Império* (henceforth, *ASI*), Tome I, pp. 85–6.

62. This assessment, of course, involved giving priority to external (exchange rate) stability, to the detriment of internal balance. The Bank of Brazil thought differently, as it was not willing to cause further hardship to the market by raising the rate of discount.
63. PRO, Foreign Office, 13/352, Scarlett to the Earl of Clarendon, Rio de Janeiro, No. 73, 13 July 1857. Speaking in the Senate on 17 May 1858, Itaboraí apologized to his colleagues for not having resigned immediately after the cabinet of May 1857 came to power and, with it, Souza Franco, 'with whose economic ideas (I) could not agree'. *ASI* 1858, Tome I, p. 82. During the same session Itaboraí and Souza Franco exchanged ironies about this point:

Itaboraí:	'I do not intend to impute all blame (for the mismanagement of the 1857 crisis) on the Bank. More appropriately, it should be ascribed to the Minister of Finance'.
Souza Franco:	'I impute it to Your Excellency's influence, for to this day you govern the Bank more than myself'.
Itaboraí:	'I will leave this aside to be judged by the public and the directors of the Bank'.
Souza Franco:	'Your Excellency is heard (there) more frequently than me' (ibid., p. 85).

On the following day, they resumed the exchanges:

Souza Franco:	'No matter what Your Excellency may say, at present you govern the Bank more than me'.
Itaboraí:	'Then, why is it that I censure its acts'?
Souza Franco:	'The father, even when he is his child's best friend, also slaps him when he deserves it. And I believe that it is the excessive love that the senator has for his child that makes him so severe' (*ASI* 1858, Tome I, p. 103).

64. Article 2 of the contract celebrated between the government and the Bank of Brazil on 29 August 1857 determined that government deposits earn a rate of interest equivalent to three percentage points below the going rate of discount practiced by the Bank. Additionally, Article 5 required the Bank and its provincial offices to charge this rate of interest when discounting Treasury bills (*letras*). See "Contracto com o Banco do Brasil para o deposito dos saldos disponiveis", in Banco do Brasil, *Relatorio* 1858, pp. 45–6.
65. Responsibility for defending the exchange rate was still a matter of dispute. For the Bank of Brazil, 'it (seemed) that in spite of the creation of (the

Bank), it (was) the government's duty to comply with the letter of the Law of 11 September 1846, and undertake the credit operations necessary to maintain the equilibrium of the exchange rate'. Cf. memorandum No. 10, in *RMF* 1857, p. 12.

66. Banco do Brasil, *Relatorio* 1858. Apparently, the directors of the bank were confident that the government would accept their counter-offer, as suggested by their decision to authorize the vice-president to prepare the operation with the sale of bills on London, pending confirmation from Souza Franco. Banco do Brasil, "Actas", session No. 365, 12 March 1857, AD 003/11-A.
67. The Bank's reluctance to cooperate was stressed by Cavalcanti (1893) and by the British *Chargé d'Affaires* in Rio, who blamed this attitude on its 'feeble Direction'. PRO, Foreign Office, 13/362, Scarlett to the Earl of Malmesbury, Rio de Janeiro, No. 38, 14 May 1858.
68. Anticipating that the amount put by the Treasury at his disposal would not be enough to sustain (let alone appreciate) the rate of exchange, the Barão gave instructions to his London office to procure more resources. Finally, he went as far as putting his own (substantial) private fortune at the service of the operation, if need be (ibid.).
69. The coffee harvest would begin in June, when the Mauá, MacGregor Bank sold the last drafts on London. Levy (1972, pp. 23–4).
70. See Table A5 in the Statistical Appendix.
71. Coffee shipments to Rio occurred throughout the year, but peaked between August and November. Sweigart (1987, p. 111).
72. An adversary of the *Conciliação* initiative, ironically, Teixeira Jr. would later marry a daughter of the Marquês de Paraná, chief architect of the attempt at reconciliation between Conservatives and Liberals in the mid-1850s. See de Lyra (1978, p. 174).
73. Speaking in the Chamber of Deputies, on 29 May, Mauá took the opportunity to reveal that before embarking on the operation to raise the rate of exchange he personally made three last-minute efforts to convince the Bank of Brazil into accepting Souza Franco's final offer to no avail (ibid., p. 150).
74. Born in the city of Rio de Janeiro in 1812, Francisco de Sales Torres Homem graduated from medical school and became a journalist under the protection of the highly respected man of the press, Evaristo da Veiga. During a stay in Europe, he was exposed to the literature on Political Economy, a topic in which he would later stand out in the Brazilian political scene, more for his raging speeches than for technical command. Originally, a fervent Liberal, author of a pamphlet (*Libelo do Povo*) which attacked the Emperor's Moderating Power like no one before, Torres Homem would switch sides and join the Conservatives in the mid-1850s,

going on to become one of the leading politicians in his new party. See de Lyra (1978, pp. 266–7).

75. Banks created by decree began issuing notes in 1858. By the end of the year, these issues amounted to 8.6 thousand *contos* or 8% of total note circulation (Treasury notes + banknotes) at the time.
76. For Cavalcanti, however, opposition to the banks created by decree arose out of 'subservience to the Bank of Brazil, a misunderstanding as to the (alleged) perils of plurality of issue or, as seems more likely, partisan reaction'. See Cavalcanti (1893, Vol. 2, p. 128). Later events lend credence to the interpretation of a political motivation behind many of the attacks on the banks of issue or, more specifically, on Souza Franco.
77. In a private letter to a friend, the Emperor clearly stated that '(he was) against the economic ideas of Souza Franco'. Pedro Calmon, cited in Caldeira (1995, p. 354).
78. Rather surprisingly, this decision did not seem to disturb the inspectors of the Bank of Brazil. As stated in their 1859 annual report, the drop in the volume of Bank notes in circulation should not be imputed to the new limit set by the government, but rather to the competition that had come about with plurality of issue. Banco do Brasil, *Relatorio dos Fiscaes* 1859, p. 5.
79. In this respect, the government was addressing, even if unwittingly, the problem posed by the drain of Treasury notes to the provinces where there were no banking institutions, as reported in Banco do Brasil, *Relatorio dos Fiscaes* 1859, p. 2. This blatant contradiction on the part of Torres Homem—who, while opposed to banks of issue, saw no harm in chartering deposit and discount banks—will be explored later in the book.
80. On the occasion, Torres Homem was criticized for presenting the bill in his capacity as a national deputy, not as Minister of Finance. As such, the bill did not need to be accompanied by any supporting documentation and explanations as to its merits. See session of 30 June, in *ACD* 1859, Tome II, p. 232.
81. Session of 6 June 1859, in *ACE*, Vol. V, pp. 95–104.
82. That was Jequitinhonha's position (ibid., p. 100). One of the longest exposés came from General João Paulo dos Santos Barreto, who offered a passionate defense of free trade, including in the realm of banking. He nevertheless admitted his ignorance about the subject under discussion, adding that most of the information he had obtained came from his son-in-law, a stockbroker in Rio (ibid., pp. 103–4).
83. Ibid., p. 101. This statement lends support to the idea that members of the Council more often than not professed a vision of the State in their meetings, rather than taking the opportunity to put forth parochial interests. In this case, Uruguai sided with hard money when clearly soft money would have helped alleviate at least part of the problems in the coffee sector.

84. The report clearly acknowledged the dual aspect of inflation on the government budget. If, on the one hand, rising prices reduced government expenditure in real terms it also corroded the real value of its tax revenues (ibid.).
85. In a sample of the monetarist tone of most early-twentieth-century authors, it was remarked that the Torres Homem bill 'soon met the greatest and rudest opposition from the advocates of inflation and a depreciated currency, who have always been numerous in Brazil'. See Ortigão (1914, p. 59).
86. In a striking "Keynesian" insight into the matter, a contemporary remarked that 'the provisions of the (Torres Homem) bill, however much they lacked the capacity to increase the value of our circulating medium directly, should bring about this desired result in an indirect way, through general impoverishment, the ruin of public and private fortune, and the retreat of industry and commerce'. Cf. Milet (1875, p. 37).
87. In the first of three voting sessions required by the statutes of the Chamber of Deputies, the bill received 61 votes in favor and 51 against. See Andrada (1923, p. 116). The Conservatives at the time held 92 seats in the lower House. As regards the discussion of the bill in Parliament, a contemporary noted that 'the support which sixty deputies and some of the most distinguished characters in the Senate have lent to the ideas of Mr. Torres Homem, in spite of the immediate harm which they bring [...], serves to show that the bill will be rejected as inopportune and in breach of the rights of the existing banks, rather than for its ineffectiveness and for being contrary to the principles of political economy' (ibid., p. 31).
88. Rio's main financial paper commented that 'the expected reaction' (to the Torres Homem bill) took place in the Chamber. 'Interests hurt by the bill reacted with the strongest possible force. Liberal opinion maintained its opposition in the name of the principles of its school, of the faith in contracts, and acquired rights. Many Conservative deputies who had supported the previous (Olinda) cabinet were convinced that they should reject the bill, as being ill suited to cure the current evils. The financial question was linked to the question of conciliation and centralization (...), as well as the dispute between the cabinet that had ceased to exist in December 1859 and its opponents'. *Jornal do Commercio*, 7 January 1861.
89. *Caixas econômicas*, or savings banks, operated by making depositors shareholders in the enterprise. In the case of those created in the province of Bahia, capital was invested mostly in urban mortgages and stocks. Interest received from these operations, net of administrative charges, was distributed semi-annually among shareholders (or depositors), in proportion to their capital. *Parecer sobre Caixas Econômicas* (1882).

90. *Metalistas* would come to designate advocates of convertibility and, more generally, of hard money, that is, monetary restraint and a high exchange. Conversely, their ideological foes, *papelistas*, sided with expansionist monetary policies, a slipping exchange, and, at times, fiduciary paper. The differences between *metalistas* and *papelistas* will be explored further in Chap. 5.
91. Ibid. The trade deficit for the 1857/58 financial year stood at £3.8 million, up £2.5 million from the year before, while service of the foreign debt remained constant at 3.7 thousand *contos* (approx. £420,000). Data on foreign trade in Brasil, IBGE (1990, p. 522). Figures (in *contos*) for foreign debt payments from *Balanços da Receita e Despeza do Imperio.*
92. There is, of course, the possibility that high interest rates and a large supply of money may coexist, given imperfections in the capital market.
93. Law 1083 of 22 August 1860. The nickname is attributed to a French author (Joseph Garnier) who, writing in 1860, first referred to it as the *Loi d'Entraves.* See Cavalcanti (1893, Vol. 2, p. 265).

References

Banco do Brasil. 1854–1870. *Relatorio Apresentado á Assembléa Geral dos Accionistas do Banco do Brasil pelo Presidente do Banco*, 1854–70.

———. 1854–1870. *Relatorio dos Fiscaes do Banco do Brasil Apresentado á Assembléa Geral dos Accionistas do Banco do Brasil*, various issues, 1854–70.

Barman, Roderick J. 1981. Business and Government in Imperial Brazil: The Experience of Viscount Mauá. *Journal of Latin American Studies* 13 (2): 239–264.

Brasil, Câmara dos Deputados, *Annaes da Camara dos Deputados*, 1850–89.

Brasil, IBGE. 1990. *Estatísticas Históricas do Brasil.* Vol. 3, 2nd ed. (séries econômicas, demográficas e sociais, 1550–1985). Rio de Janeiro: IBGE.

Brasil, Leis e Decretos, *Coleção de Leis e Decretos*, various volumes.

Brasil, Ministério da Fazenda, *Balanços da Receita e Despeza do Imperio*, 1850–89.

Brasil, Ministerio da Fazenda, *Proposta e Relatorio Apresentados á Assembléa-Geral Legislativa Pelo Ministro e Secretario d'Estado dos Negócios da Fazenda*, 1850–90.

Brasil, Senado, *Annaes do Senado do Império do Brasil*, 1850–89.

Caldeira, Jorge. 1995. *Mauá: empresário do Império.* São Paulo: Companhia das Letras.

Carreira, Liberato de C. 1980. *História Financeira e Orçamentária do Império do Brasil.* Brasília: Senado Federal/Casa de Rui Barbosa.

Cavalcanti, Amaro. 1893. *O Meio Circulante Nacional.* Rio de Janeiro: Imprensa Nacional.

de Andrada, Antonio Carlos R. 1923. *Bancos de Emissão no Brasil.* Rio de Janeiro: Editora Leite Ribeiro.

de Carvalho, José Murilo. 1980. *A Construção da Ordem: a elite política imperial.* Rio de Janeiro: Campus.

———. 1988. *Teatro de Sombras: a política imperial.* Rio de Janeiro: Vértice/IUPERJ.

de Lyra, Augusto T. 1978. *Instituições Políticas do Império.* Brasília: Senado Federal, Editora da Universidade de Brasília.

Fallas do Throno Desde o Anno de 1823 até o Anno de 1872, acompanhadas dos respectivos votos de graças da câmara temporária e de differentes informações e esclarecimentos colligidas na secretaria da Câmara dos Senhores Deputados. 1872. Rio de Janeiro: Typographia Nacional.

Foreman-Peck, James. 1983. *A History of the World Economy: International Relations Since 1850.* London: Harvester Wheatsheaf.

Franco, Afonso A. de M., and Claudio Pacheco. 1979. *História do Banco do Brasil.* Brasília: Banco do Brasil.

Gambi, Thiago F.R. 2013. *O Banco da Ordem: política e finanças no Império brasileiro (1853–1866).* São Paulo: Alameda.

———. 2017. Bancos Nacionais do Brasil: os casos de 1808 e 1853. In *Historia Bancaria y Monetaria de América Latina (siglos XIX y XX): nuevas perspectivas*, ed. Carlos Marichal and Thiago Gambi, 63–100. Santander: Editorial de la Universidad de Cantabria.

Guimarães, Carlos Gabriel. 1998. *Bancos, Economia e Poder no Segundo Reinado: o caso da Sociedade Bancária Mauá, MacGregor & Companhia (1854–1866).* Ph.D. dissertation, Universidade de São Paulo.

———. 2012. *A Presença Inglesa nas Finanças e no Comércio do Brasil Imperial: os casos da Sociedade Bancária Mauá, MacGregor & Cia. (1854–1866) e da firma inglesa Samuel Phillips & Cia. (1808–1840).* São Paulo: Alameda.

Iglésias, Francisco. 1972. Vida Política, 1848/1868. In *História Geral da Civilização Brasileira*, Tome II, ed. Sergio B. de Holanda, vol. 5, 9–132. São Paulo: Difel.

Imperiaes Resoluções do Conselho de Estado na Secção de Fazenda, desde o anno em que começou a funccionar o mesmo conselho até o presente. Rio de Janeiro, Typographia Nacional, 12 vols.

Jornal do Commercio. Rio de Janeiro.

Junta de Corretores de Fundos Públicos da Cidade do Rio de Janeiro. Livro de Registro Official de Cotações de Títulos e Valores, 1850–70.

Kindleberger, Charles P. 1996. *Manias, Panics and Crashes: A History of Financial Crises.* 3rd ed. London: Macmillan.

Legislação Sobre Papel Moeda. 1923. Rio de Janeiro: Imprensa Nacional.

Levy, Maria Barbara. 1972. *História dos Bancos Comerciais no Brasil (estudo preliminar).* Rio de Janeiro: IBMEC, mimeo.

Levy, Maria Barbara, and Ana Maria R. de Andrade. 1993. El Sector Financiero y El Desarollo Bancario en Río de Janeiro (1850–1888). In *La Economia*

Financiera y la Formación de la Banca Central en España y Latinoamerica, ed. Carlos Marichal and Pedro Tedde. Madrid: Banco de España.

Maldonado, Rodrigo, and Fernando Antunes. 2018. *Livro de Todas as Emissões do Papel-Moeda no Brasil (Colônia, Reino Unido, Império e República)*. Naples: Bentes.

Milet, Henrique Augusto. 1875. *O Meio Circulante e a Questão Bancária*. 2nd ed. Recife: Typographia do Jornal do Recife.

Nabuco, Joaquim. 1997. *Um Estadista do Império*. 5th ed. Rio de Janeiro: Topbooks.

Ortigão, Ramalho. 1914. *A Moeda Circulante no Brazil*. Rio de Janeiro: Typographia do Jornal do Commercio.

Pacheco, Claudio. 1979. *História do Banco do Brasil*. Brasília: Banco do Brasil.

Parecer sobre Caixas Econômicas e Montes de Socorro. 1882. Rio de Janeiro: Typographia Nacional.

Peláez, Carlos Manuel, and Wilson Suzigan. 1976. *História Monetária do Brasil*. 2nd ed. Brasília: Editora da Universidade de Brasília.

Prado, Luis Carlos T. D. 1991. Commercial Capital, Domestic Market and Manufacturing in Imperial Brazil: The Failure of Economic Development in the XIXth Century. Ph.D. dissertation, University of London.

Relatorio da Commissão de Inquerito Nomeada por Aviso do Ministério da Fazenda, de 10 de Outubro de 1859, undated.

Relatorio da Commissão Encarregada pelo Governo Imperial por Aviso do Primeiro de Outubro e 28 de Dezembro de 1864, de Proceder a um Inquerito Sobre as Causas Principais e Accidentaes da Crise do Mez de Setembro de 1864. 1865. Rio de Janeiro: Typographia Nacional.

Ribeiro, Benedito, and Mário M. Guimarães. 1967. *História dos Bancos e do Desenvolvimento Financeiro do Brasil*. São Paulo: Pró-Service.

Rodrigues, José H., ed. 1978. *Atas do Conselho de Estado*. Brasília: Senado Federal.

Soares, Sebastião Ferreira. 1865. *Esboço ou Primeiros Traços da Crise Commercial da Cidade do Rio de Janeiro em 10 de Setembro de 1864*. Rio de Janeiro: Laemmert.

Sweigart, Joseph E. 1987. *Coffee Factorage and the Emergence of a Brazilian Capital Market, 1850–1888*. New York: Garland Publishing.

Villela, André A. 2000. Brazil in Mid-Empire: The Council of State and the Banking Question, 1850–1870. *Estudos Economicos* 30 (4): 629–651.

CHAPTER 3

From the "Law of Impediments" to Restoration of Monopoly: 1860–6

3.1 *Metalistas* Win the Day: The 1860 Law

As seen in the previous chapter, the cabinet that replaced the *Conciliação* proceeded to reverse the liberal banking policies promoted in 1857 by Souza Franco. To that effect, the new Minister of Finance, Torres Homem, presented a bill to the Chamber directed at reducing the existing issue of banknotes and restoring convertibility. His decision to file the bill in his capacity as a national deputy, rather than as an initiative of the new cabinet, did not go down well in Parliament. Deputies, many of them from the Conservative majority, felt that the Legislative had been side-lined in its duty to examine measures emanating from the Executive. On 15 June 1859, the Chamber held a vote on a petition requiring that the bill be sent to the Civil Justice Commission. Filed by Martinho Campos, a Liberal deputy from Rio de Janeiro, it won by 36 votes to 33. The Conservative majority, taken aback by the result, accused the opposition of procrastination (*ACD* 1859, Tome II, p. 136).[1] Deputy Fernandes da Cunha (Bahia) replied by stating that the Torres Homem bill was nothing but a 'party law' (ibid., p. 79).[2] Parliamentary resistance to the banking bill ultimately led to the downfall of the Abaeté cabinet. Ângelo Muniz da Silva Ferraz was called in to form a new government.

Despite opposition, the Torres Homem bill was eventually approved in the Chamber and was sent over to the Senate, where it was amended. As well as the article concerning banks of issue, the new version of the bill included

A. A. Villela, *The Political Economy of Money and Banking in Imperial Brazil, 1850–1889*, Palgrave Studies in the History of Finance, https://doi.org/10.1007/978-3-030-32774-3_3

measures dealing with joint-stock companies, savings banks, and the minting of a new family of copper coins.[3] Back in the lower House of Parliament, Deputy Martinho Campos maintained his opposition to the bill, even in its revised version. He argued that it was no more than an attempt to alter the Commercial Code disguised as an amendment to the Torres Homem bill (*ACD* 1860, Tome III, p. 66).[4] Yet, overall, reaction in the Chamber this time was less hostile. Deputies who had voted against the Torres Homem proposal now claimed to be happy to support the amended bill, which had become more "palatable".[5] The new bill did away with the demand that convertibility of banknotes be resumed within three years. In addition, while the original proposal unilaterally imposed reductions in outstanding note issues, the new version provided for an agreement between banks and the government as to the rate of withdrawal, thus respecting banks' rights. In the end, the bill was approved by a comfortable margin of forty-nine votes (seventy votes to twenty-one) to become the Law of Impediments.[6]

Law 1083 was promulgated on 22 August 1860. It contained 'measures concerning banks of issue, the circulating medium and various corporations and partnerships'. In an attempt to reaffirm provisions from the 1850 Commercial Code, the Law determined that joint-stock companies would be heavily fined if found to be operating without official authorization (Art. 2). The Law of Impediments also regulated the operations of *caixas econômicas* and philanthropic pension societies (*monte-pios*), as well as providing for the replacement of copper coins in circulation.

The main items in Law 1083 relating specifically to the operation of the banks of issue mirrored the spirit of the earlier Torres Homem bill that had caused so much controversy in the Assembly. For example, on the question of the limits imposed on banks' outstanding issues, the new law considered an average of the first semester of 1860, instead of the average obtained in the February–May 1859 period, in the Torres Homem version. Paragraph 7, imposing a government-appointed inspector to the banks of issue, also mirrored the 1859 bill. Similarly, the Law retained the objective set out in paragraph 7 of the earlier bill, which aimed at clearing up the controversial question of primacy in approving legislation governing banks of issue. This was an attempt to avoid a repetition of the episodes of 1857, when the Executive power alone legislated on the creation of new establishments. Paragraph 5 of the Law of Impediments, in turn, introduced the threat of bankruptcy for issuing banks that failed to ensure note redemption, a provision long established in the United States.[7] Finally, paragraph 10 determined that it would be up to Parliament alone to grant banks, other businesses or individuals the right to issue 'notes, bills, *vales*, paper or bond of any kind payable to the bearer'.

Decree 2685 laid down a timetable for banks to adapt to the new issuing limits. Banks created by decree in 1857 and 1858 were required to conform to the average issue observed in the first semester of 1860 (totaling just over 14,300 *contos*), unless they succeeded in resuming convertibility. The Bank of Brazil (head office + *caixas filiais*), in turn, was limited to its average issues counting from the day it started operations, that is, to 38,953 *contos*. The former had five months from the date of Decree 2685 to adjust their issues to the limits shown in Article 1, paragraph 4. As to the Bank of Brazil, if by February 1861 its paper was still inconvertible, it would be forced to retire from circulation notes of smaller denomination (Art. 4).[8] Finally, if convertibility had not been restored after nine months, all banks would have to negotiate with the government a timetable for reduction of their note issues (Art. 6).

The new legislation, essentially, sought to restore a fully gold-backed circulation as soon as possible. With that in mind, Law 1083 and Decree 2685 capped the issue of private banknotes for as long as they remained inconvertible. In other words, should banks be capable of restoring convertibility into gold (and not gold or Treasury notes, as had been the case before) these limits would not apply.

One way to assess the impact of the Law of Impediments and Decree 2685 on the issues of banknotes is by comparing the new limits to the outstanding note circulation at the time. In December 1860, one month after Decree 2685 laid down the precise limits to note issues, the total volume of banknotes outstanding was 51.8 thousand *contos*, which was less than the 53.3 thousand *contos* allowed by the new Decree (39 thousand *contos* for the Bank of Brazil and the remaining 14.3 thousand *contos* in notes issued by the smaller banks). In other words, banks could still issue an additional 1500 *contos* in inconvertible notes and remain within the legal limits imposed by the government. Instead, eight months later (in August 1861), total banknotes outstanding had dropped to 46,000 *contos*.

At the time the Law of Impediments was implemented (August 1860), total notes outstanding (which included both banknotes and Treasury paper) were just short of 90,000 *contos*, with private notes accounting for more than half of this amount.[9] By December 1860, total note circulation had changed very little, as the minor drop in Treasury notes in circulation was compensated for by the increase in the volume of banknotes. It was only in 1861 that total notes outstanding fell (by some 9% to 82,000 *contos*) (Table 3.1).

Table 3.1 Brazil: total notes outstanding, by issuer: 1858–61. (in *contos*)

	Dec 1858	*Aug 1859*	*Dec 1859*	*Aug 1860*	*Dec 1860*	*Aug 1861*	*Dec 1861*
Bank of Brazil	41,936.8	39,086.6	40,861.9	36,457.0	38,816.2	32,762.1	33,390.1
Head office	22,125.5	20,172.7	21,889.8	19,331.2	22,626.3	17,245.2	18,131.9
caixas filiais	19,811.3	18,913.9	18,972.1	17,125.8	16,189.9	15,516.9	15,258.2
Comm. & Agric.	5790.2	7137.9	7237.9	7237.9	7237.9	7237.9	7237.9
B. da Bahia	1287.5	3012.5	3200.0	2405.8	2.207.8	2316.5	2560.3
Novo Banco de Pernambuco	1460.0	2000.0	1466.0	1490.0	1490.0	1485.9	1474.2
B. do Maranhão	430.0	680.0	680.0	400.0	200.0	249.0	256.0
B. do R. Grande do Sul	–	14.0	0.8	X	X	X	X
B. Rural & Hypot.	–	2000.0	1926.0	1966.0	1903.0	1988.5	1984.7
Total Banks (a)	50,904.5	53,931.0	55,372.6	49,956.7	51,854.9	46,039.9	46,903.2
Treasury (b)	41,664.7	41,200.0[a]	40,700.6	39,400.0[a]	37,599.9	36,300.0[a]	35,108.4
Total (a + b)	92,569.2	95,131.0[a]	96,073.2	89,356.7[a]	89,454.8	82,339.9[a]	82,011.6

Sources: For Bank of Brazil: Banco do Brasil, ***Relatorio da Commissão de Inquerito de*** 1859 (undated); and ***Relatorio da Commissão de Inquerito de 1864*** (1865). Treasury notes in ***Legislação Sobre Papel Moeda*** (1923)

Note: X Issues of the Banco do Rio Grande do Sul had declined to just 10$000

[a]Estimates

Contemporaries had real grounds to oppose the government's attempt at restoring convertibility—the ultimate objective of Law 1083 and Decree 2685. The reason was that the rules imposed on the existing banks of issue were virtually impossible to comply with in practice, given the scarcity of gold. In fact, apart from the Bank of Brazil and, later, the Novo Banco de Pernambuco, no other bank would opt for declaring full convertibility of their notes. As a result, they were either forced to undertake a gradual reduction of their outstanding circulation or forego their issuing rights altogether. Most of those that opted out of instituting a fully gold-back circulation did so for good reasons. Convertibility would have meant that these banks, while still being required to accept Treasury notes, would not be allowed to give Treasury paper in exchange for banknotes presented to them for redemption. In giving gold in exchange for their notes, issuing banks would have to make increasing use of metallic currency, leading to a depreciation of Treasury paper.[10]

As expected, the Bank of Brazil was thoroughly unhappy with the new legislation. Its board of directors commissioned five of its major shareholders, including Mauá and the private banker Antônio José Alves Souto, to look into the matter. The presence of Mauá and Souto in the commission—two advocates of expansionist monetary policies—showed up in the final report published in 1861.[11] The main point in the report referred to the illegal nature of the 1860 legislation, given that it unilaterally altered crucial provisions of the 1853 contract signed between the government and the Bank. Furthermore, the authors noted that among the changes implemented by the government was the requirement that the Bank move toward introducing convertibility of its notes exclusively into gold, when its statutes expressly authorized it to redeem its notes into either gold or paper money.

The fundamental contradiction inherent in the 1860 Law was clearly perceived by the shareholder commission. As just noted, while the government required convertibility of Bank of Brazil notes into gold, its own currency (Treasury notes) remained inconvertible.[12] In essence, the government was demanding that the Bank help it bring the rate of exchange back to par, although approximately 40% of the currency in circulation was made up of notes issued by the Treasury, not the Bank (Banco do Brasil, *Parecer Apresentado á Assembléa* 1861, p. 13).[13] Clearly, the Bank would be at a disadvantage if forced to accept (government) paper money while being required to give gold in exchange for its own notes (ibid., pp. 6–7). Finally, on the question of the privileges and obligations with which the Bank was entrusted in 1853, the commission admitted that the establishment had benefited from having its notes accepted in tax offices, as well as being exempt from the payment of stamp duty. On the negative side, however, the Bank claimed that the requirement that it withdraw from circulation 10,000 *contos* in Treasury notes, interest-free, for the duration of its thirty-year contract, amounted to a foregone revenue estimated at 46,000 *contos* at the going rates of interest (ibid., p. 10).

The government was not convinced by these arguments and the 1860 *Relatorio da Fazenda* was happy to inform that all existing banks of issue immediately adjusted their operations to comply with the limits set out in Decree 2685. Banks created by government decree in 1857 and 1858 took advantage of Article 5 of the new decree and proceeded to swap the railway shares which served as guarantees to their issues for *apólices*. Ultimately, these bonds could be sold by the banks and used to purchase gold in order to build up their metallic fund (*RMF* 1860, p. 17).

In April 1861, the Bank of Brazil finished withdrawing the last lot of Treasury notes, as mandated by the 1853 Law. These 10,000 *contos*, as already noted, would be repaid, interest-free, upon expiry of the Bank's charter. From then on, each additional instalment (of 2000 *contos* annually) would correspond to a loan to the government, receiving quarterly interest. The burden of phasing out the remaining Treasury paper in circulation would now fall on the government. It would have either to rely on budget surpluses or resort to the issue of *apólices* in order to pay the Bank for this service (*RMF* 1861, p. 26).

In the meantime, the Rural & Hypothecario and the Commercial & Agrícola, under great pains to comply with the limits set out in Decree 2685, began talks with the Bank of Brazil with a view to transferring their issuing powers to the larger bank. If successful, this would make the Bank of Brazil the sole issuer in the capital.

Plans to reinstate the monopoly of note issue (at least in Rio) began circulating in the Bank of Brazil in April 1861, but failed to draw much enthusiasm from its directors (Pacheco 1979, Vol. II, pp. 170–1). Meanwhile, and as mandated by the new legislation, the Bank was required to start retiring its notes at a rate of 3% a year from August 1861 onward.[14] This was a result of its incapacity to resume convertibility of its notes due to the shortage of specie in the provinces.[15]

In early 1862, the question of a merger with the Banco Commercial & Agrícola, which would partly compensate the reduction of the Bank's note circulation, was again brought up. This time the directors of the Bank of Brazil nominated a commission to look into an offer to be made to the two other issuing banks in the capital (the Rural & Hypothecario and the Commercial & Agrícola) to cede their issuing rights to the Bank.[16]

The commissioners were keen to point out the advantages that would accrue to the Bank of Brazil in having the Commercial & Agrícola leave the market:

> The Bank frees itself of a competitor that immediately retires from circulation 7.237:900$. And since neither the government, nor any private establishment, can issue notes that might fill the vacuum left by the notes of the Banco Agrícola, then clearly it is 7.237:900$ that the Bank of Brazil must issue and circulate, thus augmenting its own portfolio.
>
> Without discussing the great questions related to banking unity and looking at the agreement [...] solely from the point of view of the Bank's interests, it is evident that it has a lot to gain from the liquidation of the Banco Agrícola. It is of the Bank's interest, and duty, to constitute itself, as far as possible, as the regulator of the circulating medium and, in this regard, the difficulties arising from competition are as manifest as the advantages that come with liberty of action.[17]

Having decided in favor of acquiring the issuing rights of the other two banks, the directors forwarded a proposal to the government. After hearing both the Finance Standing Committee of the Council of State and, afterward, the Conselho Pleno, it was decided that the Legislative branch should give the final blessing to any such deal (*ACE*, Vol. V, pp. 278–94).[18] A bill was thus presented to the Chamber of Deputies and approved with few changes and virtually without debate. In the Senate, however, it attracted harsh criticisms from Souza Franco, who claimed that it only served to lend credence to allegations that the recent legislation was meant to drive the competitors of the Bank of Brazil out of the market (Pacheco 1979, Vol. II, pp. 177–80).[19]

These allegations notwithstanding, the proposal was approved after two more sessions of debates in the Senate, and the final decree regulating the deal was issued on 9 September 1862.[20] In essence, it entailed an increase in the Bank's capital (from 30,000 to 33,000 *contos*), the liquidation of the Commercial & Agrícola, the cession of the issuing rights of the Rural & Hypothecario to the Bank of Brazil, and the withdrawal of the notes of the two smaller banks from circulation. In return, the Commercial & Agrícola received Bank of Brazil shares, and the Rural & Hypothecario would be paid 400 *contos* to relinquish its note-issuing activities, although it would continue to operate as a deposit and discount bank (Peláez and Suzigan 1976, p. 103).

Just as the decree was being signed, in September 1862, the city of Rio experienced a dress rehearsal of what would later turn out to be the major commercial crisis in the history of the Empire. A seasonal drain of specie, once again, was credited with causing illiquidity in the capital's money market. Resources were being channeled to finance the booming cotton sector in the province of Maranhão, which had benefited from the outbreak of the American Civil War and the disruption it caused to US exports of the staple (Schulz 1996, pp. 41–2). Several private banks (*casas bancárias*) in Rio went under, and those that survived required the assistance of more liquid institutions in the market (ibid., p. 42).[21]

In the meantime, the deal struck between the Bank of Brazil and its competitors in Rio gave it some breathing space but not enough of it to allow complacency. On 23 October 1862, the Bank finally resumed convertibility. However, given its difficulty in procuring gold for the reserve fund, and in view of the increasing volume of Treasury bills (*letras*) it was being asked to discount, the limits on its issues were fast being approached.[22] At the end of 1862, the Bank once again sought permission from the government to increase its leverage from 2:1 to 3:1, to no immediate effect.[23]

As feared, on 31 December the combined issues of the head office and the *caixas filiais* in Ouro Preto and São Paulo stood at 25.8 thousand *contos*, 1.3 thousand more than permitted.[24] This excess would remain until 28 February 1863, when Decree 3054 finally allowed the Bank to expand total issues to three times the reserve fund.[25] The government insisted that this was a temporary measure, to last for six months, until conditions improved. At the same time, the decree forbade the Bank from increasing the rate of discount so as not to cause further distress to the market. This was a marked shift from earlier occasions, when interest-rate hikes were invariably prescribed to deal with monetary pressures.

The Bank gladly welcomed the first part of the decree, concerning the expansion of its issuing limit, but staunchly opposed any official curb on its autonomy to set interest rates (Pacheco (1979, Vol. II, pp. 188–9). After all, it considered the fixing of discount rates primarily as a commercial decision, which had to be taken with the interests of its shareholders in mind and, secondarily, in light of the needs of the market. This position did not go down well with the government and, because of it, the Emperor referred the matter to the Council of State's 12-member Conselho Pleno.

The three points on which the councilors were asked to deliberate were: (i) should restrictions on the interest rates charged by the Bank be lifted; (ii) if not, would an increase in interest rates be the best way to discourage redemption of the notes of the Bank; and (iii) should the Bank be allowed to suspend convertibility in order to diffuse the current pressure on its reserve fund?[26] All of the councilors, including Cândido Batista (President of the Bank), were opposed to suspension of convertibility, insisting that it should only be used in an emergency. Points (i) and (ii) were, in essence, linked, and most members voted for the outright revoking of Decree 3054, thus taking the Bank back to its original 2:1 limit, on 16 March.[27]

After tempers cooled, the Bank once again approached the government, pointing out the difficulties that a prompt return to the lower limit on its note issues would cause to the market. At the same time, the Bank insisted on obtaining the proposed increase in its issuing powers. In response, the government showed sympathy to the idea of proceeding back to the lower limit slowly. However, it adamantly refused to accede to the renewed demands for the 3:1 ratio, lest this jeopardize the strategy of eventually achieving a fully backed circulation in the Empire once all inconvertible Treasury notes had been retired.[28] Shortly afterward, the Bank was back within the legal limits on its note issues as a consignment of gold coins imported from Britain bolstered its reserve fund (Banco do Brasil, *Relatorio* 1863, p. 7).

February 1863 saw the arrival of the first foreign bank in Brazil, the London and Brazilian Bank, followed in July of the same year by the Brazilian and Portuguese Bank (later renamed as the English Bank of Rio de Janeiro).[29] Even though these banks did not engage in issuing notes, they would play an important role in the Brazilian market. As pioneers of "modern" and comparatively conservative banking principles in a backward market, they emphasized high cash reserves and the need for self-liquidating loans[30]:

> Discounts were to be confined to paper with no more than three months to run, bearing two good names and a guarantee from a third party. The renewal of bills beyond their normal tenure was prohibited. Under no circumstances were advances to be made against growing crops, and if goods were pledged as securities, no advance was to exceed two-thirds of their market value. (Joslin 1963, p. 67)

This overcautious approach to business, in an environment where personal relations (and a "man's word") were common practice, definitely helped to estrange foreign bankers from most of the local community. More importantly, it frustrated the hopes of those contemporaries who expected a lot from these banks. Contrary to what many had anticipated, foreign banks brought little outside capital into the country and, once established, proceeded to attract business from existing banks. Finally, their short-term lending, in line with the best practice of British commercial banks, was deemed unfit for the needs of a capital-poor economy like Brazil.[31]

On 18 May 1863, shortly after the London and Brazilian Bank began its operations, additional signs of what would be a major financial crisis were looming on the horizon. The *casa bancária* of Antônio José Alves Souto & Cia. (Casa Souto), Rio's largest non-corporate private bank, sent an urgent request to the Bank of Brazil. It asked for the 'necessary amount (of money) to satisfy the commitments of that day, given that the resources with which it was counting were not forthcoming'.[32] In spite of the reluctance of some directors, who pointed to Souto's virtual insolvency, the Bank raised their credit limit from 14 thousand to 20 thousand *contos* (from £1.6 to £2.3 million).[33]

For much of the remainder of 1863 and well into 1864 the minutes of the meetings of the directors of the Bank of Brazil reveal little but discussions over the day-to-day operations of the Bank, the exception being allegations of mismanagement in the operation of some of its *caixas filiais*.[34] This state of relative tranquility was reflected in the introductory remarks to the report of the commission that investigated the subsequent events of September 1864[35]:

> Commerce in general had been undergoing a liquidation of sorts, and after continuous suffering and losses, it had adopted a more solid system, and arrived at a relatively more prosperous state. Alongside moderate imports, there were sufficient exports; arrears were on the decline and commerce displayed a satisfactory aspect. Our general import and export trade with foreign countries increased 13.92% in 1863–4, compared to 1862–3. Public taxes collected in the Court and province of Rio de Janeiro in 1863–4 [...] amounted to 28 thousand *contos*, an increase of 3.5 thousand on the year before. Prices of foodstuffs had not increased. If there was not money in abundance (to use the popular expression), at least no shortage of capital was being felt.[36]

At least on the surface things appeared calm as far as the economy was concerned. At the political level, however, the remarkable ministerial instability that followed the end of the *Conciliação* period continued. After a humiliating defeat for the Conservatives in the parliamentary elections of January 1864, when they were left with just a single deputy in the Chamber, the Olinda cabinet resigned. This opened the way for the return to power of Zacarias de Góis e Vasconcellos (in the so-called Progressive League). This time, his tenure in office lasted eight months, after which a Liberal government was installed, on 31 August, under the leadership of Francisco José Furtado.

3.2 The Souto Crisis and Its Aftermath

Shortly after the Furtado cabinet had taken office, the city of Rio de Janeiro was hit by the worst commercial crisis in its history. At around 10 a.m. on 10 September, and without prior notice, José Antônio Alves de Souto suspended operations at his bank, in the center of town. The news soon spread to the rest of the city, leading to a run on other *casas bancárias*. At 3:00 p.m., a mass of people had gathered in the financial district of Rio de Janeiro, at the Rua Direita, demanding prompt redemption of bills issued by the main banks. Police were called to ensure the safety of bankers and prevent disturbances.[37]

The Bank of Brazil, unlike most other houses, was not subject to a run. Gold withdrawals from its reserve fund on 10 September amounted to just over five *contos*. On that day it did, however, act as a lender of last resort, helping *casas bancárias* to the tune of 2870 *contos*, most of which was taken up by the house of Montenegro, Lima & Co.[38] Unlike the events of 1857, the Bank of Brazil was keenly aware of its crucial position in the Rio money market. Accordingly, it spared no efforts in providing discounting facilities for institutions experiencing hardship. At the same time, it sought support from the government in allowing a relaxation of the limits on note issues and the suspension of convertibility (Banco do Brasil, *Relatorio* 1865, pp. 5–12).

Contemporaries initially claimed that the Bank of Brazil precipitated the crisis by refusing to advance Souto a 'mere 900 *contos*' to help it settle its commitments on that fateful September day (*Relatorio da Commissão de Inquerito de 1864* (1865, Annex, p. 52). This is not an accurate description of the events. The minutes of the extraordinary meeting of the board of directors of the Bank of Brazil, convened on 10 September at 2:00 p.m., reveal that the house of Souto had never asked the Bank to advance that amount. Instead, they show that Souto had simply approached an inspector of the Bank (Mr. Coelho de Castro) and sought his advice on how to proceed in face of its adversities, to which Castro replied with the recommendation that Souto suspend operations.[39] The extraordinary board meeting decided that the Bank suggest to the government the liquidation of the Casa Souto, under the supervision of its main creditors. The Bank felt that small investors should have priority in receiving their money, after which the remaining creditors would attempt to agree on conditions for the final liquidation. To that end, the Bank would be willing to receive on deposit the outstanding bills of small investors, paying interest at 5% p.a. Should creditors instead prefer prompt payment, it would advance them the money, so long as the government guaranteed the Bank the corresponding 5% interest. Finally, the Bank said that it was only awaiting a signal from the government before proceeding to help smaller creditors (Pacheco 1979, Vol. II, p. 215).

The next day, the president of the Bank of Brazil presented this proposition to the recently appointed Prime Minister, Francisco José Furtado. After hearing the joint session of the Finance and Justice standing committees of the Council of State, the government stated that it was in principle sympathetic to the idea and would do its utmost to help the Bank. However, it claimed that it could not go ahead with the liquidation, for this would give rise to a conflict among the 'constituted powers'.[40] Later that night, the Ministers of Finance and Agriculture went over to the headquarters of the Bank of Brazil. Although acknowledging the gravity of the situation, they argued that the government could not commit itself to any "extra-legal" rescue operation unless the Bank could assure them of the final success. Obviously, it could not guarantee such a thing, and the meeting ended at 2:00 a.m. on 12 September without any decision being made.[41]

During the course of that day, renewed appeals were made to the imperial government to take action to quell the panic. Once again, the official position was one of indecision. The next day, crowds gathered at the doors of the Bank of Brazil and demanded prompt redemption of its notes in gold. In a further sign of the extent of the panic, several *casas bancárias* were forced to shut down that day, signaling their incapacity to honor payments any longer. At the sight of the throng outside, which prevented the entrance of its president, and in the face of a clamor for gold that threatened its reserves, the Bank once again turned to the government. This time it requested the 'suspension of all payments in this market for 30 days, in view of the extraordinary and abnormal circumstances, so as to allow for, in the meantime, the adoption of the necessary measures demanded by commerce'.[42]

The Bank of Brazil claimed that the sheer amount of discounts it had performed over the previous two days (close to 13,000 *contos*) could not be kept up for long without a severe loss of gold.[43] Furthermore, and in order to allow it to carry on its rediscounting operations for the *casas bancárias*, the Bank also sought an extension of its issuing limit to three times the value of the reserve fund.[44] The government allowed an increase in the Bank's leverage, through Decree 3306, of 13 September.[45] On 14 September, suspension of convertibility was also decreed for the time being, and Bank of Brazil notes were made legal tender in the provinces where they had been issued.[46]

On 15 September, the Bank of Brazil and the Rural & Hypothecario sent a joint petition to the Emperor. They proposed that while the Legislative did not convene extraordinarily, the government supervise the process of liquidating banks with liabilities in excess of 10,000 *contos* and that had closed their doors (*Relatorio da Commissão de Inquerito de 1864* 1865, Annex, p. 36). In other words, both banks were urging the government to take an administrative act in order to tackle the crisis of confidence in the market. On the same day, the views of the Justice and Finance standing committees of the Council of State were heard informally by the Emperor (Nabuco 1997, Vol. I, p. 468). On the occasion, commissioners refused to sanction a step that would have implied going against commercial law, which established that it was up to the courts to rule on similar matters.

As tension in the market (and on the streets of Rio) rose, the Emperor decided to turn once again to his councilors in search of guidance. This time, the Justice and Finance Committee agreed with the suggestions put forth by the Bank of Brazil and the Rural & Hypothecario. The Conselho Pleno was held on the same day (16 September) at 9 p.m. and endorsed the opinion of the Committee. It involved enacting provisional rules for the liquidation of private banks, the appointment of inspectors to oversee liquidations, and the adoption of a thirty- to sixty-day moratorium on both bankruptcies and the payment of bills, *vales*, and other commercial paper (*ACE*, Vol. V, pp. 393–7). Accordingly, on 17 September, the government issued Decree 3308, mandating a sixty-day moratorium on all payments in the Court and province of Rio de Janeiro.

This was one of the most controversial measures taken by the government because it ran counter to the letter of the Commercial Code. In practice, it prevented creditors from claiming their assets, while sheltering both bona fide and unscrupulous bankers from these very claims.[47]

Subsequently, Decree 3309, of 20 September, regulated bankruptcies of both joint-stock banks (*bancos*) and, especially, private banks (*casas bancárias*).[48] The usual provisions of the Commercial Code did not cover the latter, which goes to show that the new legislation was attempting to address the special needs of the hour.

On 26 September, the Bank of Brazil raised its discount rate from 8% to 9%, then to 10% on 8 October, where it remained until 12 April 1865.[49] In parallel, this time it unequivocally embarked on a monetary expansion. Unlike events during the 1857 crisis, suspension of convertibility and liberal lending became the official strategy in 1864.[50] As a result, between August and September, the total amount of Bank of Brazil notes in circulation increased by 30%, to 62.7 thousand *contos* (Table 3.2).

Most of the increase in outstanding note issues was accounted for by the operations of the head office of the Bank, which also discounted the bulk of commercial paper.[51] The private bank of Bahia & Irmãos, for example, discounted approximately 10,000 *contos* with the Bank. The Rural & Hypothecario, Mauá, MacGregor, and Gomes & Filhos received, each, more than 5000 *contos* from the Bank in order to meet the run on

Table 3.2 Bank of Brazil: notes in circulation and portfolio balances, July 1864–June 1865 (in *contos*)

Date	*Head office*		Caixas Filiais		*Total*	
	Notes in circulation	*Portfolio balances*	*Notes in circulation*	*Portfolio balances*	*Notes in circulation*	*Portfolio balances*
31 Jul 1864	25,260.5	37,831.3	23,785.1	4447.3	49,045.6	42,278.6
31 Aug	25,167.3	38,310.4	23,152.8	4326.3	48,320.1	42,636.7
30 Sep	42,333.4	67,082.3	20,394.4	4450.8	62,727.8	71,533.1
31 Oct	45,790.9	68,430.7	20,866.2	5028.3	66,657.1	73,513.0
30 Nov	45,035.5	68,408.6	22,042.2	5341.2	67,077.7	73,749.8
31 Dec	43,168.0	63,975.6	23,270.5	6025.0	66,438.5	70,000.6
31 Jan 1865	40,126.2	59,536.0	25,443.2	5876.4	65,569.4	65,412.4
28 Feb	39,605.6	62,232.9	26,216.1	5772.7	65,821.7	68,005.6
31 Mar	41,636.6	65,722.1	26,913.4	6483.2	68,550.0	72,205.3
30 Apr	44,523.2	69,158.0	27,424.2	5819.0	71,947.4	74,977.0
31 May	44,437.4	69,260.7	27,753.6	5554.3	72,191.0	74,815.0
30 Jun	45,139.4	74,237.6	n.a.	n.a.	n.a.	n.a.

Source: Banco do Brasil, *Relatorio Apresentado á Assembléa Geral dos Accionistas*, 1865 and 1866

Note: n.a. = data not available

their own tills (*Relatorio da Commissão de Inquerito de 1864* 1865, p. 73).[52] The Bank's portfolio, as a result, increased by nearly 70% between August and September 1864, from 42.6 thousand *contos* to 71.5 thousand *contos*. According to an observer, the massive increase in its discounting operations forced the Bank's directors to spend the night of 14 September signing fresh notes to be put in circulation the following morning.[53]

Contemporaries could not agree on the impact of the government measures. For some, they succeeded in 'helping dissipate the panic considerably, while things got slowly back to normal'.[54] Others argued that 'the government's arbitrary measures provided a temporary truce', which in the end only benefited poorly managed banks.[55] Finally, it was claimed that 'the increased issues of the Bank and suspension of convertibility made the panic go away, and the crisis died from exhaustion'.[56]

These mixed appraisals of the effectiveness of the measures adopted to deal with the crisis were to be expected. In essence, they reflected a priori views on the role of the market in punishing malpractice, against the opinion of those who deemed government intervention necessary in such cases. With hindsight, it appears that concerted action by Bank and government did indeed provide an environment where solvent, but illiquid, institutions could survive the turmoil. Be that as it may, the toll from the crisis was substantial, claiming some of the largest private banks in Rio.

The four private banks listed in Table 3.3 were the biggest among the five *casas bancárias* thought to have gone under in 1864, and accounted for approximately 80% of losses incurred by the banking sector during the crisis.[57] At the time, the assets of the Souto were second only to those of the Bank of Brazil (81,000 *contos* in 1864), which serves to show the scale of the operation of *casas bancárias*. Furthermore, the huge combined liabilities (equivalent to £ 8.7 million) of the four major private banks that failed in 1864 attest to the fact that the Rio money market was far larger than indicated by the operations of the joint-stock banks alone.

The origins of the crisis were subject to an investigation by a commission set up by Minister of Finance Carlos Carneiro de Campos shortly after the events, in late 1864.[58] To chair the proceedings, Campos appointed Angelo Muniz da Silva Ferraz, former Prime Minister and Minister of Finance responsible for the 1860 Law of Impediments. The two other members were José Pedro Dias de Carvalho, who had very briefly occupied the Finance portfolio in the past, and Francisco de Assis Vieira Bueno.[59]

Table 3.3 Souto crisis: major failures among private banks

Private bank	*Assets* (*in* contos)	*Liabilities* (*in* contos)	*Observations*
Souto & Cia.	30,445.8	41,187.9	Administrative liquidation on 23 September 1864
Gomes & Filhos	18,568.2	20,219.0	Receivership on 16 March 1865
Montenegro & Filhos	9864.3	11,831.3	Receivership on 28 April 1865
Oliveira & Bello	1028.1	4069.7	Receivership on 23 March 1865

Source: *Relatorio da Commissão de Inquerito de 1864* (1865, Table 22B)

In an attempt to ascertain if the 1864 crisis might have been influenced by events overseas, the Commission asked to what extent similar difficulties in Europe and the American Civil War were to blame. The interviewees were unanimous in exculpating these foreign events, in support of which they pointed out the fact that coffee exports had not been affected and that cotton was actually benefiting from the conflict in the United States (*Relatorio da Commissão de Inquerito de 1864* 1865, p. 74). On the crucial point ("What influence did the Law of August 1860 have on the crisis of September 1864?"), the Commission gladly reported that 'all those heard unanimously stated that the legislation of August 1860 in no way whatsoever contributed to the crisis' (ibid.). It is only natural, then, to learn that 'the Law (of Impediments) actually prevented a more severe crisis' (ibid.). In support of this claim, the commissioners observed that the issuing limits imposed by that law were never reached and, therefore, could not have provoked a monetary contraction.

The above conclusions are hardly surprising, given that Ferraz, the architect of the 1860 Law, was heading the investigation. Moreover, looked at from the banks' perspective, in the impossibility of resuming convertibility of their notes, the limits imposed in 1860 represented a cap on any increase in issues and, hence, discounting. Finally, the banks did not exceed the limits precisely because they were limits, and infringement would have brought heavy penalties.

Below is a summary of the main questions asked by the Commission, and excerpts from the replies given:

1. Q: What is the nature of the economic events that occurred on the 9th, 10th, and following days in September 1864?

   A: The crisis of September is easily explainable. Bankers had contracted enormous obligations payable on demand, and had invested these sums in operations that could only be liquidated after a long period of time.
2. Q: What are the means by which capital is supplied to agriculture, and what influence did these operations have on the economic events of September 1864?

   A: Such advancements were usually made by *casas bancárias*, by means of bills of more than four-month maturity, as well as through a system of current accounts. It seems to us that these operations had a major influence on the events of September 1864, in light of the substantial amount of such bills found in the portfolios of the banks that failed at the time. The financial embarrassment arising from these operations will become evident when the time comes to settle debts, for it implies immobilizing capital that is lent, to the detriment of circulating capital.
3. Q: Were the *bilhetes* and *vales* issued by the private banks in return for money treated as deposit receipts given in conjunction with current accounts, or a veiled issue of notes, as in a system of banks of issue?

   A: The receipts issued to bearer by the banks that failed were in practice a covert form of issue, many times more dangerous and harmful to the public than those from circulating banks. This is because while they performed the role of currency in commercial transactions, they were not bound by any limit whatsoever, except the individual credit of the signatures they contained. In other words, this was an illicit means put in practice in order to circumvent the letter of the Law of 22 August 1860.
4. Q: Was the circulation of such bills, or receipts, limited, or did it replace, or compete, with government currency and notes of the Bank of Brazil?

A: The receipts that businesses draw on bankers, and which constitute actual checks, do replace ordinary circulating medium insofar as they pass from hand to hand, before being cashed. However, this does not occur but to a very limited extent, because the commerce of Rio de Janeiro has not achieved a state of development where such a useful and simple means of payment is widespread.

As to the possibility of preventing similar crises in the Empire, the report came up with a comprehensive list of elements that indicated possible sources of instability in the Rio market, to wit:

(i) The need to transfer funds to Europe, either because of our commitments related to the external debt, and other public expenditures, or as a result of considerable (overseas) travel expenses, or, yet, due to the constant remittances [...] which immigrants (*colonos*) and other foreigners resident in the Empire make to their countries;
(ii) The regular shipment of funds to the River Plate to supply and help the issuing banks established there by businessmen from this market, and which last year amounted to 5695:064$ (...);
(iii) Our defective monetary system;
(iv) The imbalance between revenues and expenditures of the state, and the considerable expenses that the war in which we find ourselves currently demands (...);
(v) Mismanagement in some banks;
(vi) The legal tender status given to Bank of Brazil notes and the excessive circulation of inconvertible fiduciary paper (ibid., p. 89).[60]

In short, the commissioners recognized a host of factors—some more important than others—that had a bearing on the stability of Rio's commercial and financial system. Although not all of the factors were of a monetary nature, in the end the report preferred to stick to the *metalista* litany that permeated most documents of the time.[61] "Over issue", "abuse of credit", and "speculation"—in other words, the usual suspects—were paraded and judged guilty by the commissioners. And this verdict was right—at least in part.

In fact, there had apparently been excesses in the recent past, but joint-stock banks had not committed these. They had been restrained ever since the Law of Impediments and accompanying legislation imposed clear limits on their business. Limits not only on the amount of notes they were allowed to issue, but also on their day-to-day operations, which were closely monitored by an inspector. The agents of "over issue", if any, were from a less visible part of the banking sector, the *casas bancárias*. Their activities did not even merit the attention of the Minister of Finance in his annual report to the Assembly. In fact, as noted by Pacheco, the section on "Banks and the Circulating Medium" in the *Relatorio da Fazenda* devoted a few paragraphs to small savings and loans houses (*caixas econômicas*) and philanthropic pension societies (*monte-pios*). Yet, strangely, it did not bother to examine the activities of the much larger private banks, such as the Casa Souto, Montenegro, Lima & Co., and Alves & Filho (Pacheco 1979, Vol. II, p. 232).[62]

Before the Souto crisis, hardly any mention was made to non-corporate banks in official documents, newspaper articles, or parliamentary debates. Indeed, in the long-running controversies[63] that spanned the Second Reign, opposing proponents of a liberal banking system and advocates of a more restricted framework, attentions were concentrated on joint-stock banks alone and, more specifically, on banks of issue. At the time, banks of issue were wrongly thought to be the only ones capable of influencing the money supply. These banks were not alone in this capacity, of course. Deposit and discount banks and, even more dramatically, given their sheer size, private banks, had an important impact on the general level of liquidity in the economy. This fact is reflected in the replies to questions 1–4. *Casas bancárias*, like joint-stock banks, could increase the money supply both directly, via the issue of *vales*, and indirectly, through the operation of the money multiplier, a possibility that seems to have escaped policymakers until the events of 1864.[64]

According to some estimates, total deposits in the private banks amounted to 50,000 *contos* in 1864 (Peláez and Suzigan 1976, p. 105).[65] This was more than the volume of demand deposits held by joint-stock banks at the time—estimated at 43,000 *contos* (Brasil, IBGE 1990, p. 534). Supposing that a fraction of the deposits in the *casas bancárias* were counted as part of the money supply in the early 1860s, then the story that emerges is very different from the usual one. First, the monetary stock in 1860 would have been far higher than indicated in the traditional estimates. Second, it is to be expected that in light of the restrictions imposed by the Law of Impediments private banks could have stepped in to fill the gap left by joint-stock banks. Conversely, the failure of several private banks in 1864 also meant the disappearance of substantial amounts of money, both in the form of deposits and *vales* and, hence, a subsequent monetary contraction not captured by the Peláez and Suzigan figures used in the literature and throughout the present book (Goldsmith 1986, pp. 44 ff.).[66]

Table 3.4 reveals yet another aspect overlooked in the historiography in connection with the effects of the Law of Impediments on the money supply. Even if the behavior of the private banks is left aside, the fact remains

Table 3.4 Brazil: selected monetary indicators, 1860–4 (in *contos* '000)

	High-powered money	*Currency held by the public (a)*	*Demand deposits (b)*	*M1 (c) = a+b*
1860	87.0	77.4	19.2	96.6
1861	80.4	58.6	23.6	82.2
1862	76.7	58.5	25.9	84.4
1863	78.0	62.3	29.3	91.6
1864 I	82.8	70.3	25.9	96.2
II	82.8	68.1	29.9	98.0
III	95.4	75.6	33.2	108.8
IV	98.7	84.2	28.5	112.7

Source: Brasil, IBGE (1990, p. 535)

Note: Figures are yearly averages, except for 1864

that policymakers at the time were seldom aware of the existence of the monetary multiplier, that is, the capacity of the banking system to provide credit and, in the process, expand the money supply. As a result, monetary controls in an era of plurality of issue took the shape of imposing limits exclusively on the creation of monetary base, or high-powered money. "Manufacture of money" by means of deposit creation remained untrammeled (by minimum reserve requirements, for instance). When the multiplier is taken into account, the picture that emerges is more nuanced.

In 1863, that is, a full year before the Souto crisis broke out, average money supply (M1)—leaving aside the *casas bancárias*—was a touch below its level in 1860. In fact, although the issue of monetary base fell by approximately 10% in the period, M1 declined by just 5%. This was due to a 50% expansion (from 19.2 to 29.3 thousand *contos*) in the volume of demand deposits held in joint-stock banks, giving proof of the incipient process of modernization of the Brazilian banking system.[67] By the first quarter of 1864, money supply—again, disregarding the behavior of the *casas bancárias*—was at a similar level as in 1860. As a result, when the Souto crisis erupted, in September, there are no signs of the monetary contraction that is often assumed based on the stock of outstanding note issues (by joint-stock banks) alone.[68]

Still, it must be stressed that even the extent of the drop in the volume of high-powered money itself (measured by the stock of notes in circulation) was less severe than one would expect from the Law of Impediments. Admittedly, in the first three years after the 1860 Law, high-powered money contracted palpably (−12% between 1860.III and 1863.III). However, as discussed earlier, in September 1862, the Bank of Brazil took over the issuing rights from the Rural & Hypothecario. One month later, it resumed convertibility of its notes so that its issuing limits were no longer bound by Decree 2685. The acquisition of bullion in Britain, in mid-1863, by increasing its reserve fund, made possible a further expansion of its note issue. This served to partly offset the drop in the outstanding note issues of the Treasury and the other joint-stock banks, so that by June 1864—that is, less than three months before the Souto crisis erupted—total Bank of Brazil issues amounted to 49,100 *contos*. This was a full 30% increase over the amount outstanding in November 1860 (37,300 *contos*), just before Decree 2685 was announced. In the end, money supply as measured by M1 and M2 expanded by just over 20% in the period, while total deposits in the corporate banking system increased by an even greater extent (41.3%) to reach 44.8 thousand *contos* in June 1864.[69]

In short, the essence of the problems leading up to the Souto crisis was not, as often claimed, a severe monetary contraction following the Law of Impediments.[70] The existence of a contraction at all is unlikely, given the activities (both deposit holding and issuance of *vales*) of the *casas bancárias*, which are not computed in the widely used figures compiled by Peláez and Suzigan. Instead, the crux of the matter lay at the absence of official surveillance of an important component of the financial system—the private banks.[71]

The conduct of business by Casa Souto was symptomatic of the old-style mores still prevalent in a sizeable part of the Rio money market. The bank had been created as an association between Souto, his relatives, and close friends. Yet, despite its reputation and the huge amount of business conducted, it never bothered to register a contract with the Commercial Board (Junta Commercial). It is thought that Souto's bookkeeping was primitive and inconstant with many operations going unrecorded. Credit was granted on a personal basis to friends, relatives, politicians, often with little regard for their commercial merits. Its portfolio was over-stretched with long-term loans to the agricultural sector, while the issue of *vales* and acceptance of current accounts demanded a degree of liquidity that it could hardly sustain (Levy 1972, pp. 28–30).[72] As soon as panic set in, the inevitable occurred and Souto, and four other private banks, went under.

Parliament was not late in criticizing the behavior of *casas bancárias*. Speaking in the Senate on 10 and 27 June 1865, former Prime Minister Zacarias de Góis e Vasconcellos attacked the government for single-handedly legislating on the crucial question of bankruptcies and receiverships (*moratórias*). Although acknowledging the exceptional circumstances of the time, he claimed that ultimate blame for the crisis rested with the private banks in Rio de Janeiro, which, 'operating without attention to the rules of banking art (sic) and science, would inevitably fail. The reverse would have been a miracle, a real exception to the laws of Economics'.[73]

Meanwhile, attacks on the Bank of Brazil were mounting. The government argued that the increase in the Bank's inconvertible note issue was generating generous profits for its shareholders.[74] Still, many commentators came to the rescue of the Bank, among them Mauá. In a letter sent from London, he observed that an inspection of the accounts of the Bank at the end of 1864 revealed that at that point it was in a position to consider resumption of convertibility. Yet, its ability to do so had been compromised by the government, which began to place heavy strains on its operations, by issuing short-term *letras*, some of which ultimately ended up in the Bank's portfolio. Inevitably, Mauá pointed out, Bank issues would have to increase to accommodate the discounting of government paper, an operation that it never failed to undertake (Pacheco 1979, Vol. II, p. 258).

To address the question of financing the government's budget deficit, the Council of State was heard on 21 January 1865, during the Legislative recess (*ACE*, Vol. VI, pp. 5–16). Given that an extraordinary summoning of members of Parliament would take at least three months, councillors suggested that the government issue more Treasury bills in order to help fund the war against Paraguay, which had broken out in December 1864.[75] Council members were quick to cite reasons of State for allowing extraordinary measures. These reasons clearly dominated the legal impediment to such an act, which would have required prior approval by the General Assembly.

In the midst of financial problems caused by the mounting demands of the Paraguayan War on the imperial budget, the handling of the Souto crisis still reverberated. In January 1866, the government sent a communication to the Finance Standing Committee of the Council of State, asking for their opinion on the following questions: (i) were Decrees 3306 and 3307, which granted the Bank of Brazil permission to increase its note issue to three times the reserve fund, and suspended convertibility of its notes, compatible with any measures designed to improve the circulating medium; (ii) if so, what would those measures be; (iii) if not, should the said decrees be revoked? (*ACE*, Vol. VI, pp. 35–48).

The Seção de Fazenda was of the opinion that the decrees and the 'reckless' monetary expansion undertaken by the Bank in its wake were at the root of the current situation, characterized by excessive circulation and a slipping milréis. Nevertheless, to revoke the articles would have resulted in the Bank being well in excess of the legal limit on its outstanding note issues and, hence, liable to liquidation. Thus, the signatories opined that a more sensible solution would be to remove the issuing powers from the Bank altogether, and require that it gradually withdraw its notes from circulation (ibid., p. 37).

As this would have meant an important change of course, with numerous political and legal implications, the Emperor thought best to obtain the views of the Conselho Pleno. Most of the councillors, including both Itaboraí and Souza Franco, seconded the opinion of the Finance Standing Committee. The only dissonant voice was that of Jequitinhonha, who pleaded for the salvation of 'the sole credit establishment in the country' (ibid., p. 44). He was isolated, however, and the opinion that prevailed was that the Bank of Brazil should cease to be an issuing bank.[76] Should the Committee's recommendations be heeded, this would imply an end to twelve years of a rich experiment in plurality of note issues. As the next chapter will show in more detail, the government would not hesitate to go ahead with the changes to its agreement with the Bank of Brazil.

Notes

1. Session of 15 June 1859.
2. Session of 25 July 1859. The Minister had already acknowledged this point himself three weeks earlier when he had presented the whole question as one of confidence in the cabinet. Session of 6 July 1859, in *ACD*, Tome III, p. 45.
3. In the Speech from the Throne in 1860, the Emperor had already made known the wish of the cabinet to review 'legislation on associations and corporations, both civil and commercial'. *Fallas do Throno*, p. 519.
4. Session of 6 August 1860.
5. See the speech by deputy Gomes de Souza, ibid., p. 70.
6. de Aguiar (1960). The striking contrast with the results of the vote on the Torres Homem bill can be ascribed to the changes introduced by Ferraz to the original proposal. Additionally, the fact that the incoming cabinet was avowedly "parliamentarian"—all its members were either senators or national deputies—probably helped pave the way for its final approval.

7. A comparison with a summary of the main provisions of the 1844 Joint-Stock Bank Act—which imposed several restrictions on the formation and operation of new joint-stock banks in Britain—reveals the similarity of the Law of Impediments with comparable legislation elsewhere at the time. 'The minimum nominal capital was to be £100,000, no share was to be of lower denomination than £100, and no company thus formed could begin business until all the shares had been subscribed and at least one-half of their nominal amount paid up. It was required that the deed of partnership should be in a form approved by the Privy Council and that it should contain, among other clauses, provisions forbidding the company to purchase or lend upon the security of its own shares, requiring a statement of assets and liabilities to be published once a month, and arranging for the annual accounts to be examined by auditors elected by shareholders'. Cf. W. F. Crick and W. E. Wadsworth, *A Hundred Years of Joint-Stock Banking* (London, Hodder and Stoughton, 1936), quoted in Collins (1988, p. 73).
8. Notes of small denomination (1$000 to 30$000) issued by the Treasury and banks amounted to slightly over 50% of a total outstanding issue of 96,000 *contos* in mid-1859. Session of 19 July 1859, in *ACD*, Tome III, pp. 177–9.
9. Although official figures for Treasury notes refer to end of year only, the combined sum represented by notes withdrawn from circulation by the Bank of Brazil (2000 *contos* per annum in several instalments), and the loss owing to their natural wear and tear suggests a decrease in government paper money of roughly 1300 *contos* every six months.
10. This point was made in the petition sent by the Bank of Bahia to the Chamber of Deputies on 28 June 1859, transcribed in Azevedo and Lins (1969, p. 145).
11. Banco do Brasil, *Parecer Apresentado á Assembléa Geral dos Accionistas* (1861).
12. On this basic shortcoming of the 1860 Law, see also Dunlop (1881, p. 38). Actually, this contradiction had been in place ever since the Bank was created, although until 1860 it had the option, which it exercised, of giving Treasury notes, instead of gold, in exchange for its own notes. With the Law, the Bank was required to redeem its paper into gold whenever demanded by noteholders. See Jacobina (1881, p. 8).
13. Having stabilized at near par between the end of the 1857 crisis (in August 1858) and early 1859, when the Bank of Brazil once again left gold, the value of the *milréis* oscillated around a declining trend for the next six months. It reached a low of 24d on the eve of the Law of Impediments, giving the government all the motivation it needed to take action and seek to restore the milréis to the 27d parity. Hence, Article 6 of Decree 2685, stipulating the goal of a fully gold-backed circulating medium.

14. Banco do Brasil, "Actas", session No. 571, 18 February 1861, AD 005/11-A.
15. In a memorandum sent to Minister Ferraz on 22 February 1861, the president of the Bank asserted that the head office was already in a state where it could resume convertibility of its notes, although that was not yet the case with the provincial offices. Rather than have only part of the Bank on gold, which would have been illegal, it was decided that the Bank would have to abide by Article 1, paragraph 2, of the 1860 Law and, therefore, start retiring notes of smaller denomination in both Rio and the provinces. *RMF* 1860, p. 16.
16. *Parecer da Commissão Especial Nomeada Pela Directoria do Banco do Brasil* (1862).
17. Ibid., p. 9
18. Session of 10 July 1862.
19. During debates held at the Council of State on 10 July 1862, Souza Franco had already manifested fear of the Bank of Brazil abusing its monopolist position. On that occasion, he branded as an 'odious privilege' the Bank's plea to retain monopoly of issue for the next twenty years in the places where it operated. See *ACE*, Vol. V, p. 287.
20. Decree 2970. For details, Pacheco (1979, Vol. II, pp. 180 ff.).
21. The number of bankruptcies in Rio more than doubled from an average of 45 between 1859 and 1861 to 104 in 1862. Data in Calógeras (1910, p. 142).
22. In the 1862 *Relatorio da Fazenda*, Minister of Finance Marquês de Abrantes acknowledged that part of the difficulties that the Bank had been experiencing lately derived from 'the needs of the Treasury, not only in December, but also in January, to which the Bank responded immediately, confident in obtaining (permission to) increase its issues to three times (its reserve fund), requested on 4 December 1862'. *RMF* 1862, p. 23.
23. On that occasion, the government heard the Seção de Fazenda of the Council of State, as well as businessmen operating in Rio, but decided that in order to preserve the spirit of the 1860 Law the Bank's request should not be met, 'lest the risks and perils (of the days) before the Law return' (ibid., p. 20).
24. Ibid., p. 23.
25. Relaxation of the issuing limit, as noted, ran counter to the recommendations of the Finance Standing Committee, which had convened earlier to examine the Bank's request. On that occasion, Itaboraí and the Visconde de Jequitinhonha opposed granting permission for the Bank to increase its note issue to three times the reserve fund. Itaboraí, who was the *rapporteur* for this case, suggested instead that the Bank rely on other measures to increase its circulation, such as a capital expansion and the acceptance of

interest-bearing deposits. The third member of the Committee, Cândido Batista de Oliveira, who at the time was also the president of the Bank, unsurprisingly, pressed the case for the need to change the limit on note issues. In support, he pointed out earlier instances when relaxation of the limit had been granted under more favorable circumstances, that is, when Bank of Brazil notes were not required to be convertible into gold, as they now were. The Finance Standing Committee, by two votes to one, decided against the Bank's request, but this did not stop the government from issuing Decree 3054, thus expanding the limit for note issues to three times the Bank's reserve fund. Resolution No. 726, in *SFCE*, Vol. V, pp. 359–68. For a detailed analysis of the debates and decisions on monetary and banking matters in the Seção de Fazenda of the Council of State, see Villela (2000a).

26. *ACE*, Vol. V, pp. 348–61.
27. Decree 3062.
28. At the end of 1862, outstanding Treasury notes amounted to 31.3 thousand *contos*, while banknotes had reached a value of 45.7 thousand *contos*. See IBGE (1990, p. 544).
29. The classic account of the operation of the English banks in Brazil is Joslin (1963). The London and Brazilian Bank had been incorporated in London in June, with a capital of £1,000,000. A few months later, it took over the business of the Anglo-Portuguese Bank in Portugal. See *Banker's Magazine*, Vol. 22, June 1862, p. 393. The Brazilian and Portuguese Bank was also formed with a capital of £1,000,000 on 3 July 1863. *Banker's Magazine*, Vol. 23, August 1863, pp. 638–9.
30. On the conservative practices of the English banks, and the resentment generated in Latin American countries where they operated, see Jones (1977).
31. Still, British banks occasionally invested in planter drafts, as noted by Sweigart (1987, p. 176, footnote 19). Crucially, they did not seek to become banks of issue, but rather to operate with deposits and discounts. Their subsequent success served to show that gaining the right to issue notes was not a prerequisite for expanding business, nor the only available means to support commercial activity. See Jones (1977, pp. 36 ff).
32. Meeting of the Board of Directors of the Bank of Brazil on 18 May 1863, cited in Pacheco (1979, Vol. II, p. 197).
33. Ibid.
34. Ibid., pp. 197–8.
35. *Relatorio da Commissão de Inquerito de 1864* (1865, Introduction).
36. Ibid., cited in Cavalcanti (1893, Vol. 2, pp. 274–5).
37. *Relatorio da Comissão de Inquerito de 1864*, cited in Pacheco (1979, Vol. II, p. 212).

38. Ibid.
39. Banco do Brasil, "Actas", session No. 811, 10 September 1864, AD 007/11-A. Contemporary estimates put Souto's debts with the Bank of Brazil alone at the outbreak of the crisis at 14,000 *contos* (£1.6 million). Soares (1865, p. 51).
40. Banco do Brasil, "Actas", session No. 812, 12 September 1864, AD 007/11-A. It is not exactly clear what those 'constituted powers' were, if the interests of other commercial houses and investors, or the Legislative—most likely, the latter.
41. Ibid.
42. Memorandum sent by the Bank of Brazil to the imperial government on 13 September, cited in Pacheco, (1979, Vol. II, p. 217). At the time, the Bank had clearly exceeded the limits on its issues, its reserve fund amounting to 10.9 thousand *contos*, while outstanding issues exceeded 35.9 thousand *contos* (ibid., pp. 217–8).
43. Between 12 and 14 September, the *fundo disponível* lost almost 3000 *contos* in specie. Figures from "Banco do Brasil: Quadro do Troco Realizado em Moeda Metálica em Setembro de 1864", in the Annex to *Relatorio da Commissão de Inquerito de 1864* (1865). Later, it emerged that some 90% of the gold losses (2800 *contos*) had been due to shipments made by the Mauá, MacGregor Bank to its branches in the River Plate, apparently in a move to pre-empt a run on them upon arrival of the news of the crisis in Rio.
44. The run on the *casas bancárias* in Rio put them in a very delicate position, given that while they had borrowed short their assets were often immobilized in long-term rural loans. This left them to rely on the Bank of Brazil to provide the necessary liquidity to meet the demands from panic-stricken clients. See *RMF* 1864, p. 13.
45. Note that although the decree did not refer to the *caixas filiais*, the Bank interpreted it as extending the new limit to its provincial offices as well.
46. Decree 3307.
47. Together with Decree 3308, the other piece of legislation to arouse most opposition was the appointment, by the government, of inspectors, who would oversee the liquidation of the major *casas bancárias* in difficulty (Decree 3322, of 22 October 1864). Not only would these inspectors be handsomely paid (by the businesses undergoing liquidation) but also they were often leading politicians of the time. Thus, Souza Franco was chosen to supervise Casa Souto, Ferraz took the house of Gomes & Filhos, and Paranhos (Visconde de Rio Branco), Montenegro, Lima & Cia. and Oliveira & Bello. Nabuco (1997, Vol. I, p. 471, footnote 2). Incidentally, both decrees (3308 and 3322) were for the most part drafted by Senator José Thomas Nabuco de Araújo, by then a highly respected jurist, but not

a member of the cabinet in power. Nabuco's crucial participation in the events that followed the 1864 commercial crisis went unnoticed to most contemporaries, until they were unearthed by his son, Joaquim Nabuco, when writing the biography of Senator José Thomas, which remains, after more than a century, one of the best histories of the Brazilian Empire.

48. Overall, 95 firms (in all sectors) declared bankruptcy in Rio between 10 September 1864 and 31 March 1865. Also significant was the number of bankruptcies *prior* to the house of Souto closing its doors on September 10 (112 in all). This indicates the extent of the hardship under which the capital's market was under throughout the year. Data on bankruptcies from Calógeras (1910, p. 142).
49. Figures are from the statistical Annex to *Relatorio da Commissão de Inquerito de 1864* (1865).
50. For a comparison of the reactions to the 1857 and 1864 crises in Brazil, see Villela (2000b).
51. Provincial offices played a less prominent role in the provision of liquidity to the market, reflecting the marginal impact of the crisis outside Rio de Janeiro.
52. The house of Bahia & Irmãos and the Rural & Hypothecario endured the largest withdrawal of deposits during the crisis—16,000 and 15,000 *contos*, respectively (ibid.).
53. *Banker's Magazine*, Vol. 24, November 1864, p. 1006.
54. *Jornal do Commercio*, cited in Pacheco (1979, Vol. II, p. 221).
55. Ibid. The extent of the controversy generated by the official measures implemented to tackle the crisis can be gauged by a one-page daily bulletin that began circulating on 12 September. The *Boletim Commercial* maintained a rabid anti-government, anti-Portuguese (and anti-Semitic) tone throughout its short life of some twenty issues. The leaflet was adamantly opposed to the extra-legal measures decreed by the government, as well as the decision to expand liquidity and suspend convertibility. See *Boletim Commercial*, No. 18, 1 October 1864.
56. Testimony collected by the enquiry into the crisis of 1864, cited in Pacheco (1979, Vol. II, p. 222). Unsurprisingly, the 1865 *Relatorio da Fazenda* congratulated itself (and the Bank of Brazil) for reacting to the crisis in the right manner, that is, by suspending convertibility and lending liberally. See *RMF* 1864, p. 13.
57. Villa (2016).
58. *Relatorio da Commissão de Inquerito de 1864* (1865). The organization of the 1864 report was in many ways similar to that of its 1859 predecessor, although the final text is not as illuminating, perhaps because only 19 of the 79 individuals invited by the Commission ended up being interviewed.

59. Vieira Bueno would serve as President of the Bank of Brazil from January to April 1866.
60. Although far from being a synthesis of the testimonies heard on the occasion, the commissioners added that the 1864 crisis was (rather implausibly) the result of the "monetary excesses" that followed the events of 1857. Later commentators, who more often than not just repeated the conclusions of contemporary reports, shared this diagnosis. See, for example, Ortigão (1914, p. 73).
61. See, for example, the account of the crisis given by the Minister of Finance, in *RMF* 1864, pp. 12–5.
62. As a result of this official neglect, private banks were not required to file financial statements to the government and, therefore, have left very little record of their operations. A similar problem also besets the study of the early financial history of the United States. For a discussion, see Sylla (1976) and comments by L. Davis and T. Cochrane in the same volume.
63. These debates will be briefly revisited in Chap. 5. For a more detailed discussion of the monetary controversies at the time, see Villela (2001).
64. Contemporaries put the combined issue of *vales* by the banks that failed in 1864 at 30,000 *contos*. *Relatorio da Commissão de Inquerito de 1864* (1865, Annex C, p. 52).
65. It is estimated that another eight *casas bancárias* (for which no data has been unearthed so far) survived the crash, which indicates that this segment of the banking sector attracted an even larger share of total deposits in the capital. See Villa (2016).
66. These points will be taken up again in Chap. 5 in connection with a discussion of long-term trends in monetary policy during the Second Reign.
67. In part, this process was boosted by the operation of the English banks, which arrived in Rio in the first half of 1863. See Jones (1977). By 1865, total (sight + interest-bearing) deposits accounted for 30% of the money supply (M2), up from 20% in 1855. Calculated from data in Brasil, IBGE (1990, p. 535).
68. Of course, a nominal money supply at the same level as four years earlier may have constituted a real (inflation-adjusted) contraction, especially if both the price level and the economy were growing.
69. See Table A1 in the Appendix for yearly data on outstanding note issues, by issuer.
70. This is, for instance, Cavalcanti's view, according to whom the root of the crises lay in the contraction of the money supply attempted through the 1860 legislation. 'In one word, it was the abuse of the public powers against the abuse of credit, by restricting the circulating medium at a time when business was expanding fast, which caused the suppression of the

partial movements [...] of the great economic mechanism, which was thus forced to an abrupt halt'. See Cavalcanti (1893, Vol. 2, p. 279).

71. Other contributing factors to the crisis, according to Schulz, were the increase in Bank (of England) Rate—mostly as defense against a reduction in Britain's foreign reserves—and fears surrounding Brazil's military involvement in the River Plate, prompting hectic speculation in the Rio money market. See Schulz (1996, pp. 42–3).
72. See also Vianna (1864, p. 5).
73. Cited in Pacheco (1979, Vol. II, p. 241).
74. The point was made bluntly by the Minister of Finance in May 1865. 'It is undisputedly pernicious to industry and the finances of the State that the circulation of values be made by [...] inconvertible paper, especially when this issue is entrusted to a private entity, which finds in the expansion of the faculty to issue a source of profits'. *RMF* 1864, p. 14. The government's message was clear: 'it is [...] absolutely paramount that the Bank of Brazil put itself as soon as possible in a condition such that its circulation becomes solid, relying exclusively on the trust it deserves, and resume convertibility; otherwise, and especially if the amount of paper increases, its value will no longer be equivalent to the metal it represents' (ibid.).
75. On the Paraguayan War, Marques (org.) (1995), Costa (1996), and Doratioto (2002).
76. The first casualty of the decision of the Committee would be Minister of Finance Dias de Carvalho, a long-time director of the Bank, who resigned in protest on 7 March.

References

Banco do Brasil. 1854–70. *Relatorio Apresentado á Assembléa Geral dos Accionistas do Banco do Brasil pelo Presidente do Banco.*

———. 1861. *Parecer Apresentado á Assembléa Geral dos Accionistas do Banco do Brasil pela Commissão Especial Eleita em 2 de Maio de 1861.* Rio de Janeiro: Villeneuve.

———. 1862. *Parecer da Commissão Especial Nomeada Pela Directoria do Banco do Brasil d'Entre Seus Membros, Sobre a Conveniencia de Negociar-se com os Bancos Commercial e Agrícola e Rural e Hipotecário, a Cessão ao Banco do Brasil do Direito que Aquelles Bancos Tem de Emittir Notas à Vista e ao Portador.* Rio de Janeiro: Typographia do Correio Mercantil.

Banker's Magazine. 1862–70. London.

Boletim Commercial. 1864. Rio de Janeiro.

Brasil, Câmara dos Deputados. *Annaes da Câmara dos Deputados,* various issues.

———, Ministério da Fazenda. *Proposta e Relatorio Apresentados á Assembléa-Geral Legislativa Pelo Ministro e Secretario d'Estado dos Negócios da Fazenda,* various years.

Brasil, IBGE. 1990. *Estatísticas Históricas do Brasil*, séries econômicas, demográficas e sociais, 1550–1985. Vol. 3. 2nd ed. Rio de Janeiro: IBGE.

Calógeras, João P. 1910. *La Politique Monetaire du Brésil*. Rio de Janeiro: Imprensa Nacional.

Cavalcanti, Amaro. 1893. *O Meio Circulante Nacional*. Rio de Janeiro: Imprensa Nacional, 2 vols.

Collins, Michael. 1988. *Money and Banking in the United Kingdom: A history*. London: Croon Helm.

Costa, Wilma P. 1996. *A Espada de Dâmocles: o Exército, a Guerra do Paraguai e a Crise do Império*. São Paulo: Hucitec/Ed. da Unicamp.

de Aguiar, Manoel P. 1960. *Ensaios de História e Economia*. Livraria Progresso Editora: Salvador.

de Azevedo, Thales, and Edilberto Q.V. Lins. 1969. *História do Banco da Bahia*, 1858–1958. Rio de Janeiro: José Olympio.

Doratioto, Francisco. 2002. *Maldita Guerra: uma nova história da Guerra do Paraguai*. São Paulo: Companhia das Letras.

Dunlop, Júlio Roberto. 1881. *Curso Forçado*. Rio de Janeiro: Typographia Nacional.

Fallas do Throno Desde o Anno de 1823 até o Anno de 1872, acompanhadas dos respectivos votos de graças da câmara temporária e de differentes informações e esclarecimentos colligidas na secretaria da Câmara dos Senhores Deputados. 1872. Rio de Janeiro: Typographia Nacional.

Goldsmith, Raymond W. 1986. *Brasil, 1850–1984: desenvolvimento financeiro sob um século de inflação*. São Paulo: Harper & Row.

Imperiaes Resoluções do Conselho de Estado na Secção de Fazenda, desde o anno em que começou a funccionar o mesmo conselho até o presente. Rio de Janeiro: Typographia Nacional, 12 vols.

Jacobina, Antonio de A.F. 1881. *Esboço de Estudo para a Volta dos Pagamentos em Ouro no Brazil ou Conversão do Papel-Moeda*. Rio de Janeiro: Laemmert.

Jones, Charles. 1977. Commercial Banks and Mortgage Companies. In *Business Imperialism, 1840–1930: an inquiry based on British experience in Latin America*, ed. D.C.M. Platt, 17–52. Oxford: Clarendon Press.

Joslin, David. 1963. *A Century of Banking in Latin America*. London: Oxford University Press.

Legislação Sobre Papel Moeda. 1923. Rio de Janeiro: Imprensa Nacional.

Levy, Maria Bárbara. 1972. *História dos Bancos Comerciais no Brasil (estudo preliminar)*. Rio de Janeiro: IBMEC, mimeo.

Marques, Maria Eduarda C.M. 1995. *A Guerra do Paraguai: 130 anos depois*. Rio de Janeiro: Relume Dumará.

Nabuco, Joaquim. 1997. *Um Estadista do Império*. 5th ed. Rio de Janeiro: Topbooks.

Ortigão, Ramalho. 1914. *A Moeda Circulante no Brazil*. Rio de Janeiro: Typographia do Jornal do Commercio.

Pacheco, Claudio. 1979. *História do Banco do Brasil*. Brasília: Banco do Brasil, 4 vols.

Peláez, Carlos Manuel, and Wilson Suzigan. 1976. *História Monetária do Brasil*. 2nd ed. Brasília: Ed. da Universidade de Brasília.

Relatorio da Commissão de Inquerito Nomeada por Aviso do Ministério da Fazenda, de 10 de Outubro de 1859. Undated.

Relatorio da Commissão Encarregada pelo Governo Imperial por Aviso do Primeiro de Outubro e 28 de Dezembro de 1864, de Proceder a um Inquerito Sobre as Causas Principais e Accidentaes da Crise do Mez de Setembro de 1864. 1865. Rio de Janeiro: Typographia Nacional.

Rodrigues, José H., ed. 1978. *Atas do Conselho de Estado*. Brasília: Senado Federal, 14 vols.

Schulz, John. 1996. *A Crise Financeira da Abolição*. São Paulo: Edusp/Instituto Fernand Braudel.

Soares, Sebastião Ferreira. 1865. *Esboço ou Primeiros Traços da Crise Commercial da Cidade do Rio de Janeiro em 10 de Setembro de 1864*. Rio de Janeiro: Laemmert.

Sweigart, Joseph E. 1987. *Coffee Factorage and the Emergence of a Brazilian Capital Market, 1850–1888*. New York: Garland Publishing.

Sylla, Richard. 1976. Forgotten Men of Money: Private Bankers in Early U.S. History. *Journal of Economic History* XXXVI (1): 173–188.

Vianna, Pedro Antonio F. 1864. *A Crise Commercial do Rio de Janeiro em 1864*. Rio de Janeiro: Garnier.

Villa, Carlos Eduardo V. 2016. Pequeños Acreedores de Grandes Deudores: clientes y acreedores de las casas bancarias cariocas en la quiebra de 1864. In *Crédito e Descrédito: Relações Sociais de Empréstimos na América – séculos XVIII ao XX*, ed. Carlos Gabriel Guimarães and Luiz Fernando Saraiva, 86–121. Niterói: Editora da UFF.

Villela, André A. 2000a. Brazil in Mid-Empire: The Council of State and the Banking Question, 1850–1870. *Estudos Economicos* 30 (4): 629–651.

———. 2000b. Trying Times: Reactions to the 1857 and 1864 Crises in Brazil. *Economia* 1 (2): 241–266.

———. 2001. The Quest for Gold: Monetary Debates in Nineteenth-Century Brazil. *Revista de Economia Política* 21 (4): 79–92.

CHAPTER 4

The Treasury as a Monopolist Note-Issuer: 1866–89

4.1 Revising the Agreement with the Bank of Brazil

At the start of the 1866 legislative session, in May, the new Minister of Finance, João da Silva Carrão, presented a bill designed to curb the Bank of Brazil's right of issue and to restore stability to the monetary system through a return to gold.[1] His proposal aimed at requiring the Bank to withdraw part of the stock of notes in circulation until it reached twice its reserve fund (or 50,000 *contos*, whichever was lower). At this point, the Bank was to resume convertibility of its notes. The joint Finance and Special Committee of the Chamber of Deputies endorsed the main points of the bill (Cavalcanti 1893, Vol. 2, pp. 281–9).

Simultaneously with the Minister's proposal, two petitions were sent to the Chamber of Deputies, one from the directors of the Bank of Brazil, the other by representatives of *fazendeiros* from the province of Rio de Janeiro.[2] The Bank attempted to justify the state of the monetary circulation at the time by arguing that had it acted selfishly at the outbreak of the Souto crisis, it could have easily sat back, suspended its discounting operations, while continuing to redeem its notes on demand (presumably, in Treasury notes). However, perceiving the gravity of the situation, and conscious of its weight in the Rio money market, the Bank had decided to ask the government for permission to increase its issues.[3] With this, it sought to provide the necessary liquidity to institutions in distress, thus performing the role of a lender

A. A. Villela, *The Political Economy of Money and Banking in Imperial Brazil, 1850–1889*, Palgrave Studies in the History of Finance, https://doi.org/10.1007/978-3-030-32774-3_4

of last resort. The Bank was confident that, soon after that 'abnormal state' had passed, the volume of notes in circulation would resume the levels reached prior to the crisis, had it not been for the onset of the Paraguayan War and the accompanying demands of the Treasury.[4]

For its part, the petition signed by *fazendeiros* of the province of Rio de Janeiro, very short on specifics, urged the Bank to reduce to 6% the rate of discount it charged *comissários*. The latter, in return, would commit to lending the money to the agricultural sector at 9%.[5]

The Bank's petition was dismissed. Yet, planters' pleas were partially addressed by the new arrangement envisioned for the Bank, which would set up a mortgage department.[6] In the meantime, the Minister of Finance appointed Jequitinhonha to head the Bank of Brazil, on 22 April 1866. This was an attempt to rein in an institution thought to have become increasingly unruly (Pacheco 1979, Vol. II, pp. 276 ff.). Under the prodding of Jequitinhonha, and in face of opposition from part of its directorate, the Bank found itself in a corner. At the same time that the government demanded that the Bank show restraint in its issuing activities and effect a quick return to convertibility, it also required the institution to discount increasingly large amounts of Treasury bills. Additionally, and against the Bank's will, the government asked for help in obtaining essential hard currency needed to purchase war matériel abroad.

Throughout the month of June, the government displayed the same ambiguity, as news of the crash of Overend, Gurney & Co., in Britain, brought nervousness to the major markets of the Empire. This led to a run on many institutions, including the London & Brazilian Bank, which turned to both the government and the Bank of Brazil for help.[7] At that time, the Bank was operating at the limit of its issuing powers and, therefore, sought advice from the government on how to proceed. On 14 June, Minister of Finance Carrão replied that he was awaiting the outcome of a bill under discussion in Parliament, which would have allowed an increase in the Bank's rights of issue.[8] Five days later, Carrão gave his consent to an assistance to the London and Brazilian Bank, while urging the Bank of Brazil to do its utmost to keep issues within the assigned 3:1 ratio (Pacheco 1979, Vol. II, 285–7).[9] Shortly afterward, and upon hearing the opinion of the financial community in Rio, the government temporarily relaxed the limits on the issues of the Bank. From then on, both the Bank and the Treasury were able to provide discount facilities against solid securities, thus enabling the London and Brazilian Bank to meet its demands for discounts.[10]

Amid the turbulence of the day, the Olinda cabinet began to show the first signs of internal strife. On 11 June 1866, the Minister of Agriculture, Antônio Francisco de Paula e Sousa, had taken the initiative, 'in a private capacity, as a deputy', to present to the Chamber his own bill aimed at dealing with the 'events of June' (i.e., the fallout from the Overend, Gurney crisis).[11] The main points of the new proposal consisted of allowing the Bank of Brazil and the government to jointly issue up to 12,000 *contos*, while giving the former unlimited powers to discount Treasury bills in excess of its normal limits (Pacheco 1979, Vol. II, 284–5).

The opposition in Parliament could not fail to point out the sheer contradiction of the bill, coming as it did through the hands of a cabinet member, and at odds with the earlier bill submitted by Carrão (ibid., pp. 145–7).[12] To make matters worse, earlier in April the Minister of War (and author of the 1860 banking and corporate law), Ferraz, had called for the "regeneration" of the Bank of Brazil, in the Chamber of Deputies (Nabuco 1997, Vol. I, p. 633, footnote 4).[13] Clearly, ministers were not speaking with one voice on an important issue at a critical juncture. Nevertheless, by 30 June, before any decision had been taken on either bill, the Bank was already exceeding its issuing limits by more than 9600 *contos* (Nabuco 1997, Vol. I, p. 635, footnote 7).

On 3 July, and while the texts from the Ministry of Finance and Paula e Sousa (Agriculture) were being debated in the Chamber of Deputies, senator Silveira da Mota (Liberal for the province of Goiás) took an allegedly individual initiative to submit a different bill to the upper House. Essentially, he proposed a revision to the contract signed between the government and the Bank of Brazil in 1853. If turned into law, it would imply a termination of the right of the Bank to issue notes, turning it into a bank of deposits, discounts, and mortgages only.[14] In addition, the bill envisaged that the Bank be required to sell its metallic reserves to the government. After some deliberation, and in spite of the disapproval of the then Minister of Finance (Carrão), the Finance Committee of the Senate endorsed the Silveira da Mota text, with a few modifications.[15]

It is noteworthy that the final draft of the Senate bill bore the imprint of the two leading financial experts of the day—Itaboraí and Souza Franco—both of whom were the spiritual leaders of the opposing "schools" of thought on banking and monetary affairs. At that point, the two men showed signs of fatigue after more than a decade of disputes between *metalistas* and *papelistas*. Both had modified their earlier positions and, in a way, moved toward a common middle ground. Itaboraí, by admitting an end to the issuing powers of his own brainchild.[16] Souza Franco, in turn, having seen his worst fears about circulating banks running amok come true, thought best to do away with the issuing powers of the Bank. If the price for the restoration of a sound currency was the institution of a government monopoly of issue, they reasoned, so be it. Their joint statement summarized the final opinions of the Finance Committee of the Senate on the Silveira da Mota bill. In addition, it signaled a truce between monopolists and advocates of plurality of issue after years of bitter dispute:

> Invested, for more than two years, with legal tender status, and during this period having increased the issues of its head office by almost twice (the amount) in early September 1864; with two-thirds of its portfolio composed of bills which cannot be discounted in the short-run, or of difficult and doubtful liquidation, the Bank of Brazil can no longer satisfy the essential conditions of when it was created. If its right to issue notes is not revoked, it will remain, as now, merely a paper-money factory, steered at the whim of its directorate, without support nor intervention from the General Legislative Assembly, and subject only to governmental inspection, which has, unfortunately, encouraged, instead of prevented, the abuses which led the monetary circulation to its present state.[17]

The opinions uttered by the two financial statesmen delivered the final blow to a crumbling cabinet. Paula e Sousa, the Minister of Agriculture, saw much in common in the bill finally approved by the Senate and his own, and came to its support. Minister of Finance Carrão, as already noted, was opposed to the Silveira da Mota proposal finally embraced by the Senate. Prime Minister Olinda, in turn, showed increasing signs of failing health. All ingredients were in place for an administrative reshuffle. This came about in the early days of August 1866 when, upon the resignation of the 1865 cabinet, the Emperor summoned once again Zacarias to occupy the chair of President of the Council of Ministers.

Deeming control of the Bank of Brazil strategic for his efforts to tackle the financial difficulties facing the government, Zacarias soon sacked the Visconde de Jequitinhonha as head of the Bank. Former Minister of Finance, and leading *metalista*, Torres Homem, replaced him. Jequitinhonha did not leave silently. Speaking soon afterward, in the Senate, he would criticize the government for its ongoing attacks against the Bank, positioning himself against the Silveira da Mota bill. Jequitinhonha insisted that the only reasons why the Bank failed to remain within the limits on its note issue had been precisely its operation as a lender of last resort during the Souto crisis and, ever since, its discounting of government paper. Zacarias was unimpressed. On 9 August, he formally endorsed the modified version of the Silveira da Mota bill being debated in the Senate, insisting that it was better than the one presented by his predecessor, Carrão. Not only did it propose measures to revamp the Bank of Brazil but, crucially, 'afforded the government the means to face the deficit' (Pacheco 1979, Vol. II, p. 318).[18] The real motive behind the coming Law 1349 could not have been presented more candidly.

Debates in the Senate continued until late August, when the proposal was approved and sent to the Chamber of Deputies. In the lower House, discussion was less vibrant and shorter. In the end, and with minor modifications, the bill from the Finance Committee of the Senate left Parliament to receive Imperial sanction, becoming Law 1349 on 12 September 1866.

The new law turned the clock back to the 1830s, when the Treasury was the sole issuer of paper currency in the Empire. Apart from revoking the right of the third Bank of Brazil to issue notes (Article 1, paragraph 1), it allowed for the purchase of its metallic fund (paragraph 2), a crucial resource in the war effort. The determination to replace the Bank's issues with Treasury notes was provided for with paragraphs 4 and 6, the latter having established a timetable for conducting the retirement of Bank of Brazil paper. The creation of a mortgage department (paragraphs 1 and 2), in turn, arose out of the belief that it would be able to address the demands of the rural sector. Finally, the exceptional nature of the measures, at least as regards the issue of government fiat money, was acknowledged in paragraph 8, which envisaged a gradual retirement of this type of paper after the war against Paraguay was over.[19]

In practice, Law 1349 implied the retirement of one class of paper and its replacement by another: unbacked Treasury notes would gradually take the place of notes issued by the Bank of Brazil (which at the time were also inconvertible). Thus, with the outlay of 40.6 thousand *contos* made by the Treasury, an equivalent amount of Bank notes would be removed from circulation.[20] Yet, the government's objective was more prosaic than this swap of (then) inconvertible private notes for official paper money. First, the law allowed it to get hold of the metallic reserves of the Bank. Second, by taking over the Bank's issuing powers, the government could henceforth finance itself directly, instead of having to rely exclusively on debt, as had been the case until then. This latter point was crucial, in light of the widening budget deficit (Table 4.1).

Table 4.1 Revenue and expenditure of the imperial government, 1860–1 to 1870–1 (in *contos*)

Financial year	*Revenue*	*Expenditure*	*Balance*
1860–1	50,052	52,358	−2306
1861–2	52,489	53,050	−561
1862–3	48,342	57,000	−8658
1863–4	54,801	56,494	−1693
1864–5	56,996	83,346	−26,350
1865–6	58,523	121,856	−63,333
1866–7	64,777	120,890	−56,113
1867–8	71,201	165,985	−94,784
1868–9	87,543	150,895	−63,352
1869–70	94,847	141,594	−46,747
1870–1	95,885	100,074	−4189

Source: Table A6, in the Appendix

At the time the Law of Impediments was implemented, in 1860, the budget deficit was still manageable, with expenditures not exceeding revenues by a large margin. However, by the mid-1860s, as the Paraguayan War broke out and the need for additional resources arose, it widened considerably. Combined expenditures of the Ministries of War and Navy jumped from an average of 40% of the total in the mid-1850s to 60% of a much larger budget at the height of the conflict in 1867–8.[21] Clearly, the government had to find other sources of finance.

With a view to obtaining the necessary resources to pay for the increasing expenditures of the imperial government, Zacarias turned to Parliament for permission to go ahead with an issue of 45,000 to 50,000 *contos* in Treasury notes. The usual opposition to "over issue", "recklessness", and "abuse" was mustered in both Houses, dragging the discussion well into the legislative year.[22] Finally, on 28 September 1867, Law 1508 authorized the government to issue up to 50,000 *contos*, which it promptly did.[23]

The exchange rate, meanwhile, felt the blow. Between December 1867 and early 1868 it dropped sharply, from around 19d to a low of 14d in mid-February, ahead of the arrival of news of the decisive military victory at Humaitá.[24] Subsequently, it recovered its earlier level and stabilized at 19–20d in April.[25] By then, Zacarias's hold on his post showed the first signs of weakening. Three months later, he was replaced as Prime Minister.

The Emperor, breaking with all tradition in a parliamentary system, invited Itaboraí, old-time Conservative, to preside over a new cabinet amid a Liberal-controlled Assembly. Itaboraí was also entrusted, as Minister of Finance, with solving the financial difficulties in which the Empire found itself because of a long and costly military conflict. The remaining cabinet members were experienced politicians as well. The new administration included Paranhos at the Ministry of Foreign Affairs and José Antônio Pimenta Bueno (Marquês de São Vicente) as Minister of the Empire (Interior).

In order to increase his room for maneuvre, Itaboraí asked the Emperor to dismiss the Chamber of Deputies, to which the monarch agreed. Taking advantage of the dissolution of the lower House, and before a new one could convene, the Executive passed Decree 4232 on 5 August 1868, authorizing an additional issue of up to 40,000 *contos* in Treasury notes in order to meet pressing needs linked to the war effort.[26]

In the preamble to this decree, Itaboraí admitted that the Executive was acting beyond its powers, but had decided to go ahead in view of the urgency of the situation (Pacheco 1979, Vol. II, pp. 416–9).[27] Shortly afterward—and on top of the earlier note issue—a new Decree (No. 4244, of 15 September) gave permission to the Ministry of Finance to contract a domestic "gold" (exchange-rate-indexed) loan of up to 30,000 *contos*. This was intended as a means to extend the maturity of debt—deemed excessively reliant on short-term (less than one year) *letras*—and reduce the need for the issue of paper money.

Subscription to this issue of the National Loan (Empréstimo Nacional) exceeded all expectations and reached 120,000 *contos*, a sixth of which came from the Bank of Brazil (*SAJ*, 7 November 1868, p. 12). This significant demand suggested both the existence of substantial resources in the economy, awaiting profitable investment opportunities, and the good reputation of the imperial government.[28] In the end, a proportional distribution was made in order to accommodate all investors, who bought the Treasury bonds (*apólices*) at 90% of their face value and were guaranteed 6% interest annually. From then on, issues of bonds of the consolidated imperial debt would become the main source of deficit financing. Accordingly, payments of interest on the domestic debt would take up a growing share of government expenditures, the cost having increased from 4800 *contos* in the 1864–5 financial year (5.8% of total expenditures) to 17,200 *contos* in 1870–1 (17.2% of outlays).[29]

Table 4.2 Liabilities of the imperial treasury, 1864–71 (in *contos*)

	Long-term debt (apólices)	*Short-term debt* (letras)	*Treasury notes*
1864	76,777.4	8248.5	28,300
1865	80,376.4	29,174.0	28,100
1866	90,442.2	38,986.8	38,900
1867	106,350.6	59,572.7	72,000
1868	125,206.7	72,705.6	115,900
1869	191,076.5	64,575.3	143,900
1870	234,312.0	42,586.1	150,700
1871	280,456.9	18,632.5	150,900

Sources: For *apólices* and *letras, RMF,* various issues; Treasury notes, from Brasil, IBGE (1990, p. 544)

Notes: Figures for *apólices* are as of March. Other data refer to end of year

The short-term effect of Decrees 4232 and 4244 on the structure of imperial government liabilities was a decrease, after 1868, in the share composed of *letras* and the growing reliance on *apólices* to finance current expenditures (Table 4.2).[30]

The reverse side of the decline in the use of *letras* was a ballooning of the outstanding stock of *apólices* and notes. The consolidated domestic debt reached a staggering 280,000 *contos* in March 1871 (a 250% increase on the amount outstanding at the outbreak of the War). Meanwhile, the end to the issuing rights of the Bank of Brazil, in 1866, made way for a four-fold increase in outstanding Treasury notes, which totaled more than 150,000 *contos* as of December 1871.[31] Total note issue (Treasury + private banks), in turn, grew by more than 60% (or approximately 75,000 *contos*) between December 1866 and December 1870 (Table 4.3).[32]

The War of the Triple Alliance ended on 1 March 1870, with the death of the Paraguayan leader, Solano López. Months before, deeming that the conflict could not last for much longer, parliamentary debates were increasingly directed to the issue of the emancipation of slaves. Speaking in the Senate on 17 June 1869, Nabuco de Araújo demanded from the government a clear position on the subject. He claimed that, in spite of its inclusion in the Speech from the Throne for two consecutive years, no proposal was forthcoming from the Conservative administration (Nabuco 1997, Vol. II, p. 789).

One year later, Nabuco insisted on the gravity of the situation, pointing out to the Emperor that the Liberals, then in opposition, did not have the

Table 4.3 Brazil: total notes outstanding, 1866–71 (in *contos*)

	Treasury notes	*%*	*Banknotes*	*%*	*Total*
1866	33,253.8	28.2	84,580.4	71.8	117,834.2
1867	60,164.7	49.1	62,357.7	50.9	122,522.4
1868	120,629.7	68.1	56,512.0	21.9	177,141.7
1869	150,687.4	77.7	43,133.3	22.3	193,820.7
1870	151,916.1	78.9	40,727.6	21.8	192,643.7
1871	150,833.5	79.7	38,329.5	20.3	189,163.0

Source: *RMF* 1871, p. 17

Note: Figures for Treasury notes differ from those in Table 4.2 due to the different sources used

power to push through the gradual abolition of slavery. However, he believed that there were moderate Conservative backbenchers up to the task. The message was clear: the current Itaboraí cabinet, as a representative of the older (*saquarema*) generation of Conservatives, was not truly committed to emancipation.

The turning point came with yet another Nabuco initiative—the introduction, on 19 September, of an amendment to the imperial budget determining that the government set aside 1000 *contos* every year to provide for the manumission of slaves. Itaboraí and part of his cabinet refused to accept this Liberal initiative, which nevertheless was welcomed by other ministers. Among them, Paranhos, just returned from Paraguay and resuming his post as Minister of Foreign Affairs. In view of the split in the Conservative ranks, Itaboraí resigned, making way for a new cabinet, led by João Antônio Pimenta Bueno (the future Marquês de São Vicente) and with Torres Homem as Minister of Finance, to be inaugurated in September 1870.

Shortly after taking office, the new government made an issue of 25,000 *contos* in *apólices* with the stated objective of starting to withdraw part of the floating debt (*letras*) of the Empire, which, by December 1869, had reached nearly 65 thousand *contos*. Moreover, in February 1871 the government floated a £3 million loan in London at 89% and 5% interest amounting to a nominal value of £3,459,000 (Bouças 1955, p. 164). With the resources thus obtained, it sought to consolidate the short-term Treasury debt, finance the extension of the Pedro II railroad, and to cover budget deficits arising from extraordinary outlays by both the War and Navy ministries.

These loans would turn out to be one of the few notable measures taken by this short-lived cabinet. Barely a fortnight after signing the foreign loan, the João Alfredo government would be replaced by the longest-serving cabinet of the Second Reign, headed by Paranhos (since June 1870 Visconde do Rio Branco), who would also act as Minister of Finance.

4.2 The Rio Branco Government and the 1875 Crisis

The whole 1870–89 period is often heralded in the historiography as the "age of reform" and, more broadly, commitment to change in imperial Brazil.[33] Few imperial cabinets displayed such reformist initiative as the one led by Paranhos from March 1871 to June 1875. Among other things, it introduced the metric system in the Empire,[34] successfully carried out the first general population census in Brazil—both in 1872—and, most notably, managed to pass in Parliament in September 1871 the so-called Free Womb Law.[35] This, in turn, would bring the "labor question" (*questão da mão-de-obra*) to the forefront of the political debate in the closing decades of the Empire. A constant supply of labor for the expanding coffee frontier, alongside cheaper capital (credit), would be the two major rallying cries of the planter class in the 1870s and 1880s.

In the 1871 Report of the Minister of Finance presented to the Assembly, Paranhos had no doubt in stating that, as regards economic affairs, 'the abnormal state of the monetary circulation' constituted the 'most important matter worthy of study and the dictates of the (lawmakers') wisdom' (*RMF* 1871, p. 16). He would go on to remind members of Parliament of the massive increase of inconvertible paper issued during the War, comprised mostly of liabilities of the State (notes and *letras* issued by the Treasury).[36] These issues, in turn, were deemed the major factor behind what the Minister considered the 'general disturbance of all prices and a low (depreciated) and unstable rate of exchange, which chases away foreign capital while injuring the country in its foreign trade' (ibid., p. 18). Gradual withdrawal of this inconvertible paper and its replacement by specie and convertible notes was necessary, he argued, if the country were to reach a point of a 'normal (monetary) circulation' (ibid., p. 19). The latter, in turn, supposed a rate of exchange at (or near) the "mythical" parity of 27d/1$000.

Table 4.4 Average monthly rate of exchange in Rio, 1870–5 (in pence per milréis)

	1870	*1871*	*1872*	*1873*	*1874*	*1875*
Jan	19 7/8	24 3/8	24 3/8	26 1/8	26 1/8	26 1/2
Feb	19 3/4	24 1/8	24 1/8	26 1/4	25 7/8	26 11/16
Mar	21 1/8	25 1/8	24 3/8	26 11/16	26	26 3/4
Apr	23	25 1/4	24 1/2	26 1/4	25 11/16	26 5/8
May	23 1/8	25 1/8	24 1/4	25 3/4	25 1/8	26 7/8
Jun	22 1/8	25 1/4	24 1/4	25 3/4	24 15/16	27 3/16
Jul	22 7/8	22 3/4	24 1/2	25 1/2	25 5/16	26 5/8
Aug	20 5/8	24 1/4	25 1/2	25 13/16	25 15/16	27
Sep	20 1/4	24 1/4	25 3/4	26	26 1/4	27 1/8
Oct	22 1/16	23 3/4	25 3/4	25 13/16	26 7/16	27 1/2
Nov	22 7/8	24 1/8	25 7/8	26	26 3/4	27 7/16
Dec	23 7/8	24 1/2	25 13/16	25 7/8	26 5/16	24 1/16
Average	21 3/8	24 1/4	24 7/8	25 15/16	25 7/8	26 15/16

Source: *RMF*, various issues

Looking at the data in Table 4.4, two things stand out. First—and more strikingly—it is clear that the milréis had recovered significant ground in the twelve months between the end of the War, in March 1870, and the start of the Rio Branco government, in March 1871. Second, it does appear, at first glance, as if the minister succeeded in his objective of bringing the milréis to the 27d parity. Indeed, the rate of exchange over the whole period when Paranhos acted as both Prime Minister and Minister of Finance (i.e., from March 1871 to June 1875) displays a gradually appreciating trend from just over $25_{1/8}$d to $27_{3/18}$d. Nevertheless, the *government's* role in promoting this appreciation is not altogether clear.

The two tools at the minister's disposal that could have helped achieve the desired appreciation of the milréis were monetary and fiscal policy. As regards the former, high-powered money (defined exclusively as the sum of outstanding issues of both Treasury notes and private banknotes) fell by some 13,000 *contos* (or 7%) between March 1871 and June 1875 and, as such, may well have helped appreciate the milréis. However, this drop in the monetary base was accounted for, basically, by the progressive retirement of private banknotes from circulation, as mandated by the 1866 Law. Treasury issues remained practically constant (at approximately 150,000 *contos*) throughout, indicating that Paranho's plan to use budget surpluses to withdraw (government) paper money from the market was frustrated.[37]

Estimates of the money supply (M1) in the first half of the 1870s, in turn, point to a relative stability between 1870 and 1874, at around 223,000 *contos*, subsequently retreating to 215,000 *contos* by June 1875.[38] M2, in turn, increased approximately 12% over the same period.[39]

Fiscal data for the first half of the 1870s reveal that the government did expect an excess of revenues over outlays in the budgets presented by the Minister of Finance to the Assembly from 1870–1 to 1874–5. Yet, in every occasion—bar a modest surplus obtained in the 1871–2 fiscal year—realized expenditures far exceeded estimated expenditures. This, ultimately, led to substantial realized deficits and, thus, to an expansionary fiscal policy, which was *less* conducive to an appreciation of the currency (Table 4.5).

While the money supply (M1) remained stable during the first half of the decade,[40] credit conditions for the productive sector were far from ideal.[41] In an attempt to address the high cost of credit to agriculture, in early 1871, the President of the Bank of Brazil suggested to its shareholders that a proposal be submitted to the government with a view to enable the Bank to support agriculture more 'efficiently'. As the worst effects of the 1864 Crisis and the Paraguayan War had been overcome, he argued, more resources had become available in the Rio market, and this presented the Bank with an opportunity to channel part of these funds to planters. Accordingly, in April 1872, the Bank sent a formal petition to the Minister of Finance (Paranhos) where it recognized that interest and amortization rates being charged *fazendeiros* (9% and 8%, respectively), combined with short repayment periods (six years), conspired to make

Table 4.5 Estimated and realized central government budgets, 1870–1 to 1874–5 (in *contos* '000)

Fiscal year	*Estimated revenues*	*Realized revenues*	*Estimated expenditures*	*Realized expenditures*	*Estimated result*	*Realized result*
1870–1	94.1	97.7	83.3	100.1	10.8	−4.2
1871–2	95.8	105.1	85.7	101.6	10.1	0.7
1872–3	95.8	112.1	85.7	121.9	10.1	−11.2
1873–4	103.0	105.0	98.3	121.5	4.7	−18.8
1874–5	103.0	106.5	98.3	125.9	4.7	−21.2

Source: calculated from data in Brasil, Ministério da Fazenda, *Balanços da Receita e Despeza do Imperio*, various issues

loans from its mortgage department less attractive to farmers, who remained dependent on *comissários* for most of their credit needs (Pacheco 1979, vol. III, pp. 6–7).[42]

In return for a reduction of both interest and amortization rates to 6% and an increase in the repayment period to twelve years, the Bank of Brazil sought from the government a number of measures, namely: (i) an extension of its charter for another fourteen years; (ii) a reduction of the rate at which its notes were to be withdrawn (from 5% to 2.5% p. a.); and (iii) changes to mortgage legislation (in particular, to the forced adjudication mechanism,[43] which the Bank desired to do away with) and to rules governing the judicial sale of slaves given as collateral by debtors.

Overall, Paranhos was sympathetic to the Bank's requests, noting only that, in view of the benefits accruing to the Bank from a slower pace of withdrawal of its notes in circulation, the rate of interest charged customers should be even lower (5%), with amortization set at 7% annually (ibid.). The Bank's petition, turned into an Executive bill, was duly referred to Parliament in May 1872, but shortly afterward, the Chamber was dissolved.[44]

As the new Chamber convened, in 1873, the bill came under attack from several deputies. Tomás Coelho de Almeida, an influential landowner from the cane-growing region of Campos dos Goytacazes and Conservative deputy for the province of Rio de Janeiro, was one of the most vocal critics of the proposed changes to the statutes of the Bank of Brazil. In his opinion, with the new contract that was signed with the government in 1866, the Bank had actually been rescued from collapse. He added that, under the terms providing for the creation of a mortgage department within the Bank, the conversion of 35,000 *contos* of commercial loans of poor quality into an equal amount of collateralized credit to agriculture was a boon to the institution. This benefit was reinforced, he reasoned, by the permission the Bank received to withdraw its notes from circulation over more than a decade (*ACD* 1873, Tome I, pp. 231–5). Deputy Pereira da Silva, a Director of the Bank of Brazil, as expected, positioned himself in favor of the bill, while maintaining that rural credit was still hampered by several obstacles, notable among which was the institution of forced adjudication, which limited banks' incentives to offer credit backed by rural property (Pacheco 1979, vol. III, p. 19).

The bill was approved after debate in the Chamber and was sent to the Senate, where it withstood another barrage of attacks. In the end, an amended version was ultimately approved and the bill returned to the lower House. On 11 September 1873, the final version passed the vote in the Chamber and, following the Emperor's sanction, became Law 2400 on 17 September (ibid.).

The Law's main provisions included: (i) a reduction in the rate of retirement of notes issued by all banks created by decree in 1857–8, from 5% to 2.5% annually; (ii) an extension of the Bank of Brazil's charter for another fourteen years, provided its mortgage loans did not drop below 25,000 *contos*; and (iii) a cap on the rates charged by the Bank's mortgage department (at 6% interest and 5% amortization).[45]

Months before passage of the Law, news of the 1873 international crisis arrived in Brazil. In a letter dated 15 May and sent by its correspondent in London, Rio's *Jornal do Commercio* reported on the decision taken on 11 May by the Bank of England to increase its rate of discount from 4½% to 5%, with further rate increases being expected by the market.[46] The correspondent went on to explain the origin of the panic (in Vienna) and its spread to Berlin and Germany as a whole, couching the Bank of England's policy decision in terms of the need to protect its gold reserves. He also added that prices for bonds of both the Brazilian and Argentinean foreign debts were adversely hit, as expected (*Jornal do Commercio*, 12 June 1873, p. 2).[47]

In sharp contrast to events in 1857, the effect of the news on the Rio foreign exchange market was negligible. The milréis, which in early June was quoted at 26d – 26½d, lost some ground, falling to 25¾ in subsequent weeks and remaining at a similar level for the rest of the year.

The "real" economy does not seem to have been greatly affected either by news of the financial panic in Europe—and, later, in the United States. On the contrary, a number of indicators suggest that the economy was in the midst of a recovery from the difficulties arising from the long war against Paraguay.[48] For instance, the rate of railway and telegraph extensions, coffee exports and prices, and central government tax receipts all seemed to indicate a buoyant economy barely touched by news of the turmoil overseas.[49]

This apparent calm notwithstanding, in October 1873, the Mauá Bank (Banco Mauá & Cia.) approached the Bank of Brazil with a loan request for 1000 *contos* (£108,000).[50] At the time, it was still reeling from the effects of a (second) run on its branch in Montevideo, which had taken place in February 1869 and forced it to suspend payments.[51] Two years later, the Mauá Bank was still suffering from the losses incurred by its affiliate. Its deposit base (demand + time) had dropped from 47.7 thousand *contos* in December 1867 to just over 21.3 thousand *contos* in December 1869.[52] The Bank of Brazil agreed to provide the loan asked by Mauá, considering the businessman's timely payment of previous loans extended by the Bank as well as the quality of the assets being offered as collateral in the present credit operation (Pacheco 1979, vol. III, p. 34).

Still, this did not mean that all was well with Mauá's business ventures. In early March 1874, the Mauá Bank once again contacted the Bank of Brazil. This time, it sought permission to draw on £40,000 it had previously deposited in the Bank as security for a loan, giving in exchange a bill for 360 *contos* (the equivalent of the amount in sterling) due in twenty days. The hard currency, Mauá claimed, was needed to attend to an urgent necessity of his bank's branch in Montevideo (ibid., p. 36). In the end, the Bank acquiesced and granted the loan.

Six weeks later, on 25 April, the Board of Directors was informed of yet another appeal from Mauá. This time, it involved a loan of up to 2000 *contos* (£240,000) to help his business group weather the ongoing monetary crisis in Montevideo and the stagnation in export activity (coffee, mostly) in Santos, both of which, he claimed, were creating great hardship for his business. Assets offered in guarantee comprised shares in two of Mauá's companies operating in Uruguay with cattle raising and the production of beef extract. This collateral would be supplemented by a power of attorney entitling the Bank of Brazil to receive from the Treasury 1000 *contos* due Mauá on account of studies prepared by his firm for a planned railway line linking the provinces of Paraná and Mato Grosso (ibid.).

Given that the statutes of the Bank of Brazil banned the acceptance of collateral consisting of shares with no price quoted in Rio, the majority of its Board of Directors turned down the loan. The decision went against the President's recommendation, and was in no small measure influenced by Mauá's incapacity to honor the 360 *contos* bill, which had been given as guarantee for the previous loan (ibid., p. 37).

At the time, economic difficulties appeared to be confined solely to Mauá's business ventures. Indeed, the behavior of the exchange-rate market in Rio through the better part of 1874 suggests that the Brazilian economy displayed a healthy state overall. The rate of exchange—in a sense, a "barometer" of the general shape of the economy and of agents' expectations—averaged 25 7/8d, just a notch below the average quotation of the previous year. Still, momentary shocks to an otherwise stable market did occur in June, amid rumors of a possible conflict with Argentina over border disputes around Paraguay, and again in October, when the government officially recognized facing troubles in trying to float a loan in London (*RCJC* 1874, p. 38). Yet, nothing that could indicate that a crisis in the Rio market was brewing in the horizon, the origins of which were not in the industrializing economies of the North Atlantic, but in the small Republic of Uruguay.

On 15 January 1875, in the aftermath of a *coup d'état* that brought Pedro Varela to power, the Uruguayan government allowed the Junta de Crédito Público to issue 3 million pesos worth of inconvertible currency, sending shock waves through the local monetary market and producing a run against, among others, the Mauá Bank (Millot and Bertino 1991, Tome II, pp. 433–4). In anticipation of this, in early January, Mauá had instructed the manager of the head office of his bank in Rio to secure £200,000 in gold from London, which were to be sent in the next steamer to Montevideo, where it would be used to calm depositors. The operation, ultimately, fell through, as the Banco Alemão Brasileiro (Deutsche Brasilianische Bank), which would finance the operation, was unable to raise the necessary resources. As a result, the Mauá Bank in Montevideo ran out of specie and was forced to shut its doors after operating for almost two decades in the country (Caldeira 1995, pp. 497–9).

The strain on Mauá's banking empire reverberated in Rio. In a meeting of the Board of Directors of the Bank of Brazil on 23 February 1875, its Vice President mentioned the "tightness" then prevailing in the money market. In light of this, he had instructed the mortgage department to slow down the concession of new loans and, furthermore, was seeking permission from Board members to approach the government for a 2100 *contos* loan backed by *apólices* in its portfolio. Permission was duly granted (Pacheco 1979, vol. III, p. 46).[53]

On the meeting held on 4 March, the Vice President notified Board members that the abnormal circumstances of the market persisted, aggravated by 'some difficulties with discounts'. He added that the government was willing to assist the Bank, for not only did it approve the loan request, which had been made earlier, but also the Minister of Finance himself (Rio Branco) had indicated that more resources could be made available if needed in order to calm the market (ibid., p. 47).

A few days later, Mauá's troubles would be laid firmly at the Bank's doorsteps. When the Board convened on 8 March, directors were informed of a new loan application made by the financier. This time, the Mauá Bank sought 800 *contos* (£89,200) to help in dealing not only with the fallout from its operations in Montevideo but also the pressure being felt in the

Rio market. As the collateral it offered (the proceeds Mauá expected to receive from the Treasury for the feasibility study on the railway line connecting Curitiba to Miranda) was deemed insufficient, once again, the request was turned down (ibid.).

Still, the next day the Board met extraordinarily to deliberate on a *new* loan request from Mauá—now for 1500 *contos* (£167,200)—backed by a different guarantee: the endorsement of the Banco Alemão. If approved by the Board, Mauá would withdraw an equivalent amount in *apólices* deposited in the Bank as collateral for a previous operation.

This time around—and somewhat surprisingly, in light of subsequent events—the directors were unanimous in giving the go ahead to the operation. Arguments in favor of the decision highlighted the Bank's stake in approving the loan, given its position as Mauá's foremost creditor, the latter's past efforts in reducing its reliance on the Bank of Brazil, and the trust provided by the endorsement of the Banco Alemão. This bank, it was noted, had never fallen foul of its commitments toward the Bank of Brazil, with whom it maintained significant businesses (ibid., p. 48).

In May 1875, a full-blown crisis unfolded. On an extraordinary meeting held on the 5th, the Board of directors of the Bank of Brazil convened to debate a request made by the Banco Nacional for a loan for 2000 *contos* (£224,000), to be backed by commercial paper. Participants noted that the Nacional already owed the Bank 1900 *contos* and that the quality of its credit had become dubious. Furthermore, Board members remarked that the turbulence currently experienced by the market was visible and that, as such, the Bank of Brazil should proceed with the utmost prudence, especially considering the low level of its reserves (which stood at only 1500 *contos*, against demand deposits in excess of 23,000 *contos*).[54] The loan was denied (Pacheco 1979, vol. III, p. 48).

Two days later, on yet another extraordinary meeting of the Board, the acting President briefed directors on a reunion he had attended the day before at Minister Paranho's residence, and at which the presidents of other banks and the capital's main financiers were present in order to discuss 'the state of the (Rio) market'. Participants agreed that this state was "difficult", marked by retrenchment of capital and overall wariness, and that this should be attributed mainly to maturity mismatches in banks' portfolios.[55] As for solutions to these difficulties, those present urged the Treasury to advance resources at its disposal to the banks, thus acting as a lender of last resort.[56]

On the session held on 11 May, the Board debated an application made by the Banco Nacional for a new loan, this time consisting of an advance of 2000 *contos* in *apólices* against various assets in its portfolio. The request was unanimously turned down, with directors citing the Bank of Brazil's need to retain those *apólices* in view of its low cash reserves (now down to just 800 *contos*), as well as the Nacional's reckless lending activities, which had saddled it with a poor credit standing (Pacheco 1979, vol. III, p. 49). The next day the Nacional folded.

On 15 May, the directors of the Bank of Brazil convened again to discuss the latest request made by Mauá. The Barão had approached the Bank for a 3000 *contos* (£337,000) loan, to be received in *apólices*, and guaranteed by shares of Mauá's Cia. Agrícola Pastoril (Caldeira 1995, pp. 499–503). Once more, the Board of Directors decided in unison against the loan. Two days later, on 17 May 1875, the Mauá Bank suspended payments and went into receivership (Schulz 1996, pp. 45–7).[57]

Much as the month of May should be seen as the climax of the 1875 crisis, there were signs that the Rio market was already undergoing difficulties earlier in the year. And this shows up in both the financial press and in the minutes of the debates in Parliament. Regarding the former, in a column dated 24 February that appeared in the *Jornal do Commercio*, the author describes the Rio money market as being 'hampered' (*peado* in the original), 'with money hard to obtain even against solid collateral, all this indicating either excessive wariness or the exhaustion of all available resources' (*Jornal do Commercio*, 24 February 1875, p. 1).

In Parliament, the issue of a possible crisis in the Rio market was raised soon after Senate convened for the first session of the legislative year, on 19 March. In the occasion, Zacarias de Gois e Vasconcellos (who had thrice served as Prime Minister and, in his last term, also as Minister of Finance) read in the Senate floor an internal memo from the Banco Alemão, dated 27 February. In this document, the bank alluded to hardships in the Rio money market, urged the government to take 'forceful measures' in order to 'remedy that evil' and informed that it had decided that from 15 March onward it would severely limit the terms of loans advanced to its clients (*ASI* 1875, vol. I, pp. 7–9).

In the same session, Zacarias asked that the Minister of Finance be explicit about the government's stance on the matter. In other words, that he clarify whether, in the Minister's opinion, the Rio market was, indeed, suffering from a crisis and, if so, what 'forceful measures' were authorities willing to take in order to overcome it (ibid., p. 10). In his reply, Paranhos admitted that, in fact, there was a shortage of credit in the Rio market and that (commercial) transactions were not undertaken as under 'normal circumstances'. He added that it had become impossible to secure loans collateralized by either *apólices* or *letras* issued by the Treasury of late and suggested that, under the circumstances, a bank of issue that could alleviate credit conditions would be welcomed (ibid., p. 11). The matter was further debated in a number of sessions in the imperial Senate over the coming months.

The first reference to a "crisis" in the Rio market was made in the Chamber by representative Ferreira Vianna (Conservative, Rio de Janeiro) during an extraordinary session held on 20 March and while debating an altogether lateral issue with the Minister of Justice (*ACD*, Sessão Extraordinária, 1875, p. 52). The latter seconded Paranho's statement in the Senate on the previous day to the effect that the market was experiencing, at most, a modest contraction of credit, adding that, in the absence of major bankruptcies, alterations to the rate of exchange or to discount rates, there was a degree of exaggeration in labelling the situation at hand a "commercial crisis" (ibid., p. 76).

Two months later, reality could no longer be evaded. On the inaugural session of the 14th Legislature, on 14 May, Paranhos brought before the Chamber of Deputies a bill that, if approved, would authorize the government to issue a sum not exceeding 25,000 *contos* of either interest-bearing *letras* or Treasury notes, to be used toward assisting commercial banks.[58] These resources were needed, according to the Minister, to address the 'current circumstances affecting the Rio market and those amongst the most important in the Empire', and which required 'prompt and exceptional measures in order to prevent the dire consequences arising from a panic' (*ACD* 1875, vol. 1, p. 79).

After three sessions of debates in the Chamber, the bill was approved without amendments and sent to the Senate. The Finance Committee of the upper House backed the proposal and prompted senators to debate the matter urgently and endorse it. Despite vehement protestations by, among others, Senators Zacarias de Gois e Vasconcellos and Silveira da Mota, the bill was ultimately approved on 28 May and forwarded to the Emperor for sanctioning. The following day, it was published as Law 2565, and, just as in the original bill, it authorized the government to issue up to 25,000 *contos* in either Treasury bills or notes in order to assist deposit banks.

As it happened, Law 2565 sanctioned a policy that had been well under way since early March, when the Treasury made the first of 15 advances to Rio banks, totaling just over 16 thousand *contos*, and consisting exclusively of paper money (notes). Altogether, the Bank of Brazil borrowed 7.1 thousand *contos* (or 44%) of total funds loaned by the Treasury, with the German Bank and the Rural & Hypothecario receiving 5.4 thousand *contos* and 3.3 thousand *contos*, respectively (*RMF* 1876, Annex, Table 9). As part of the total amount was redirected from monies in the budget, net issues of Treasury notes totaled 9.1 thousand *contos* (see Table 5.2). Repayment of the final instalment of these emergency loans occurred in January 1876.

Lawmakers were not happy with the way the government handled the crisis. Two topics dominated subsequent debates that looked into the matter in both Houses of Parliament. First, the fact that the government had issued paper money during the Legislative recess instead of waiting for the new Chamber to convene. Second, allegations of misconduct in an operation involving the transfer of resources to London by the Mauá Bank on behalf of the Treasury. In the latter case, the personal friendship linking the fallen banker with the Prime Minister (and Minister of Finance) lent itself to political use by the Liberal opposition in Parliament (Caldeira 1995, pp. 505–9). In the end, Paranhos resigned, making way for a new, Conservative, cabinet led by the elderly war hero, Caxias, with Sinimbu as Minister of Finance.

The 1875 crisis left a mixed legacy on the Brazilian economy. Immediate casualties, of course, involved the failures of the Mauá Bank (and, ultimately, the collapse of his business empire) and of the smaller Banco Alemão and Banco Nacional.[59] Looking at specific variables, coffee prices in Rio remained stable over the course of 1875 while the average rate of exchange exhibited a moderately appreciating trend, on several occasions exceeding the 27d/1$000 mark.[60] Rates of discount in Rio increased from 7% in February to 8–10% for the rest of the year, while the volume of credit advanced by local banks contracted between 1875 and 1877, amid an increase in the cash/deposits ratio of the banking system as a whole.[61]

Unlike his predecessor in the post, Paranhos, who in his annual report sent to Parliament barely referred to the 1875 crisis or to the loans extended by the Treasury to banks,[62] João Maurício Wanderley (Barão de Cotegipe) addressed the matter over three pages in the 1876 *Relatório do Ministerio da Fazenda*. After detailing the credit operations carried out by the Treasury in support of the three Rio-based banks (and another 500 *contos* advanced to banks in the province of Bahia), Cotegipe noted the benefits accruing not only to the Rio market but also to the Treasury itself in the shape of 365 *contos* in profits from the loans (*RMF* 1876, pp. 25–7).

During the two-and-a-half years of the Caxias administration, two policy initiatives in the monetary and banking realm stand out. The first one involved the ill-fated attempt to provide a further boost to mortgage credit. Law 2687, of 6 November 1875, authorized the government to offer guaranteed annual dividends of 5% on bonds issued by a mortgage bank set up in accordance with the 1864 (mortgage) legislation. Capital for this bank would have to be raised in Europe, mandatorily, and loans were to be advanced against rural property at a maximum rate of interest of 7% and amortized at between five and thirty years. The new Law did not arouse investors' interest as these mortgage bonds were deemed less attractive than bonds of the imperial government foreign debt (ibid., p. 24).[63]

The second, and more controversial, initiative took the shape of the Treasury sale, on 23 January 1877, of 30,000 *contos* in *apólices* to the Bank of Brazil. Critics of the operation argued that, in buying those *apólices* from the Treasury, the Bank was depriving the private sector (agriculture) of sorely needed credit (Pacheco 1979, vol. III, pp. 96–7). This transaction came in the wake of issues of the domestic-funded debt amounting to 8600 *contos* made in 1876 in order to help finance the budget deficit (see Table A8, in the Appendix). This shortfall would extend over three fiscal years (from 1876–7 to 1878–9), peaking at more than 55% of ordinary revenues (65 thousand *contos*, or £6.2 million) at the end of the period (see Table A6, in the Appendix). Issues of the domestic-funded debt were complemented in the second half of 1877 by increased recourse to the floating debt: between May and December, the stock of circulating *letras do Tesouro* more than doubled to 45,000 *contos*, implying the net issue of 25,000 *contos* in short-term liabilities of the government over the same period (*RMF* 1877, Annex, Table 35).

4.3 Political Instability, Debt, and Banking Reform: The 1880s

The end of the Caxias government in January 1878 made way for the return of the Liberals to power after almost a decade in opposition, ushering in a period of frantic cabinet reshuffles that would last until the very end of the imperial era.[64]

The first Liberal cabinet, headed by Sinimbu,[65] took over amid, arguably, the worst episode of drought in Brazilian history—the *Grande Sêca* of 1877–79. Virtual absence of rainfall for an extended period led to an estimated half a million fatal casualties, with another 200 thousand affected residents fleeing to other regions of the Empire, mostly to the Amazon (Davis 2002, pp. 79–90). As part of the efforts to provide relief to the tragedy, Sinimbu requested permission from the Emperor (in the absence of the new Chamber, which had not yet convened) to issue up to 60,000 *contos* in Treasury notes during the 1877–8 and 1878–9 fiscal years.[66] This was a significant sum, as it corresponded to approximately 30% of the expected ordinary revenues over these two years. The Emperor acceded to the request and Decree 6882, of 15 April 1878, followed, granting permission to Minister of Finance Silveira Martins to carry out the operation.[67]

As expected, the decree met with harsh opposition as soon as Parliament resumed its activities, notably from the Liberal-controlled Senate. The Finance Committee of the upper House ruled the decree illegal and unfounded; nevertheless, it suggested its backing by lawmakers as 'all its consequences have materialized and the Chamber of Deputies has approved it, therefore ceasing the ministers' criminal responsibilities (for the act)' (Pacheco 1979, vol. III, p. 120). In the end, the government would issue 40,000 *contos* to help fund the increased expenditures.[68]

The most visible victim of the acrimony that followed the controversial Decree 6882 was the Minister of Finance himself, Silveira Martins, who was replaced in February 1879 by Senator Afonso Celso de Assis Figueiredo. Shortly after taking office, Afonso Celso approached the Bank of Brazil with a proposal for a contract to be celebrated between that institution and the imperial government. The essence of the contract would involve three measures:

1. The Bank would take charge of the servicing of the floating debt, thereby opening a current account for the Treasury;
2. The Bank would provide the government with the bills of exchange needed to service its foreign debt; and

3. The Bank would take over functions hitherto exercised by the Amortization Office (the issuance and withdrawal of treasury notes, especially) (Pacheco 1979, vol. III, p. 134).

In March, the shareholder's meeting approved the terms of the agreement with the government and, shortly afterward, a contract was signed for the current account to be opened by the Treasury, with credit limited to 10,000 *contos*.[69] Subsequently, shareholders approved a change to the statutes allowing the Bank to operate overseas in foreign exchange on its own behalf. On 3 May, the government issued Decree 7265 approving the said changes to the Bank's statutes (Pacheco 1979, vol. III, pp. 136–8).

The following month, Parliament authorized the issue of a second National Loan consisting of bearer bonds with interest and principal fixed in sterling. The 50,000 *contos* offer was heavily oversubscribed and was used toward meeting the budget deficit and retiring part of the floating debt. The latter, which at the time stood at just over 30,000 *contos*, would drop by half in the next twelve months (see Table A7 in the Appendix).[70]

The Sinimbu cabinet ended in March 1880,[71] owing to its failure to secure parliamentary backing for a constitutional amendment that would allow for a reform of the electoral system. Over the next five years, six Liberal cabinets would take turns at the helm of the Executive. During this period, the milréis would sustain the downward trend that had started in 1875 when it briefly stood above par (27d). Thereafter, the rate of exchange went into freefall, with the occasional respite or mild recovery. At the start of the Saraiva government, in March 1880, the milréis was quoted at 22d, and in August 1885, when the Conservative Party returned to power once again under the premiership of Cotegipe, it had fallen further, to 18d.[72]

The third Liberal cabinet in the decade, headed by Paranaguá, would last less than a year (from 3 June 1882 to 24 May 1883). Still, it would be responsible for promoting a major change in company law, turning formation of joint-stock companies into an administrative affair only and, hence, independent of official authorization, as had been the case since the 1860 Law of Impediments.[73] Charters would henceforth be required exclusively of a handful of businesses, including banks of issue (but not ordinary deposit banks), which would still have to obtain legislative approval prior to starting operations.[74]

In his capacity as Minister of Finance, Paranaguá would also secure the floatation of the first of four loans contracted by the imperial government in London in the 1880s (see Table A9, in the Appendix). The £4 million loan of 1883 was taken out with the aim of financing the government's growing expenditures with the so-called material improvements, such as railways, central sugar mills, Rio's water supply network, and so on.[75] These capital expenses, which averaged 20% of total outlays in the early 1870s, ten years later were taking up approximately 30% of the imperial budget.[76]

The Paranaguá government was brought down by a vote of no confidence and was succeeded by yet another Liberal cabinet, headed by Lafayette Rodrigues Pereira. In the section on "The Circulating Medium" in his 1883 report to the Assembly, Lafayette claimed that there was a 'superabundance' of paper money in circulation, and that this was, ultimately, the reason why the rate of exchange had been depreciating for almost a decade. In order to remedy this situation—and given the sheer impossibility of instituting a fully gold-backed monetary circulation at the time—he suggested that at least the *spirit* of the 1846 legislation (which had established the official gold parity of 27 pence to the milréis) be restored. In practice, this entailed (following Art. 2 of the said Law), withdrawing paper money from circulation until the rate of exchange reached par (*RMF* 1883, pp. 58–62).

In the same section in his report, Lafayette highlighted the recurring phenomenon of the drain of currency (both notes and specie) from Rio to the provinces at different times in the year, where it helped finance the commercialization of export crops. In his opinion, the scarcity of circulating medium that was being felt at that moment in Rio was akin to the situation prevalent in the same market when it was hit by the 1875 crisis. On the occasion, noted Lafayette, Law 2565 was passed, authorizing the government to lend funds to banks in distress. He finished by recommending that the said Law, which had been revoked by the 1879 budget law, be restored (ibid.).[77]

While not engaging in new issues of paper money, during his tenure as both Prime Minister and Minister of Finance, Lafayette presided over a momentary spike in the issuance of Treasury *letras* used to finance expenses linked to investments in "material improvements". By the time he left office, however, the amount of floating debt in circulation was back to the 46,000 *contos* where it stood when he came to power in May 1883 (*RMF* 1884, Annex, Table 26).

The final government in this so-called second Liberal quinquenium[78] came to office on 6 May 1885, lasted just over one hundred days, and was once again led by Saraiva. The political and economic atmospheres at the time were dominated by the abolitionist campaign, which added fear to coffee growers in the Paraíba Valley already having to grapple with the progressive deterioration of soil conditions in the region. Planters' predicaments had been compounded the year before by the Bank of Brazil's decision to cease advancement of new mortgage loans (Sweigart 1987, p. 158).

In an attempt to alleviate their plight, Law 3263, of 18 July 1885, was passed, authorizing the government to issue up to 25,000 *contos* in Treasury notes in order to assist deposit banks in Rio—thus reversing back to the 1875 Law championed by Paranhos. Over the next three years, the Treasury would issue 23,000 *contos* in all, which were loaned to Rio banks (most of which went to the Bank of Brazil) against the backing of both *apólices* and *letras*.[79]

The fall of the Saraiva cabinet in August 1885 and its replacement by the Conservative-led Cotegipe government resulted, largely, from the Crown's desire to garner support in the Senate for a bill promoting the definitive abolition of slavery in Brazil. During the next two-and-a-half years, Minister of Finance Francisco Belisário (nephew of the Conservative statesman Paulino José Soares de Souza, Visconde do Uruguai), would preside over a number of measures touching on monetary and fiscal policy.

Shortly after coming to office, the new cabinet oversaw the approval, in Parliament, of a "watered down" version of a bill freeing slaves who had reached the age of 60. The bill was converted into Law 3270 on 28 September 1885.[80] This would be a further step toward full emancipation of slaves, a prospect that sowed panic among coffee planters and brought their demands for cheaper credit closer to the center of the political debate. In this regard, Decree 3272, of 5 October 1885, sought to address one of the issues considered by banks as an obstacle to the expansion of mortgage credit, by doing away with the forced adjudication arrangement, which up to that point had made rural property an unattractive form of collateral in the eyes of creditors.[81]

As for monetary affairs, in the "Circulating Medium" section of the report he presented to the Assembly in May 1886, Minister Belisário remarked that

> the depreciation of our circulating medium (has been) producing disastrous consequences for all classes of society and imposes upon us the duty of no longer postponing the adoption of measures that will tend to correct such a state and prepare the country to reconquer the specie that it lost through the issuance of paper money. (*RMF* 1885, p. 16)[82]

Belisário went on to blame the excess of paper money in circulation for the depreciated rate of exchange and expressed his wish to establish in due course a metallic circulation in the country consisting of convertible banknotes, in accordance with the 1846 Law (i.e., at the 27/1$000 parity). This desideratum would be advanced, he pondered, by setting aside in the annual budget funds that would be used toward withdrawing paper money from the market and bringing the exchange back to par. Only then would the State entrust a bank, modeled on the experiences of the banks of England, Germany, and Belgium, with the task of 'regulating (monetary) circulation in the country' (ibid., p. 18).[83]

Earlier in that year, in February, the government contracted a loan for £6 million in London at 5% interest and a price of 95, with the objective of balancing the budget and providing for the consolidation of the floating debt (Bouças 1955, p. 70). One month before, the stock of *letras* in circulation reached a peak of 82,000 *contos*. With the proceeds from this loan, the latter would be gradually retired from the market and, one year later, their amount was down to 31,000 *contos*. This process was further aided by the issuance, in April 1886, of 50,000 *contos* in 5% *apólices* (instead of the usual 6% coupon) with the express purpose of consolidating the floating debt.

The question of convertibility would once again occupy part of Belisário's annual report presented to Parliament in May 1887. In the document, the minister remarked that the gradual withdrawal of paper money from circulation—as mandated by the latest budget law—was having the anticipated effect of forcing an appreciation of the currency. He then suggested that a bank of issue, after securing a foreign loan, could carry this forward by substituting its own gold-backed notes for government paper (*RMF* 1886, pp. 20–1). Finally, he wondered about the level at which convertibility of the new notes should be set, if at the notional 27d/1$000 rate of the 1846 Law or at a lower rate—24d, for instance (ibid., p. 22).[84]

In June, a bill was proposed by the Conservative Senator Teixeira Jr. (the future Visconde do Cruzeiro) in conjunction with his Liberal peers Afonso Celso and Lafayette, touching on a related matter—banking reform. In sharp contrast to the picture portrayed by Belisário in his reports, contemporaries agreed that Rio's money market was suffering not from "superabundance", but from a scarcity of circulating medium that went beyond the normal pattern that had historically been observed at the beginning and the middle of each year (Franco 1983, p. 53). The bill sought not only to address this recurrent problem but also the anticipated effects of abolition combined with the growing demand for currency brought about by the flow of tens of thousands of European immigrants into Brazil.

Essentially, the proposed legislation would restore the plurality of banks of issue that had been instituted by decree in 1857–8 under Souza Franco, and which remained in force until 1866, when the Treasury once again took over the monopoly of note issues (Schulz 2013, p. 148). Under the proposed bill, banks would be authorized to issue notes to the bearer redeemable on demand in Treasury paper. Backing for these issues (which were capped at 20,000 *contos* per bank, and 200,000 *contos* overall)[85] would consist of *apólices* to be deposited at the Caixa de Amortização. However, should the capital used to set up these banks consist of specie, gold-backed issues of up to three times the amount paid-in would be authorized.

Lacking official support from the Executive, the bill lay dormant in the Senate, following the endorsement provided by both the Finance and Legislation committees of the upper House (Pacheco 1979, vol. III, pp. 258–9). In the meantime, the Cotegipe cabinet collapsed under the weight of the visceral infighting among Conservatives over the question of the abolition of slavery.

Like many of his predecessors, the new President of the Council of Ministers, Conservative Senator João Alfredo Correia de Oliveira, who came to office on 10 March 1888, also held the Finance portfolio. As part of his strategy to prepare the economy for the imminent end of slavery, the government raised a £ 6 million loan in London in April, at 97 and 4½% interest—the best ever terms obtained by Brazil. In justifying to lawmakers the need for the loan, João Alfredo argued that for him 'it seemed urgent, at a time when the labor regime is being transformed, that the Treasury should be able to rid itself of the floating debt, to satisfy its extraordinary commitments easily, and to restrict, as much as possible, the circulation of paper money' (*RMF* 1887, p. 4).[86]

Abolition was finally approved in Parliament on 13 May 1888.[87] In June, the banking reform bill was once again brought for discussion to the Senate floor, where it would receive lukewarm support from Minister João Alfredo.[88] In his opinion, the provisions of the bill were not ideal. Instead, he preferred a single large bank of issue charged with the task of retiring government paper money from circulation, instead of the plurality of issue prescribed by the Teixeira Jr. bill. He recognized the difficulties involved in attaining that objective at the time and deemed that the banks envisioned by the Senate bill could lay the ground for a better solution in the future (Pacheco 1979, vol. III, p. 259).

After further debate, the bill was approved by the Senate and sent over to the Chamber of Deputies in September. There, it was endorsed by the House's Finance Committee, which, in support of the bill, pointed to its expected benefits, including 'the monetization of the consolidated debt, the (provision of) greater elasticity to the circulating medium (…) and in assisting in the *advent of a metallic circulation*' (emphasis added) (ibid., p. 261). The bill passed the vote in the lower House in November and was taken to the Emperor for sanction, becoming Decree 3403, of 24 November 1888, subsequently regulated by Decree 10144 of 5 January 1889.

João Alfredo resigned as President of the Council of Ministers in June 1889. After a succession of failed attempts to form a government, the Emperor turned to the Liberal Visconde de Ouro Preto. Following a vote of no confidence passed in the Conservative-controlled Chamber of Deputies, the lower House was dissolved and new elections called.

By the time Ouro Preto came to power, the Empire was in the midst of an economic boom that had started the year before, and which involved, among other things, increased numbers of European immigrants entering the country, a rising rate of incorporations in the manufacturing sector and growing inflows of direct foreign investment. Amid record trade and current account surpluses, the rate of exchange had attained the par value of 27d in October 1888, and remained at that level in subsequent months (Franco 1983, p. 61).[89]

Ouro Preto's avowed objective as head of the government was to deflate republican propaganda (in his own words, he sought to 'render the Republic worthless'). This would be accomplished, the minister hoped, by means of a program of institutional modernization of the monarchy, while at the same time securing the support of its traditional mainstay, the planter class.[90] To that effect, two policy initiatives would dominate his economic agenda: a massive program of assistance to agriculture (the Auxílios à Lavoura) and the adoption of a fully gold-backed monetary circulation.

The Auxílios promoted by the Ouro Preto government sought to help fulfill the expectations created by a host of initiatives undertaken since the 1860s in favor of rural credit. Ever since the promulgation of the mortgage reform in 1864 and the creation of the mortgage department of the

Bank of Brazil three years later, hopes of a major increase in the amount of credit (and a reduction in interest rates) extended to agriculture had been largely frustrated.[91] Law 2400, of 1873, which relaxed the pace of retirement of Bank of Brazil notes in exchange for its extension of a larger amount of credit to agriculture, had brought equally modest results.[92]

Ouro Preto's program was, effectively, a continuation—on a much larger scale—of the loans advanced by the previous administration to the Bank of Brazil and the Banco da Bahia, totaling 18,000 *contos*.[93] Over the following months, the government would sign seventeen new contracts involving a combined amount of 154,000 *contos*. The terms under which the banks would lend to agriculture were similar: the Treasury would advance a given amount of funds at zero interest to banks, which would have to lend double the amount to agriculture at 6% for periods that varied depending on the collateral offered by clients. As for the source of the government funds, they would come from yet another exchange-rate-indexed National Loan in the amount of 100,000 *contos* (Franco 1983, p. 83).

The program of assistance to agriculture carried out by both the João Alfredo and Ouro Preto administrations had a marked impact on the liquidity of the Rio banks, with a fourfold increase in their cash/deposit ratio between November 1888 and November 1889 (ibid., p. 86, Table 18). A not so welcome outcome, however, was the boost the Auxílios gave to frenzied speculation in the Rio stock exchange, as new banks were incorporated in the hope of benefiting from the subsidized credit provided by the Treasury (ibid., p. 90).[94]

The potential effects on the monetary market deriving from the credit injection under the Auxílios à Lavoura led to Ouro Preto's second major policy initiative: Decree 10262, of 6 July 1889, regulating the execution of the 1888 Decree dealing with banks of issue. In his opinion, by imposing limits on both the individual and aggregate capital base of the new banks, the regulation then in effect (laid down in January by Decree 10144) discouraged the formation of a bank of issue large enough to be capable of regulating the money supply and the rate of exchange. For the minister, formal adherence to the gold standard, as dreamed by generations of policymakers, was within reach—if only those limits were removed.

To this end, the new legislation promoted by Ouro Preto (Decree 10262) removed any limits to the capital base of gold-backed banks of issue, which would be allowed to issue convertible notes in values of up to three times their paid-in capital. Two months later, the minister reached an agreement with the Conde de Figueiredo, a leading financier and president of the Banco Internacional, the dominant player in the foreign exchange market. Under the agreement, Figueiredo's bank was converted into the Banco Nacional do Brasil on 19 September 1889, with a nominal capital of 90,000 *contos* (£9.9 million), and having the Banque de Paris et des Pays Bas as a major shareholder (Schulz 2013, pp. 164–5).

The new bank's statutes were approved on 28 September and, on 2 November, its contract with the government was signed. Under the latter, the bank was entrusted with the task of replacing within five years all Treasury notes in circulation (at the time, amounting to approximately 180,000 *contos*) with its own gold-backed currency. In exchange for its notes, the government pledged to issue 4% interest "gold" bonds (ibid., p. 164).[95]

More controversially, the contract also included a "crisis clause", authorizing the bank to suspend convertibility of its notes in case the exchange rate fell significantly below par as a result of an undefined "financial crisis". A second controversial clause of the contract signed with the Banco Nacional do Brasil involved the government's formal commitment to refrain from issuing new Treasury notes for the duration of the new bank's charter. This provision not only precluded any future recourse to deficit financing by the government but also compromised its role as lender of last resort to the banking system, as laid out in Law 3263 of 18 July 1885 (Franco 1983, pp. 92–4). Unlike the arrangement made with the "third" Bank of Brazil in 1853, this stabilizing role was not formally entrusted to the Banco Nacional do Brasil.

Twelve other banks would either be created or start issuing gold-backed notes under the provisions of Decree 10262. Most of those would have their statutes approved after 15 November 1889, when a military coup put an end to the constitutional monarchy. For the time being, though, it seemed as if the Ouro Preto banking reform was bearing fruit: the exchange remained close to its par level and a booming "real" economy appeared to be benefitting from an adequate level of liquidity provided by a banking system operating under the rules of the gold standard.

However, this impression would prove to be misleading. An even bolder banking reform was in the offing. When promulgated by the incoming republican government,[96] it would dramatically alter Brazil's monetary and banking landscape, bringing in its wake unchecked monetary expansion and the collapse of the exchange rate. Thereafter, the "mythical" 27d/milréis parity would remain just that: a myth.

Notes

1. A lecturer in Political Economy at the Law School of São Paulo, Carrão was a moderate Liberal representative for that province. In the report presented to the Assembly in May 1866, he stressed that at some 28,000 *contos* Treasury notes could not be deemed excessive, given that they had to meet the needs of the Empire as a whole, including the twelve provinces not served by the Bank of Brazil. However, he would go on to add that their 'existence, even in this amount, (could) not fail to be an evil, a fact that ha(d) been repeatedly recognized by the powers of the Empire'. For the Minister, 'present experience must have convinced all spirits that while paper money remained in circulation credit institutions with issuing (rights) must be reputed dangerous'. *RMF* 1865, pp. 6–7.
2. See "Representação da Directoria do Banco do Brasil" and "Representação dos Lavradores" in *Proposta do Poder Executivo sobre o Meio* (1866).
3. Ibid., p. 29.
4. Ibid., pp. 31 ff.
5. Ibid., p. 46. Regular interest rates charged by *commissários* to their planter clients varied between 8% and 14% p.a. See Sweigart (1987, pp. 120–1).
6. A contemporary pamphlet urged the government to follow a different path and create a new mortgage bank outside the Bank of Brazil. 'Let us effectively organize rural credit, which only exists on paper in the current mortgage legislation, and in the embryonic development of rural bonds, that presently obstruct the channels of mercantile circulation. Let mortgage credit have a powerful center, just as commercial credit has the Bank of Brazil'. *Ao Visconde de Itaborahy* (1866, p. 10).
7. According to a director of the Bank of Brazil, over a period of 'ten or fifteen days (they) were called upon to pay upward of £1000,000 in deposits'. *Banker's Magazine*, Vol. 27, February 1867, p. 166.
8. This was the Paula e Sousa bill, discussed below. The bill was credited with 'hastening by a material measure the (restoration) of confidence (in the Rio market)'. *The Brazil and River Plate Mail and South American Journal* (hereafter, *SAJ*), 23 July 1866, p. 316.
9. See also *SAJ*, 7 July 1866, p. 292.
10. *Banker's Magazine*, Vol. 27, February 1867, p. 166; and *SAJ*, 23 July 1866, p. 316.
11. Paula e Sousa was accused of serving as a figurehead for Carrão, his bill presumably bearing the handwriting of the Minister of Finance. See session of 12 June 1866, in *ACD*, Tome II, p. 88.
12. See also the "Annual Retrospect for Brazil", translated from the *Jornal do Commercio* and published in *SAJ*, 7 March 1867, pp. 8–9.

13. As pointed out by Pacheco, it was as though the Olinda cabinet had four different Ministers of Finance: Dias de Carvalho, later replaced by Carrão, Paula e Sousa (Agriculture), and Ferraz (War). See Pacheco (1979, Vol. II, pp. 296–9).
14. Pacheco disputes the version that the bill was at the sole initiative of Silveira da Mota. Instead, he claims it had been, at the very least, inspired by Silveira da Mota's conversations with Itaboraí and Torres Homem, as well as by the reading of articles that they had been publishing lately in the press. At the time, accusations of plagiarism were made against the author of the bill, charged with taking excerpts right out of earlier documents from the Council of State. See Pacheco (1979, Vol. II, pp. 308–9).
15. The Silveira da Mota bill contained six articles, while the committee's version had ten. Their essence was the same, however: to end the issuing activities of the Bank of Brazil; create a mortgage department; to promote the purchase, by the government, of the Bank's metallic fund; and the progressive withdrawal of the Bank's outstanding circulation. For the Silveira da Mota bill, see Cavalcanti (1893, Vol. 2, pp. 287–8); for the text of the Committee's bill, see Pacheco (1979, Vol. II, pp. 310–4).
16. The smaller Banco da Bahia, Banco Novo de Pernambuco, and Banco do Maranhão would retain a residual note circulation until the end of the Empire. However, given the volume of their total outstanding notes (less than 4000 *contos* in February 1867), and the fact that they were not accepted in payment of taxes and debts to the State, their impact on the money supply was marginal.
17. Quoted in Nabuco (1997, Vol, I, p. 636, footnote 9).
18. See also the "Annual Financial Retrospect for Brazil - 1866", in *SAJ*, 22 March 1867, pp. 6–7.
19. Decree 3720, of 18 October 1866, laid down the finer points for the proper execution of Law 1349 as regards the issues of the Bank of Brazil and the repayment of Treasury debts. On 23 November, the Bank's new statutes were approved (Decree 3739). For details, see *RMF* 1866, pp. 17–9; and Pacheco (1979, Vol. II, pp. 353–4). Zacarias, in charge of the Ministry of Finance during the early days of implementation of the 1866 Law, preferred to stress what he saw as the beneficial effects of the innovation of the agreement between Bank and government. Removal of the Bank's issuing powers, he argued, far from being a liability, actually ushered in a new era for the establishment. Free from the 'false idea that an issuing bank had as its main task the rescue of every victim of the forced expansion of credit, at the expense of its own private fortune', the Bank would henceforth be in a genuine position 'to meet the needs of commerce and agriculture'. See *RMF* 1866, p. 19. Under the new statutes of the Bank of Brazil, its president would no longer be appointed by the

government but, instead, would be elected by an assembly of shareholders. Accordingly, on 10 December, former Minister of Finance, Francisco Sales Torres Homem, who had been in command as the last officially appointed president, was elected.

20. The breakdown of Treasury notes issued in conjunction with Law 1349 is as follows: 3800 *contos* in payment of Treasury bills belonging to the Bank of Brazil; 25,800 *contos* for its metallic reserves; and 11,000 *contos* corresponding to government notes that the Bank had retired from circulation, in accordance with its statutes. *RMF* 1872, Annex, Table 30. The remaining note issue of the Bank, after allowing for the swap for Treasury notes (and their subsequent retirement), was estimated at 45,600 *contos* as of 16 March 1867. On that day, Decree 3814 (Art. 3) determined that the Bank withdraw each year, beginning in June, 5% of this amount, so that after twenty years none of its notes should remain in circulation. See Pacheco (1979, Vol. II, pp. 358–9).
21. Figures calculated from Table 5 in the Annex to *RMF* 1872.
22. For a summary, see Pacheco (1979, Vol. II, pp. 371 ff).
23. Additionally, a major overhaul of the tax system was undertaken. This included, inter alia, a revision of the import tariff schedule (including the introduction of payment of part of the tariffs "in gold"), a head tax, and a new system for the tax on "industries and professions". Law 1507, of 6 September 1867, provided an increase in the revenues of the imperial government in subsequent years. For details, see *RMF* 1867, pp. 41–4. Both the tax increase and the note issue received warm support from the *South American Journal.* In its leader column, it noted that 'the war with Paraguay, to which alone the present financial difficulty (was) attributable, (had) not been of Brazilian creation, and it (made) it the more incumbent on the people to second the efforts of their excellent Sovereign to bring it to an honourable and successful issue'. *SAJ*, 22 October 1867, p. 12.
24. Despite the fact that the imperial government had extended telegraph lines all the way South toward the frontline, news of the Brazilian navy's successful crossing of the bend on the Paraguay River guarded by the Humaitá fortress, which took place on 19 February 1868, was only published in the Rio papers on 3 March, having arrived by steamer. On that day, the exchange rate (ninety-day bills on London) was at 16d, inching toward 17d on 7 March and 18d a few days later. Rates in the *Jornal do Commercio*, various issues.
25. In his report to the Assembly, Zacarias downplayed the influence of the recent (and substantial) issues of Treasury notes on the depreciation of the milréis. Instead, he attributed the drop in the rate of exchange to the exhaustion of the resources obtained with the 1865 foreign loan for £5000,000. See *RMF* 1867, p. 8. The 1865 loan had been contracted

under the most adverse terms for the Brazilian Treasury, facing a discount of 26% and paying interest of 5%. The money thus obtained (68,850 *contos*) was entirely used in financing the military campaign in Paraguay. For details, see Bouças (1955, pp. 157–61).

26. This decree would only be made public one month later, thereby drawing intense criticism from Parliament and the press. See de Holanda (1972, vol. 3, Tome II, p. 106).
27. See also *RMF* 1868, p. 8. In the end, the government issued 23,390 *contos* out of the 40,000 *contos* authorized by the decree.
28. Indeed, even "gold" issues, such as this one, were subject to default. The massive oversubscription to the 30,000 *contos* loan indicates that investors did not deem this likely. On the imperial government's excellent reputation as a debtor among both domestic and foreign creditors, see Summerhill (2015).
29. Interest payments on the foreign debt would also experience a marked increase in the period—to 10,000 *contos*—from an average of 4000 *contos* in the first half of the 1860s. This reflected both the growth of outlays in sterling and the drop in the rate of exchange (depreciation) during the Paraguayan War. Fiscal figures from Brasil, Ministério da Fazenda, *Balanço da Receita e Despesa*, various issues.
30. The issue of 25,000 *contos* in 6% *apólices* on 28 June 1870, with a view to consolidate part of the floating debt, would further reduce the stock of *letras* outstanding.
31. This dramatic rise in the value of the liabilities of the imperial government, as noted, went toward financing the costs of the Paraguayan War. At the time, two highly discrepant estimates were made of the total financial cost of the conflict. The lesser one, by the Ministry of Finance, came up with the final figure of 461,000 *contos*, while Treasury estimates put the total cost at 614,000 *contos*. The main difference in the two estimates refers to the actual amount of taxes directed to financing the war effort. Either way, in both cases, the issue of Treasury notes figures prominently. Treasury estimates from Peláez and Suzigan (1976, p. 114); Ministry of Finance data in *RMF* 1871, Table 15A, Annex.
32. In light of the inflation of the war years, the *real* rate of growth of all variables discussed above would have been more modest. There are no reliable estimates of inflation in Brazil for the pre-1870 period. A composite index of the cost of living, which consists of an average of crude indices found in the literature, indicates an average inflation of 5.3% p.a. during the second half of the 1860s. See Goldsmith (1986, p. 29).
33. Costa (1993). One has only to consider the campaigns in the period in favor of, inter alia, electoral reform, abolition, federalism, and the republican movement.

34. Not without consequences, though, as attested by the outbreak of the *Quebra-Quilos* ("kilo-smashers") revolt in the Northeast in the early/mid 1870s, with looting and popular unrest taking place in several municipalities in the region.
35. According to the latter, new-born children of slave mothers would be free, although their masters were required to maintain them until their eighth birthday. From then on, the children could either be handed over to the state in exchange for financial compensation or provide labor to their masters until they were 21. Unsurprisingly, most slave owners opted for the latter, but the survival of slavery as a vital institution for the Brazilian economy and society was henceforth undermined.
36. As remarked by Rio Branco in his first report submitted to the Assembly in 1871 as Minister of Finance, such large amounts of outstanding bills posed a burden on the Treasury, as they required that it keep in its vaults enough funds to honor payments which at any given month could amount to 6–8 thousand *contos*. This state of affairs made consolidation of the floating debt all the more necessary, leaving recourse to Treasury bills exclusively to 'extraordinary and unpredictable emergencies'. See *RMF* 1870, p. 10.
37. Still, Treasury bills (*letras*), which acted as a partial substitute to paper money, saw their amount in circulation decrease by half during Paranho's tenure as Minister of Finance from 40,000 to 20,000 *contos*. As such, this may have helped appreciate the currency.
38. Money held by the public fell by approximately 10% during the whole period, being offset by the growth in the volume of sight deposits held in commercial banks. See Table A3 in Peláez and Suzigan (1976).
39. As will be discussed in greater detail in Chap. 5, estimates of the traditional monetary aggregates such as high-powered money (or monetary base), M1 and M2 for the second half of the nineteenth century in Brazil must be approached with extreme caution. The estimates of the monetary base made by Peláez and Suzigan (1976) and cited in this paragraph refer to a subset (consisting of Treasury and banknotes) of the total monetary base. As such, they leave aside metallic circulation and promissory notes (*vales*) issued by a host of market agents. Depending on the period, specie and *vales* in circulation could reach a significant amount, rendering the Peláez and Suzigan figures as an indication of a lower bound for the total amount of money put into circulation.
40. Money supply (M1) averaged 220,000 *contos* from 1870 until the first quarter of 1875, after which it would drop by almost 10%. This monetary contraction was a direct consequence of the 1875 financial crisis to be discussed below. Data in Brasil, IBGE (1990, p. 534).
41. Average rates of discount charged by Rio-based banks in 1870 were 10.5%, while non-bank loans carried average rates of 12.4%. By 1880, these rates

had dropped to 6.8% and 11.6%, respectively. Figures in Ryan Jr. (2007, Tables 3.1 and 4.1).

42. See also Sweigart (1987, p. 138).
43. Sweigart (1987, pp. 194–5) thus explains this mechanism: 'If a creditor wanted to foreclosure on a mortgage, he called for a judge to establish an open auction in the county in which the property was located. The judge first appointed appraisers to establish the property's value, yet the appraisal could never be less than the value of the original loan. If bids were not high enough to cover the appraised value, the creditor had to buy the property at four-fifths of the appraised value. Control over the appraisal lay with the judge who appointed the evaluators, often landowners and evaluators themselves, sympathetic and easily influenced by the debtor, who was often a relative. Planters arranged for their properties to be appraised well above their true value, and came out ahead in the settlement, after reimbursing their creditor for the original loan and any penalties assessed for late payments. (…) Since the creditor lost control over the adjudication process as soon as he initiated proceedings, coffee factors and mortgage banks avoided foreclosure altogether, and preferred to refinance the debtor's original loan indefinitely, in hopes of retrieving their initial investment through the proceeds of future coffee sales'.
44. Over the course of the Second Reign (1849–1889), there were 18 different Legislatures, of which 11 were dissolved. On three of those occasions, the Emperor followed the wish of the incumbent Prime Minister and called for new elections in an attempt to secure a parliamentary majority for the party in office. The dissolution of the 11th Legislature in May 1872 was one such occasion. See Ferraz (2017, p. 76, footnote 18).
45. In December 1874, the Bank of Brazil would start issuing mortgage-backed bonds, prompting an increase in its loans to the rural sector, which would peak in 1880. Thereafter, and amid depressed coffee prices and the momentum gained by the abolitionist campaign, mortgage loans outstanding reached a plateau and started to contract. See Sweigart (1987, pp. 190–2).
46. Bank rate would go on to peak at 9% in 1873. See Homer and Sylla (2005, p. 206, Table 23).
47. On the 1873 crisis, see Foreman-Peck (1983) and Kindleberger (1990).
48. Further (qualitative) evidence of the modest impact of the 1873 panic in Brazil is given by the fact that not a word about the crisis in Europe and the United States appeared in the 1873 report (published in May 1874) of the Minister of Finance to the Assembly. Annual reports of the Ministério da Fazenda would always begin with a summary of the main events in the economy in the previous year.

49. Foreign trade data, however, suggest a possible channel linking the crisis in Europe to the Brazilian economy, as export earnings (in sterling) decreased by 8% between 1872–3 and 1873–4. Still, most of this resulted from a 30%-plus drop in sugar exports (totaling just over £ 1 million), therefore, not reflecting export activity as a whole. See Holanda (1972, Tome II, vol. 5, p. 153). Coffee exports and prices in Sweigart (1987, Table E.2). Central government (ordinary) receipts did contract 6% between the 1872–3 and 1873–4 fiscal years, but this was accounted for, basically, by a fall in the collection of import duties brought about by a new, more liberal, tariff schedule. In the same period (1872–3 to 1873–4), the value of imports in sterling remained roughly constant, having increased 5% in mil-réis. See Brasil, IBGE (1990, p. 569). Meanwhile, taxes collected on internal activities—and which tended to be correlated with the overall state of the economy—remained constant in 1873–4 compared to the previous fiscal year. See Diniz (2002, Annex D.1).
50. Irineu Evangelista de Souza set up the The Mauá Bank in January 1867 in place of his earlier partnership (Mauá, McGregor), founded in 1854 in the aftermath of the merger of his Banco do Brasil with the Banco Commercial do Rio de Janeiro. In the occasion, this made for the creation of the “third” Bank of Brazil. By 1873, the Mauá Bank maintained seven branches in Brazil, one in London and six in the River Plate region. For a discussion of Mauá’s banking activities in the River Plate, see Kunioshi (2005); his interests in Uruguay, see Millot and Bertino (1991, Tome II); his (flawed) business strategy, see Bertero and Iwai (2005).
51. In the occasion, Mauá was able to obtain some support from the Bank of Brazil (to the tune of 700 *contos*, or £55,000) giving as collateral his (and his wife’s) private assets. This amount was supplemented by 600 *contos* secured by the Ponta de Areia ironworks (also belonging to the Mauá concern) from the Bank of Brazil in September 1869. See Mauá (1942, p. 248, footnote 228).
52. Ibid., p. 249.
53. The most detailed account available of the events surrounding the 1875 financial crisis in Brazil is to be found in the summary of the numerous meetings of the Board of Directors of the Bank of Brazil published in Pacheco (1979, vol. III). They will be used extensively in what follows.
54. Deposits in *RMF* 1876, Annex G, p. 10.
55. Present at the reunion at Paranho’s residence, the President of the Banco Nacional reported on the hardship under which his institution was laboring, with the bank under risk of having to shut its doors. The Minister reminded those present of the possibility that the other banks might join forces to help shore up the Nacional (ibid., p. 49).

56. Ibid. In the occasion, the acting President of the Bank of Brazil raised the idea that the Bank be temporarily allowed to issue notes backed by its holdings of *apólices*. Yet, most of those present at the meeting agreed that provision of liquidity should be undertaken directly by the Treasury by means of loans to the banks. It would later emerge that the Treasury had been doing this for two months now, starting with an advance of 2101 *contos* to the Bank of Brazil on 5 March. See *RMF* 1876, Annex, Table 9.
57. The Banco Alemão closed its doors on the 15th, two days before the Banco Mauá suspended payments, its manager having gone missing. It was later learned that he had committed suicide. See Holanda (1972, p. 170). Mauá would be made *Visconde* (Viscount) barely five weeks after his bank shut its doors to the public.
58. This initiative by Rio Branco came on the eve of Mauá's final request for funds from the Bank of Brazil and three days before his bank was forced to shut its doors.
59. São Paulo's largest private bank (*casa bancária*) at the time, Gavião Peixoto, with close links to the Mauá Bank, was also forced to shut its doors in May 1875. See Saes (1986, pp. 75–6).
60. Coffee prices in *RCJC* 1877, p. 48, Table 7. Average rates of exchange in *RMF* 1876, p. 28. The firmness displayed by the foreign exchange market was to an extent helped by the government's successful floating of a £ 5 million loan in London in January.
61. Rate of discount in *RCJC* 1875 (published as a supplement to that year's *Almanak Laemmert*), p. 194. For the contraction in the volume of credit extended by Rio banks (and which would last until the end of the decade), see Ryan Jr. (2007, p. 156). Data on cash/deposits ratios in Peláez and Suzigan (1976, Table A4).
62. Indeed, in the report presented by Paranhos to Parliament on 8 May 1875, there is only passing reference to a 'shortage of currency in the Empire's major commercial centers (*praças*)', in the section dealing with the £ 5 million loan floated in London. Four days later, the crisis would be laid bare as the Banco Nacional failed, followed by the Mauá Bank and the Banco Alemão. See *RMF* 1874, p. 29.
63. The same Law provided a dividend guarantee of 7% to investments made in the establishment of central sugar mills. On the latter, see Eisemberg (1974).
64. The Emperor's decision to invite the Liberal Party to form a new government stemmed from his desire to push for a reform of the electoral system, a policy long advocated by Liberals. See Nabuco (1997, Vol. II, pp. 996–8). Given that the Conservative Party dominated the Chamber, the latter would be dissolved in April 1878 and new elections were called. As expected, the Liberals would take the majority of the seats in the new legislature.

65. Unlike most of the Presidents of the Council of Ministers in the Second Reign, Sinimbu would jointly exercise the role of Minister of Agriculture, Trade and Public Works instead of Minister of Finance. Gaspar Silveira Martins, followed by Afonso Celso de Assis Figueiredo (the future Visconde de Ouro Preto), would hold the latter portfolio. When Sinimbu took charge of the Ministry of Agriculture, it was firmly endowed with the second largest share of the imperial budget, after Finance.
66. In the memorandum presented to the Emperor in support of the requested permission, the cabinet showed alarm over the dire state of the Treasury and deemed the proposed note issue a lesser evil compared to the alternative of resorting to either a domestic or external loan. See *RMF* 1877, Annex B.
67. The obviously unconventional nature of the measure was fully acknowledged by the government, as Article 3 of the Decree stated that 'as soon as the General Assembly convenes it shall be informed (of the decision) by the Minister, who will seek approval of this measure'.
68. On a different front—and in an effort to bring the planter class closer to the reformist agenda championed by the party that he headed and away from republican propaganda—in July 1878 Sinimbu sent out an invitation to their representatives to attend an Agricultural Congress to be held in the capital. Debates in the Congress ended up being dominated by two concerns: labor (slavery) and capital (the cost of credit). Although little came out of the gathering in the way of concrete policy, the imperial government would have to engage with both issues for the rest of the monarchical period. On the 1878 Agricultural Congress, see Sweigart (1987, pp. 150–3), Schulz (2013, chapter 5), and José M. de Carvalho, "Introdução", in: *Anais do Congresso Agrícola* (1988).
69. In practice, this current account provided the government with an overdraft facility, as the Treasury had been incurring in deficits of late and, therefore, its balance was negative.
70. For details on the three National Loans issued by the imperial government (the final one would be floated in 1889), see Summerhill (2015, pp. 96–9).
71. The Budget Law for the 1879–80 and 1880–1 fiscal years, passed in the twilight of the Sinimbu government, revoked the 1875 Law 2565 that had authorized the government to issue up to 25,000 *contos* in either Treasury notes or bills with a view to assisting deposit banks in distress. See Law 2940 of 31 October 1879, Art. 24, paragraph 2.
72. Coffee prices displayed a similar trend. Having peaked at around 20 US cents/lb. in 1875, average coffee prices in New York consistently fell over the next decade, reaching 7.5 cents in 1885. Just like the milréis, it would start to recover thereafter and into the early years of the Republic. Coffee prices in New York in Sweigart (1987, Table E.2).

73. Law 3150 of 4 November 1882, regulated by Decree 8821 of 30 December 1882.
74. A further limitation on the reach of the new corporate legislation was the provision of unlimited liability of shareholders. For a discussion, see Hanley (2005, pp. 66–8). On the many obstacles to incorporation during the imperial period, see Summerhill (2015, chapter 6).
75. Proceeds from the loan would be kept in London in order to meet expected outlays in the next two years, while also not exercising undue pressure on the foreign exchange market in Rio. For the railways' significant impact on the economy of imperial Brazil, see Summerhill (2003).
76. For the dispute among regional elites for central government investments in "material improvements" in the closing decade of the Empire, see Carvalho (1988, chapter 1) and Mello (1984). Villela (2007) discusses the growing share of outlays in infrastructure projects in the central government budget in this period.
77. In this report, Lafayette would also suggest that, in light of the quotation of 6% *apólices* at above par, the government should consider a conversion of its consolidated debt to a 5% basis (ibid., pp. 29–32).
78. The first "quinquennium" corresponded to the six consecutive cabinets led by Liberals between 1862 and 1868.
79. Subsequent withdrawal of these notes from circulation meant that, after a modest increase in 1886, the stock of government paper money in circulation reverted to the same levels obtained at the start of the decade (188,000 *contos*, on average).
80. This new version of the bill would go down in history as the "Law of the Sexagenarian" (or the Saraiva-Cotegipe Law). It included the provision that slaves thus liberated would have to perform unpaid labor for another three years or until they reached the age of 65. Costa (1993, pp. 200–2).
81. See footnote 43 above.
82. Interestingly, Belisário failed to note that the milréis had made significant progress since the end of 1885 when it was quoted at 18d. In May 1886, the exchange rate was approaching the 22d mark.
83. The Budget Law submitted to Parliament in the occasion earmarked 5000 *contos* for that purpose.
84. In May 1887, as the report was presented to the Assembly, the exchange rate on London was 22d. By then, it was in the early stages of a rally that would take it to par by October 1888. For Shulz (2013, p. 41), Belisário's motivation for suggesting that convertibility be adopted at the 24d parity derived from the desire to safeguard the profitability of the coffee sector, which had been benefiting from a rebound in the commodity's international price (after an equally protracted slide in 1875–85). A milréis left to appreciate unimpeded would erode profits (in domestic currency) in the export sector—hence, the suggestion that the currency be fixed at a rate

below the "mythical" 1846 parity. If true, this motivation would anticipate by decades the rationale for Brazil's adherence to the gold standard in 1906 when the rate of exchange would also display a markedly appreciating trend. For a detailed discussion, see Fritsch (1988, chapter 2).

85. At the time, this corresponded, roughly, to the combined outstanding circulation of (Treasury) paper money and banknotes.
86. Thereafter, the stock of Treasury *letras* in circulation would decline dramatically. At the start of the João Alfredo government, in March, it stood at 31.4 thousand *contos*. One year later, it was down to just 77 *contos* (see Table A7, in the Appendix).
87. Meanwhile—and in a further effort to ease planters' burdens during the transition to wage labor—the government signed three contracts with the Bank of Brazil and the Banco da Bahia involving advances from the Treasury to bolster these banks' mortgage portfolios. See *RMF* 1888, pp. 29–30. These operations foreshadowed the ambitious loan program carried out by the next cabinet, led by Ouro Preto.
88. The *Retrospecto Commercial do Jornal do Commercio* was less than enthusiastic about the benefits that would follow from the banks of issue envisaged by the Senate bill. The foreign loan, however, was hailed as a 'laudable (…) measure' on the part of the government, especially in light of the excellent terms involved. See *RCJC* 1888, p. 4.
89. See also *RCJC* 1889, pp. 5–6. Balance of payments estimates in Franco (1991).
90. Ouro Preto's bold reformist agenda followed the program outlined earlier in May at the Liberal Party congress. This included the broadening of the political franchise, devolution of powers to the provinces, mandatory civil marriage, full freedom of worship, set mandates for the Senate, reform of the Council of State, support for large-scale (subsidized) European immigration, and the extension of credit to agriculture. See Lynch (2018).
91. On the limited impact of mortgage finance on the overall credit needs of the coffee sector, see Marcondes (2002, 2017).
92. To that list may be added the failed attempt in 1875, through Law 2687, to set up a mortgage bank funded abroad.
93. See footnote 87 above.
94. See also Shulz (2013, pp. 161–2).
95. Ouro Preto also succeeded in securing Brazil's largest foreign loan until then. Totaling £ 19,837,000, it allowed for the conversion of bonds of the 1865, 1871, 1875, and 1886 loans (all bearing 5% coupons) into new 4% bonds. For details, see Bouças (1955, pp. 172–4), Abreu (1985), and Summerhill (2015, pp. 64–6).
96. The new minister's (Rui Barbosa) policies are discussed in detail in Franco (1983, chapter 4), Triner and Wandshneider (2005), and Schulz (2013, chapter 7).

References

Abreu, Marcelo de P. 1985. A Dívida Pública Externa do Brasil, 1824–1931. *Estudos Economicos* 15 (2): 167–189.

Anais do Congresso Agrícola do Rio de Janeiro, 1878. 1988. Rio de Janeiro: Fundação Casa de Rui Barbosa.

Ao Visconde de Itaborahy: carta de Erasmo sobre a Crise Financeira. 1866. Rio de Janeiro: Typ. de Pinheiro & Companhia.

Banker's Magazine. 1862–70. London.

Bertero, Carlos Osmar, and Tatiana Iwai. 2005. Uma Visita ao Barão. *Revista de Administração Contemporânea* 9 (2): 1–17. https://doi.org/10.1590/S1415-65552005000600002.

Bouças, Valentim F. 1955. *Finanças do Brasil*, Dívida Externa, 1824–1945. Vol. XIX. Rio de Janeiro: Ministério da Fazenda.

Brasil, Câmara dos Deputados. *Annaes da Camara dos Deputados*, various years.

———, Ministério da Fazenda. *Proposta e Relatorio Apresentados á Assembléa-Geral Legislativa Pelo Ministro e Secretario d'Estado dos Negócios da Fazenda*, various years.

Brasil, IBGE. 1990. *Estatísticas Históricas do Brasil*, séries econômicas, demográficas e sociais, 1550–1985. Vol. 3. 2nd ed. Rio de Janeiro: IBGE.

Brasil, Ministério da Fazenda. 1850–89. *Balanços da Receita e Despeza do Imperio*, various years.

Brasil, Senado. *Annaes do Senado do Império do Brasil*, various years.

Caldeira, Jorge. 1995. *Mauá: empresário do Império*. São Paulo: Companhia das Letras.

Cavalcanti, Amaro. 1893. *O Meio Circulante Nacional*. Rio de Janeiro: Imprensa Nacional, 2 vols.

da Costa, Emília V. 1993. 1870–1889. In *Brazil, Empire and Republic, 1822–1930*, ed. L. Bethell, 161–213. Cambridge: Cambridge University Press.

Davis, Mike. 2002. *Late Victorian Holocausts: El Niño Famines and the Making of the Third World*. New York/London: Verso.

de Carvalho, José M. 1988. *Teatro de Sombras: A política imperial*. Rio de Janeiro: Vértice/IUPERJ.

de Holanda, Sergio B. 1972. *História Geral da Civilização Brasileira*. Tome II, vol. 1. São Paulo: Difel.

de Mauá, Barão. 1942. O Meio Circulante no Brasil. In *Visconde de Mauá, Autobiografia (Exposição aos Credores e ao Público) seguida de O Meio Circulante no Brasil*, ed. C. Ganns, 2nd ed., 93–309. Rio de Janeiro: Zélio Valverde. (originally published in 1878).

de Mello, Evaldo C. 1984. *O Norte Agrário e o Império, 1871–1889*. Rio de Janeiro: Nova Fronteira.

de Saes, Flavio M. 1986. *Crédito e Bancos no Desenvolvimento da Economia Paulista, 1850–1930*. São Paulo: IPE/USP.

Diniz, Adalton F. 2002. *Centralização Política e Apropriação de Riqueza: análise das finanças do Império brasileiro (1821–1889)*. Ph.D. dissertation, Universidade de São Paulo.

Eisemberg, Peter. 1974. *The Sugar Industry in Pernambuco, 1840–1910*. Berkeley: University of California Press.

Ferraz, Sérgio Eduardo. 2017. A Dinâmica Política do Império: instabilidade, gabinetes e Câmara dos Deputados (1840–1889). *Revista de Sociologia e Política* 25 (62): 63–91.

Foreman-Peck, James. 1983. *A History of the World Economy: international relations since 1850*. London: Harvester Wheatsheaf.

Franco, Gustavo Henrique B. 1983. *Reforma Monetária e Instabilidade Financeira Durante a Transição Republicana*. Rio de Janeiro: BNDES.

———. 1991. *A Década Republicana: o Brasil e a economia internacional – 1880/1900*. Rio de Janeiro: Ipea. (Série PNPE, n. 27).

Fritsch, Winston. 1988. *External Constraints on Economic Policy in Brazil, 1889–1930*. London: Macmillan.

Goldsmith, Raymond W. 1986. *Brasil, 1850–1984: desenvolvimento financeiro sob um século de inflação*. São Paulo: Harper & Row.

Hanley, Anne G. 2005. *Native Capital: Financial Institutions and Economic Development in São Paulo, Brazil, 1850–1920*. Stanford: Stanford University Press.

Homer, Sidney, and Richard Sylla. 2005. *A History of Interest Rates*. 4th ed. Hoboken: Wiley.

Jornal do Commercio. Rio de Janeiro.

Kindleberger, Charles P. 1990. *Historical Economics: Art or Science?* Berkeley: University of California Press.

Kuniochi, Marcia N. 2005. A Intermediação Mercantil e Bancária na Fronteira Meridional do Brasil. *História e Economia* 1 (1): 67–85.

Lynch, Christian Edward C. 2018. Necessidade, Contingência e Contrafactualidade. A Queda do Império Reconsiderada. *Topoi* 19 (38): 190–216.

Marcondes, Renato L. 2002. O Financiamento Hipotecário da Cafeicultura no Vale do Paraíba Paulista (1865–87). *Revista Brasileira de Economia* 56 (1): 147–170.

———. 2017. Hipotecas, Mudanças Institucionais e o Banco do Brasil na Segunda Metade do Século XIX. XII Congresso Brasileiro de História Econômica/13ª Conferência Internacional de História de Empresas, Niterói.

Millot, Julio, and Magdalena Bertino. 1991. *Historia Económica del Uruguay*. Montevideo: Fundación de Cultura Universitária.

Nabuco, Joaquim. 1997. *Um Estadista do Império*. 5th ed. Rio de Janeiro: Topbooks.

Pacheco, Claudio. 1979. *História do Banco do Brasil*. Brasília: Banco do Brasil, 4 vols.

Peláez, Carlos Manuel, and Wilson Suzigan. 1976. *História Monetária do Brasil*. 2nd ed. Brasília: Editora da Universidade de Brasília.

Proposta do Poder Executivo sobre o Meio Circulante e Documentos Relativos Mandados Publicar para Serem Presentes á Assembléa Geral Legislativa. 1866. Rio de Janeiro: Typographia Nacional.

Retrospecto Commercial do Rio de Janeiro. Rio de Janeiro, various years.

Ryan Jr, Joseph J. 2007. *Credit Where Credit Is Due: Lending and Borrowing in Rio de Janeiro, 1820–1900*. Ph.D. dissertation, University of California at Los Angeles.

Schulz, John. 1996. *A Crise Financeira da Abolição*. 1st ed. São Paulo: Edusp/ Instituto Fernand Braudel.

———. 2013. *A Crise Financeira da Abolição*. 2nd ed. São Paulo: Edusp.

Summerhill, William R. 2003. *Order Against Progress: Government, Foreign Investment, and Railroads in Brazil, 1854–1913*. Stanford: Stanford University Press.

———. 2015. *Inglorious Revolution: Political Institutions, Sovereign Debt, and Financial Underdevelopment in Imperial Brazil*. New Haven: Yale University Press.

Sweigart, Joseph E. 1987. *Coffee Factorage and the Emergence of a Brazilian Capital Market, 1850–1888*. New York: Garland Publishing.

The Brazil and River Plate Mail and South American Journal. London, various years.

Triner, Gail, and Kirsten Wandschneider. 2005. The Baring Crisis and the Brazilian Encilhamento, 1889–1891: An Early Example of Contagion Among Emerging Capital Markets. *Financial History Review* 12 (2): 199–225.

Villela, André A. 2007. Distribuição Regional de Receitas e Despesas do Governo Central no II Reinado, 1844–1889. *Estudos Economicos* 37 (2): 247–274.

CHAPTER 5

Taking Stock: Monetary and Banking Policy in the Second Reign

5.1 The Long-Term Behavior of the Money Supply

The previous chapters documented in detail the evolution of government policy and legislation dealing with monetary and financial matters over the course of almost four decades in nineteenth-century Brazil. As one would expect, such a trajectory was far from linear, combining periods when responsibility for issuing notes was exclusively held by the Treasury with phases when the issue of private banknotes prevailed. Throughout, commercial banks—even those not entitled with issuing rights—would also affect the money supply by means of their regular operations involving the provision of loans against their deposits. The same held true for *casas bancárias* (private banks), partnerships whose size often rivalled that of the corporate banks, and which would exercise significant influence on overall monetary conditions in the Brazilian economy until 1875.

As for the *rationale* behind the frequent shifts in monetary policy discussed in Chaps. 2, 3 and 4, it can best be grasped by briefly stepping back and shifting focus from the day-to-day conduct of policy toward a broader look into the evolution of a number of aggregate indicators (both monetary and fiscal) of the Brazilian economy that seek to capture the motivations and results of those policies.

Although officials dutifully collected figures for the central government budget at the time, contemporaries did not keep track of the ordinary monetary aggregates that are calculated by modern central banks, such as

A. A. Villela, *The Political Economy of Money and Banking in Imperial Brazil, 1850–1889*, Palgrave Studies in the History of Finance, https://doi.org/10.1007/978-3-030-32774-3_5

high-powered money, M1, M2, and so on. Still, post-War scholarship has endeavored to estimate some of those aggregates for the nineteenth century based on detailed study of a diverse body of primary sources, including official publications, newspapers, bank reports, and so on. The landmark contribution in this literature was the pioneering work of Friedman and Schwartz, *A Monetary History of the United States, 1867–1960*,[1] which went on to inspire a number of similar projects in other countries, including Brazil.

Brazil has a long history of monetary histories.[2] One of its best-known works is Peláez and Suzigan's 1976 book, which follows in the path opened by Friedman and Schwartz's classic. Mirroring the latter, it brings together the most extensive and widely used estimates of the main monetary aggregates (and their determinants) of the Brazilian economy for the nineteenth and early twentieth centuries, weaving them into the country's broader economic history.[3]

As the authors themselves readily admit, their estimates of the monetary aggregates for the start of the series (i.e., the second half of the nineteenth century, thus coinciding with the period discussed in the present book) are not comprehensive (Peláez and Suzigan 1976, p. 8). Three major shortcomings combine to cause their figures for the volume of money in the economy in the 1850–89 period to be underestimated; consequently, rates of growth of the money supply were, at times, considerably different from what their numbers indicate.

The first limitation of the Peláez and Suzigan data lies in the coverage—thought to be in the order of 85%–90% of the total universe—of the balance sheets of the commercial banks that were consolidated in order to provide estimates of total deposits in the economy (Suzigan 1990, p. 520). The second source of underestimation of the total money supply concerns specie. Although it is generally accepted that significant amounts of metallic currency circulated only during certain intervals in Imperial Brazil, there were occasions when they did comprise more than half of the money supply as measured by notes and bank deposits alone.[4] The final distortion in the Peláez and Suzigan series refers to the omission of data on the non-corporate banking houses (*casas bancárias*). As indicated in Chaps. 3 and 4, when discussing the 1864 (Souto) and 1875 (Mauá) crises, the individual size of such institutions could rival that of the largest joint-stock banks and, collectively, they accounted for a significant part of the deposit base of the economy—and, hence, the money supply—before 1875.

In an effort to provide a more accurate estimate of the money supply (M2, defined as currency held by the public + demand deposits + time deposits) in the 1850–89 period, Goldsmith indicates tentative ranges for two of the magnitudes mentioned above, namely, specie[5] and deposits held at *casas bancárias* and the Mauá Bank, a deposit and discount bank. His proposed corrections to the M2 series compiled by Peláez and Suzigan revises upward the figures for the money supply in the first half of the period—especially, in the years prior to the 1864 Souto crisis (see the last column in Table 5.1). Goldsmith's inclusion of an estimate of the stock of metallic currency in circulation and deposits held at banking houses in 1849 combine to increase the Peláez and Suzigan figures for that year by up to 70%. A broadly similar difference applies to his estimate of the money supply in 1864. Thereafter and, in particular, after the Mauá Bank ceased its operations in 1875, Peláez and Suzigan's figures achieve a fuller coverage of the "actual" money supply at the time.

As for the rates of *growth* of the stock of money (M2) implied by the Peláez and Suzigan estimates and the revision suggested by Goldsmith, they tend to differ more, as expected, in the first half of the period under consideration. Thus, the average annual rate of growth of the money supply between 1850 and 1874, considering the corrections proposed by Goldsmith, would be 4.8%, down from 6.3% p.a. in the series compiled by Peláez and Suzigan. For the entire 1850–89 period, the two estimates differ by 1 p.p.: M2 would have grown, on average, 4.7% p.a. according to Peláez and Suzigan and 3.7% under Golsmith's revision.

Table 5.1 Estimates of the money supply (M2), selected years, 1849/89 (in *contos* '000)

			Deposits		
Year	*M2 Peláez & Suzigan*	*Specie*	Casas bancárias	*Mauá Bank*	*M2 revised*
	(1)	(2)	(3)	(4)	(1 + 2 + 3 + 4)
1849	56	10–20	10–20		76–96
1864	125	5–10	25–50	10–20	165–205
1870	238			5–10	243–248
1874	259			12–24	271–283
1889	369				369

Source: Goldsmith (1986)

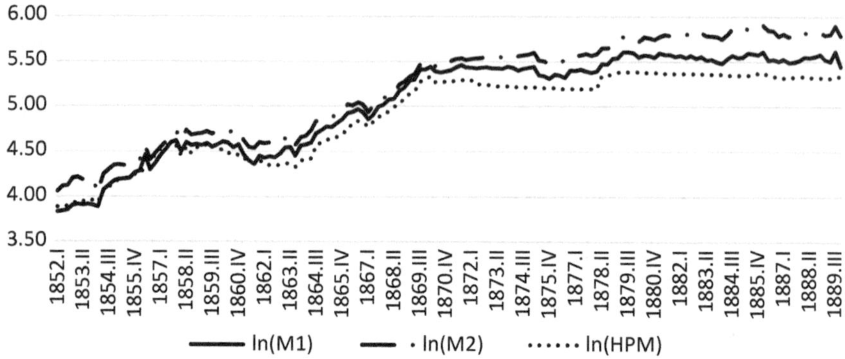

Fig. 5.1 High-powered money, M1 and M2 in Brazil, 1852–89 (in *contos* '000, log scale). (Source: Compiled from data in Brasil, IBGE (1990))

Given that the Peláez and Suzigan series provide the longest estimates of the main monetary aggregates (high-powered money, M1 and M2) in a quarterly basis, as well as their close determinants (reserves/deposits and currency held by the public/money supply ratios), it has been referred to in other parts of the book and will be used again in what follows.

Figure 5.1 displays the evolution of the money supply and high-powered money in Brazil in the 1852–89 period, based on the Peláez & Suzigan figures. Over the course of almost forty years, two sub periods of higher growth stand out: 1852–7 and 1864–70. The first one corresponds to the era of plurality of note issues in the mid-1850s, while the latter includes the years when the demands of the Paraguayan War led the Treasury to engage in massive deficit financing via the issue, inter alia, of notes.

The average rate of growth of the money supply in the entire 1852–89 period was similar if measured by either M1 or M2 (4.6–4.7% p.a.). Over the same period, Brazilian population increased by an estimated 1.7% yearly, which results in an average per capita rate of growth of the money supply in the order of a little more than 3% per annum.[6] Real (i.e., inflation-adjusted) rates of growth may only be guessed, as there are no reliable price indices for the pre-1870 period.[7] Based on a simple average of four price indices found in the literature, Goldsmith (1986, pp. 30–1) hazards a figure of 2% average annual inflation for the whole 1850–89 period, with prices increasing in the initial decades—especially during the Paraguayan War—followed by probable deflation between 1870 and 1889. Taken together, the estimated nominal growth of the money supply over these four decades (4.6–4.7% p.a.), population growth of 1.7% p.a. and 2% average yearly inflation would yield *real* per capita growth of, approximately, 1% per annum in the money supply.

At the start of the period, deposits held at joint-stock banks constituted just 25%, on average, of the money supply. This share gradually increased over the following decades, reaching approximately 50% of M2 by the late 1880s. The money multiplier—an indicator of the "creation" of money by the banking sector—increased accordingly, from 1.3 at the start of the series to 1.6, on average, in the final years of the imperial period.

In spite of the existence of this multiplier effect, disputes over banks' issuing rights, as noted in Chaps. 2 and 3, were often predicated on the misconception that the only way by which these institutions could affect the money supply was by securing issuing rights and putting in circulation their own notes. As a result, ultimate responsibility for the issue of notes was subject to fierce disputes, leading to periods when providing high-powered money to the economy was the preserve of the Treasury and others when banks held this privilege.

Figure 5.2 shows the two main periods comprising faster increases in the supply of high-powered money, as measured by the stock of notes outstanding.[8] As expected, it mirrors the behavior of the growth of the money supply as shown in Fig. 5.1—that is, steeper in the mid-1850s and,

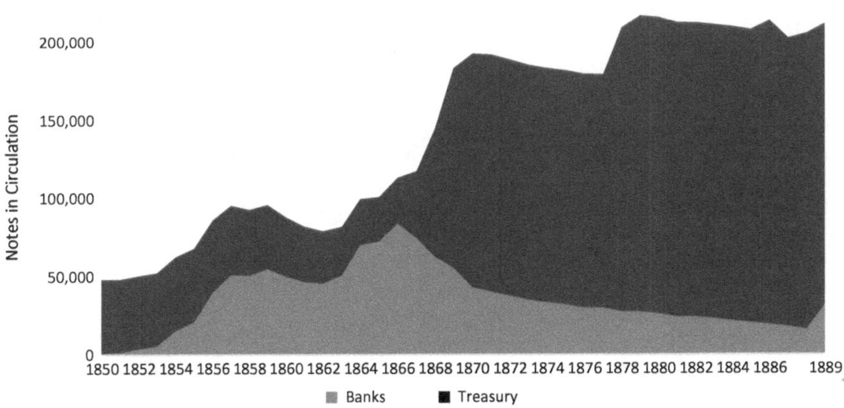

Fig. 5.2 Total notes in circulation, 1850–1889 (in *contos*). (Source: Cavalcanti 1893)

again, in the mid-1860s. Starting from a point when Treasury paper comprised the bulk of note circulation, banknotes would increase their share in the total right after the third Bank of Brazil started its operations in 1854, followed by the entry in circulation of notes issued by the banks created by government decree in 1857–8. From then on—and until 1866—, the amount of private notes in circulation would exceed the volume of government paper, with the former comprising 75% of total outstanding issues in that year.[9] After the cessation of the Bank of Brazil's issuing rights in 1866, and the ensuing massive issues of fiat money, Treasury notes would once again come to predominate in the market.[10]

The purpose of each of the six issuances of Treasury notes authorized by Parliament is detailed in Table 5.2. In four instances, this involved deficit financing, with a combined amount of approximately 154,000 *contos*.[11] The bulk of these issues derived from the emergencies presented by the Paraguayan War and the Great Drought in the late 1870s. The remaining 55.1 thousand *contos* were issued on two occasions (1875 and 1885) for the assistance provided to banks.

As regards fiscal policy, between the 1849–50 and 1889 fiscal years, the imperial government posted a surplus on only three occasions: 1852–3, 1856–7, and 1871–2 (see Table A6, in the Appendix). Still, it was able to meet shortfalls by a combination of loans (both domestic and foreign) and, to a lesser degree, seigniorage, that is, recourse to the issue of Treasury notes (Fig. 5.3).

Table 5.2 Issues of treasury notes, 1850–89 (in *contos*)

Purpose	*Amount*
Notes issued in accordance with Law 1349, of 12 September 1866, toward payment to the Bank of Brazil for Treasury notes in its reserves and purchase of its metallic fund	40,604.4
Credit opened by Law 1508, of 28 September 1867, for expenses incurred in the Paraguayan War	50,000.0
Issues made in accordance with credit of 40,000 *contos* opened by Decree 4232, of 5 August 1868, for the same purpose	23,389.5
Decree 2565 of 29 May 1875 (*Auxílio aos Bancos*)	9148.5
Decree 6882 of 16 April 1876 (drought relief)	40,000.0
Law 3263 of 18 July 1885 (*Auxílio aos Bancos*)	23,000.0
TOTAL	186,142.4

Source: *RMF* 1889, Table N. 4

Note: Data as of March 1889

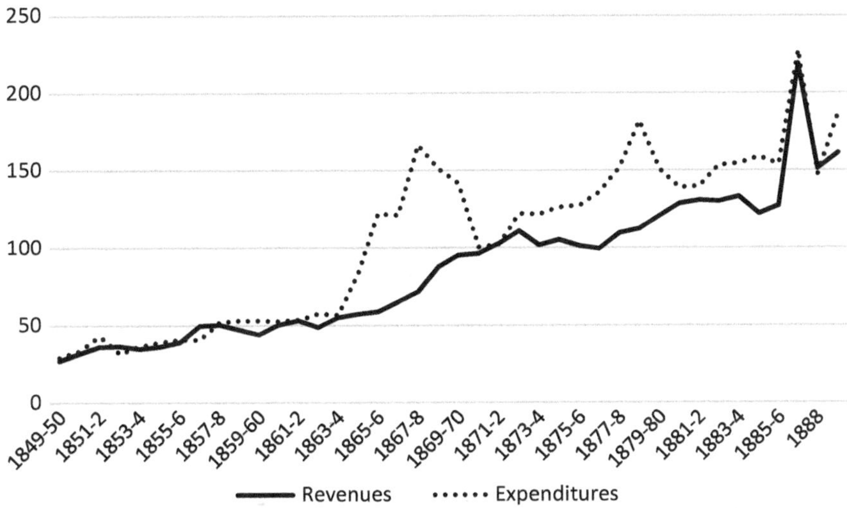

Fig. 5.3 Revenues and expenditures of the imperial government, 1850–89 (in *contos* '000). Note: Data for the 1886–7 fiscal year refer to three semesters. (Source: Compiled from original figures in Brasil, Ministério da Fazenda, *Balanços da Receita e Despeza do Imperio*, vários issues)

The imperial government funded debt was composed of loans floated domestically and overseas. The former comprised mostly bonds (*apólices*) of 6% annual coupon. These were complemented by the issuance, in 1886, of 50,000 *contos* in 5% bonds and the three exchange-rate-indexed National Loans taken out in 1868, 1879, and 1889 with a combined net value of 177,000 *contos*.[12] Between March 1850 and March 1889, total domestic funded debt in circulation went from 52.4 thousand *contos* to 434.8 thousand *contos*, amounting to a net increase equivalent to approximately £ 44 million.[13] During the same four decades, the house of N. M. Rothschild & Sons handled thirteen bond issues made by the Brazilian government overseas, involving varying discounts and coupon rates of 4.5–5%. Total amount issued reached £ 64 million, or £ 57 million net (see Table A9, in the Appendix).

Total funded debt (domestic and foreign) outstanding in March 1850 was in the order of £ 12.6 million, equally split into domestic and foreign loans (see Fig. 5.4). Throughout the 1850s, the funded debt increased slowly, reaching £ 15.2 million in December 1862. From then on, the

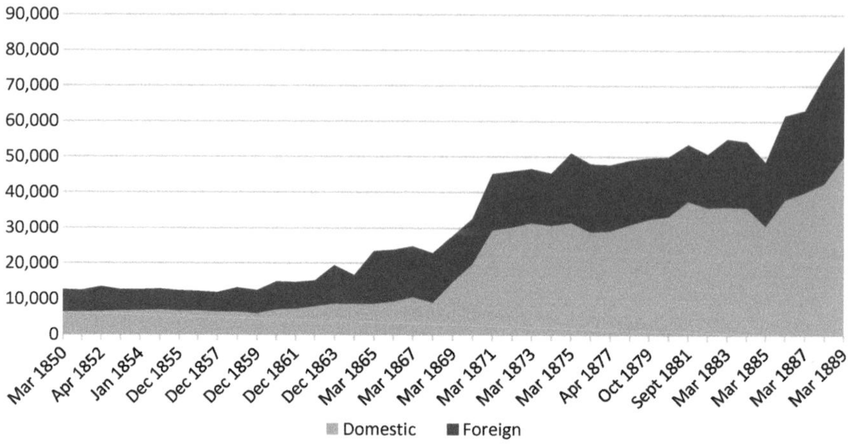

Fig. 5.4 Imperial government funded debt, 1850–89 (in £ '000). Note: Figures for domestic debt originally published in milréis and converted to sterling at the average monthly rate of exchange at each data point. (Sources: Foreign debt in *RMF*, various issues. Domestic debt in Levy 1995)

government would resort more frequently to both domestic and foreign loans, particularly during the Paraguayan War of 1864–70. By March 1871, the funded debt stood at approximately £ 45 million, of which two-thirds raised domestically. The two final decades of the Empire witnessed a renewed surge of borrowing by the imperial government, with issues of approximately 160,000 *contos* in *apólices* of 5% and 6% coupon, two National Loans bringing in another 150,000 *contos* and six foreign loans with a (net) combined value of £ 41.4 million. In March 1889, total funded debt outstanding reached £ 81.4 million, of which just over 60% was raised in Brazil.

If borrowing at home and overseas allowed the Brazilian government to finance its recurrent budget deficits with less recourse to inflationary issues of Treasury notes, shortfalls during a given fiscal year were met with Treasury bills (*letras*), issued in anticipation of revenues.

Issues of Treasury bills peaked on three occasions during the Second Reign (see Fig. 5.5). The first upsurge occurred in the second half of the 1860s and coincided with the overall increase in the budget deficit due to the Paraguayan War (see Fig. 5.3). Significant expenditures associated with drought relief in the late 1870s also show up in the second "blip" in

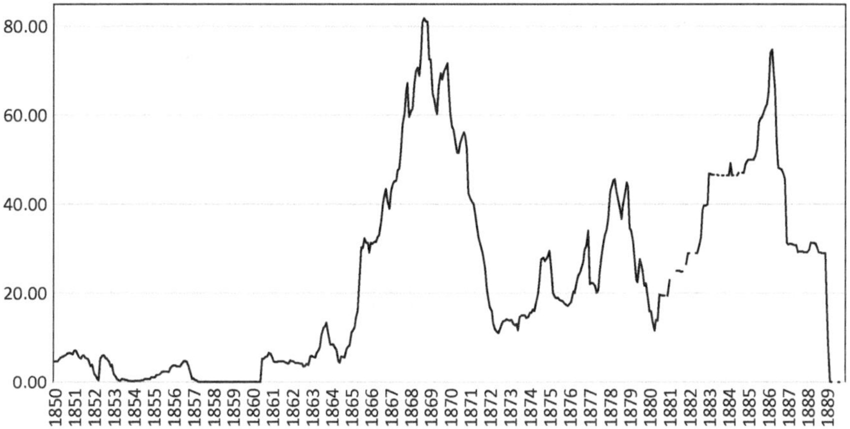

Fig. 5.5 Treasury bills (*Letras*) in circulation, 1850–89 (in *contos* '000). (Source: *RMF*, various issues)

the series, when the outstanding amount of *letras* surpassed the 40,000 *contos* mark. The final peak corresponds to the first half of the 1880s, as the government increasingly resorted to this means of financing its short-term funding needs.[14]

As mentioned earlier, apart from loans in both the domestic and foreign markets and the use of *letras* in anticipation of revenues, the imperial government occasionally resorted to the issue of Treasury notes to help plug its deficits. Still, the net increase of just over 150,000 *contos* in the stock of government paper money in circulation during the years when it held the monopoly of note issuance (i.e., between 1866 and 1889) fell way short of the amount of resources raised via the floating of domestic-funded debt (including both *apólices* and the three National Loans) over the same period. Indeed, total domestic debt outstanding between 1866 and 1889 increased by approximately 344,000 *contos*,[15] that is, more than twice the amount corresponding to the issue of Treasury notes. Considering that over the same period the government would count on a further £24 million in the form of foreign loans,[16] it becomes clear that contemporaries were reluctant to resort to the printing press to finance the Treasury's needs.

To a certain extent, this shunning of inflationary financing—in sharp contrast with Brazil's future experience for most of the republican period—derived from the overwhelming influence of "hard money" thought at the time. Repeated references to the mythical 27 pence/1$000 parity and the actual desire expressed by most contemporaries to institute a gold-backed monetary circulation attest to the power of orthodox ideas among most individuals involved in the monetary debates at the time.

In a sense, reluctance to accommodate increased issues of inconvertible paper money (both Treasury paper and banknotes) was a matter of doctrine. It stemmed from the conviction, shared by most contemporaries, that the single most important (if not the only, according to some) determinant of the rate of exchange was the money supply—crudely approximated by the amount of currency in circulation.

The long-term behavior of the exchange rate (in pence per milréis) between 1850 and 1889 is displayed on Fig. 5.6 (the dotted line indicates the 27d/1$000 parity instituted in 1846 and which was in force for the remainder of the imperial period). It shows three periods in which the milréis lost significant ground against sterling: a brief interval during the 1857 crisis, when the exchange rate fell from above par to a low of 23d (see Table A5, in the Appendix), followed by two periods where the milréis depreciated more significantly—from late 1864 to mid/late 1868 and again between early 1876 and early 1886.

Concerning the drivers of these periods of, at times, enduring depreciation of the currency, the data lend mixed support to contemporaries' conviction as to the prominent role played by an expanding money supply. In the first period (late 1857/early 1858), the stock of total notes outstand-

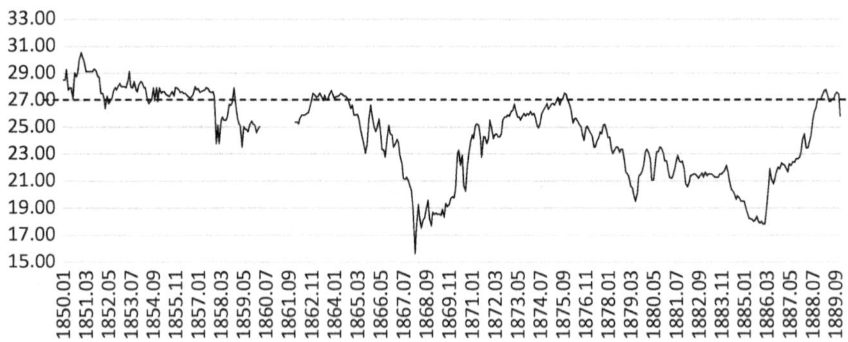

Fig. 5.6 Average monthly rate of exchange in Rio, 1850–89 (in pence/milréis). (Source: Ipeadata, Câmbio: Séries Históricas. http://www.ipeadata.gov.br/Default.aspx. Accessed 8 May 2019)

ing actually *fell* a little, as the amount of Treasury notes withdrawn from circulation (2000 *contos*) exceeded the new notes issued by private banks. In the occasion, exchange-rate depreciation was largely a consequence of the spread to Brazil of the 1857 international crisis ("contagion") rather than of excessive issues of banknotes.

However, the other two periods of significant depreciation of the milréis display a (negative) association between note issues and the exchange rate. They therefore appear to confirm the widely held belief in the existence of a direct connection between periods when the volume of notes in circulation increased and the exchange rate suffered a depreciation.

During the second phase of exchange-rate devaluation, in the second half of the 1860s, the Brazilian economy was mobilized to help finance the war against Paraguay. Moreover, private note issues (from the Bank of Brazil, in particular) had been expanding since 1864 in an effort to quell the panic sparked by the failure of the banking house of J. Souto. These issues were supplanted, from 1866 onward, by massive increases in the amount of Treasury notes in circulation. Similarly, from January 1876 to January 1886 the milréis lost 1/3 of its value, while total note circulation increased by 20%.

The direct association made by contemporaries between the stock of paper money in circulation and the trajectory of the exchange rate is fraught with problems, however. To begin with, notes in circulation constitute, at best, a partial indication of the monetary base in the economy. Moreover—and as indicated before—, the "true" levels (and, by extension, rates of growth) of the *money supply* differ from those captured by the Peláez & Suzigan series, especially in the pre-1875 years. Stocks of metallic coins in the earlier part of the post-1850 period and liabilities of the *casas bancárias* (both deposits and *vales*) would greatly increase the estimated money supply before 1875. Consequently, testing for a possible positive correlation between trends in the money supply and the behavior of the rate of exchange requires the use of improved estimates of the monetary aggregates on a regular basis and which, at present, do not exist.

Yet, these measurement issues pale in comparison with the theoretical and empirical problems posed by the association between money and the exchange rate—or, more to the point, the implied *causation* between the two variables, running from "money" to "exchange rate", as assumed by most observers in nineteenth-century Brazil. In discussing the relationship between the two variables, endogeneity problems immediately arise, as the causality between them runs in both directions. Additionally, the rate of exchange, being a price that indicates a host of variables acting on an economy's relations with the rest of the world, is bound to be influenced by factors other than just monetary policy. Foreign trade and financial flows would also affect it, something only the more discerning observers, such as Mauá, perceived clearly at the time.[17]

Given contemporaries' belief in the close relationship (causation, even) between the amount of notes in circulation and the rate of exchange, disputes over monetary and banking policy were bound to reflect different actors'/groups' preferences regarding the foreign price of the milréis. As a result, understanding the rationale behind the numerous shifts in monetary and banking policy discussed in Chaps. 2, 3 and 4 requires closer attention to the political economy of exchange-rate policy.

In practical terms, any discussion of exchange-rate politics involves differentiating supporters of a depreciated and flexible currency and advocates of a fixed rate of exchange. Indeed, a fixed currency cannot depreciate so that, in practice, those in favor of a depreciated currency will also advocate a flexible exchange-rate regime. Conversely, supporters of a fixed exchange rate will not argue, simultaneously, in favor of a currency that appreciates or depreciates (Frieden 2015, pp. 36–7).

In the context of imperial Brazil, the main actors/groups who sided with "hard money" and a fixed rate of exchange were the government and foreign creditors. Commodity exporters, foremost among which the coffee *fazendeiros*, demanded "soft money" and a corresponding flexible (and depreciated) rate of exchange.[18]

From the government's viewpoint, the main aspect to consider was the extent of its foreign-exchange liabilities. Capacity to honor its foreign debt commitments cautioned the government, particularly from the mid-1860s onward, against a depreciating rate of exchange, since a slipping value of the milréis, other things being equal, increased the domestic currency equivalent of its liabilities. On this count alone, the government in principle would favor an appreciated milréis. Yet, there was another reason for this preference. Given the great reliance on customs taxes for official revenue, an appreciated milréis, ceteris paribus, would lead to increased imports and, hence, higher proceeds from customs houses.[19] In short, if, as contemporaries overwhelmingly believed, depreciation of the exchange rate was to be blamed largely on lax monetary management, the government had strong prima facie grounds for favoring monetary restraint and an exchange rate that was (ideally) fixed and always appreciated.

Examples of this preference abound in contemporary sources. Minister of Finance Francisco José Torres Homem (Visconde de Inhomirim) put it clearly in his 1858 annual report to Parliament that

> the government is the first one to bear the consequences of a depreciating currency. On the side of tax collection, it is the most important of creditors; likewise, it is the foremost consumer from the point of view of expenditures. As a creditor, it is subject to the same fortune as the others, suffering with them the violation of contracts, and receiving in payment amounts below those anticipated. In his capacity as a consumer, it is forced to disburse more in order to purchase the same amount of goods and satisfy the same number of necessities. To these evils should be added the more or less considerable losses incurred in transferring the funds required to settle its overseas commitments. (*RMF* 1858, p. 3)

In the same vein, Joaquim José Rodrigues Torres (Visconde de Itaboraí), speaking in the Council of State in 1864, inveighed against what he thought were the dire consequences for all of an over issue of inconvertible notes by the Bank of Brazil.

> (...) it seems unquestionable that (this will result) in great depreciation and instability in the value of the circulating medium, and, with it, the reduction in the incomes of holders of the consolidated internal debt, and of all those who live on fixed wages; the diminution of the salaries and means of subsistence of the numerous working class; the disturbance in the relations between creditors and debtors; the absence of a base for calculations and predictions in commerce and industry; the increase in the State's commitments related to the payment of the foreign debt, as well as its current purchases; and, finally, the difficulty that the depreciation and uncertainty regarding the value of the currency creates for the importation of foreign capital.[20]

Foreign bankers and investors in general sided with the government in favoring monetary prudence and were unwilling to see the Brazilian government indulge in inflationary financing. They feared this would jeopardize exchange-rate stability and, consequently, increase their exchange-rate risk.[21]

On the opposite end of the spectrum in the political economy of the exchange rate, exporters at large preferred an undervalued milréis, coupled with a lax monetary policy. This soft money combination best served their interests. Indeed, ceteris paribus, a depreciated rate of exchange increased the domestic currency proceeds from the export of the main crops, the prices of which were determined internationally.[22] In this context, and provided domestic production costs (which were defrayed in depreciating local currency) increased less than revenues, *fazendeiros* benefitted from a slipping rate of exchange.[23]

Planters would seldom admit openly their preference for a weak milréis. However, they insisted that trade (or balance of payments) deficits—not excessive monetary growth—were at the root of exchange-rate depreciation.[24] Curtailment of the process of expansion of the banking system, or of the money supply, was therefore considered by exporters as a counterproductive means of attempting to regulate the rate of exchange. Ultimately, in their view, hard money only served to penalize the agricultural sector, by increasing the cost of credit. Accordingly, *fazendeiros* demanded an expansion of the circulating medium to help bring down interest rates. This position, in turn, depended on two points, one theoretical, and the other a misconception. The first point concerned the non-neutrality of money, that is, the implicit belief that at least in the short run increases in the money supply could affect real variables, not just nominal ones. As for the second, it consisted of equating money and credit, meaning that a monetary expansion automatically, and necessarily, translated into cheaper credit.

In this connection, it has sometimes been suggested that Brazilian banks in the mid-nineteenth century failed to support the agricultural sector.[25] More specifically, the financial system has been accused of short-termism, and deliberate withholding of longer-term credit from the countryside. This line of argument equates bill discounting with failure to provide medium and long-term capital. Contemporaries voiced this view, noting that 'historically, commerce (...) had access to credit, unlike agriculture, which lived in penury'.[26] Others observed that the existing system of banks of issue was incapable of providing the type of credit most suited to the needs of the rural sector. It was argued that they could not afford to be exposed very long term, while at the same time issuing instant liabilities, that is, banknotes.[27]

In a similar spirit, the predominance of short-term lending in nineteenth-century Brazil has led to claims that 'commercial and financial capital at the time, linked to unfettered speculation, (was) of a "parasitic" nature, sucking the subsistence out of the old mercantile slave system, while unable to transform it and promote profound economic changes' (Soares

1984, p. 15). Apart from the blatantly teleological nature of this assertion, it is clearly at odds with Sweigart's detailed research on the financing of the coffee industry, discussed in Chap. 4. The picture that emerges from Sweigart's work, far from portraying coffee factors as "parasites", establishes them as crucial agents bringing together commercial and financial capital at the time. As the author pointedly shows, factors were the lifeline that linked, financially and materially, the *fazendas* in the interior to Rio and, ultimately, to the international economy.[28]

According to their detractors, the degree of "parasitism" on the part of coffee factors seems to lie in the level of the interest rate they charged on their loans to planters. However, it must be stressed that, in the end, interest rates planters faced depended on the general cost of credit in the Rio market. Macroeconomic conditions and, crucially, the number of intermediaries who discounted coffee bills affected rates paid by *fazendeiros.* As such, the issue should not be presented as a moral one, pitting greedy factors against helpless planters. Rather—and in the absence of major shocks to the economy—, the cost of credit was conditioned by institutional characteristics. At the time, none was more important than the peculiar framework that regulated the foreclosure of rural property—the so-called forced adjudication mechanism discussed in Chap. 4 in connection with mortgage legislation.

It was then shown that this mechanism heavily stacked the odds against creditors by inflating the value of real property given as collateral when foreclosure was enforced.[29] In light of this, it is no wonder, then, that the credit system did in fact fail the rural sector. However, this had much more to do with what amounted to an institutional failure than to the greed of financial agents.[30] In the end, excessive legal protection given to rural property had dire consequences for the quality of collateral offered to creditors, hampering the financial-intermediation role of the banking system. True, slaves, whose value could amount to close to one-half the total value of an average plantation, were an alternative form of guarantee and were often given as collateral in credit operations. Yet, they were not the ideal type of guarantee either, in view of the risk of flight or death and in light of their declining price as final abolition drew near, in the 1880s.[31]

Clearly, there were instances of misconduct on the part of coffee factors. However, the credit-intermediation market was highly competitive, with between 100 and 200 coffee factorage and sacking firms operating in Rio in the third quarter of the nineteenth century (Sweigart 1987, p. 31). In this context, monopolistic behavior could hardly have flourished, even more so since planters managed to monitor their creditors by hiring the services of more than one factor at a time. In the end, therefore, it was in the interest of both *fazendeiros* and *comissários* to retain a good reputation, for failure to do so could lead to loss of future businesses for either party.

As argued earlier, *premia* charged on loans to the rural sector ultimately reflected the existence of an extended credit chain composed of several intermediaries, each of whom took part in the process of discounting planters' drafts. These commission charges built up into a heavy burden on *fazendeiros.* The obvious question, therefore, is why bankers did not lend directly to planters, bypassing factors altogether. Two interrelated features militated against such an arrangement: contemporary banking practice and informational problems. The general prudence in bank procedures at the time—that is, the need to maintain as liquid a portfolio as possible, in view of the risk of a run on their reserves—kept bankers away from commitments in excess of one to three months.[32] By discounting a planter's draft only after it had received the endorsement of the factor (and possibly of an additional merchant), bankers engaged on a wholly different operation from what would have been the case had they loaned directly to the planter himself. In the first case, they would be lending against the liquid assets of a city merchant. A direct loan to a planter, by contrast, would ultimately have to be guaranteed by land, slaves, or coffee, hardly the type of collateral that would meet bankers' preference for liquidity.

The other major reason why banks were reluctant to lend directly to planters stemmed from informational problems associated with rural credit operations. It was much easier for a factor than for commercial bankers to know the creditworthiness of a planter. The close ties that *comissários* developed with *fazendeiros* enabled them to have a good idea of the quality of their productive methods, the state of their coffee trees and slaves and, ultimately, their capacity to honor debts. It was only natural, then, that *comissários* should be best suited to gauge the risks involved in particular credit operations. Interest charged on loans granted to planters—a premium on the going market rate—reflected, therefore, both the risk of the operation itself and the service factors provided in assessing their clients' creditworthiness.

In short, the high cost of credit to rural producers derived from a combination of three inter-related factors: (i) mortgage legislation; (ii) banks' fears of tying up their portfolios with risky, long-term, planter bills; and (iii) the costs of monitoring *fazendeiros*' creditworthiness. Ultimately, these three factors combined to render contracts signed with planters potentially harder to enforce. This implied high transaction costs and, as such, an obstacle to the development of the capital market.[33]

There is no doubting the importance of banks for latecomers in the development process (let alone late, latecomers, like Brazil), as the French and German experiences have demonstrated.[34] In this connection, financial institutions have been shown to perform some important functions, such as i) serving as intermediaries between savers and investors; ii) supplying means of payments, through deposit creation; and iii), in a Schumpeterian vein, providing 'initiative and enterprise, as well as finance, for the creation, transformation, and expansion of industrial and other ventures' (Cameron et al., eds. 1967, pp. 7–8). Yet, this list should serve as the basis of a general defense of banks, and not necessarily of *issuing* banks, as was often the case in nineteenth-century Brazil. Some contemporaries perceived this point, as illustrated by this passage from a speech delivered by Itaboraí in the imperial Senate in 1858.

> Issuing banks do not do very much beyond substituting their notes for part of the metallic circulation, thus converting an expensive instrument into one that costs virtually nothing (...). Issuing banks, as such, do not go beyond this. In order to centralize credit, to bring together scattered capital, and entrust it to those who can employ it productively, thus promoting the interests of commerce and industry, banks of deposit are all that is needed. For in the countries where there are no issuing banks, is there not credit, loans, discounts of issues of private debt? No, (...) no one believes Brazil would be deprived of the advantages that credit produces if we did not have banks of issue.[35]

Jequitinhonha had already made a related argument a few days earlier in the Senate. Although himself a member of the same party as the then Minister of Finance, Souza Franco, Jequitinhonha did not agree with the latter's decision to allow the incorporation of six new banks of issue in 1857–8.

> The Minister sustained (...) another error, namely, the need and usefulness of having several banks of issue. To this day he seems not to perceive that the utility that may result for the country of banking establishments, especially banks of issue, does not depend on their number, but rather on the number of people who deal and make transactions with them.[36]

Jequitinhonha had gone to the crux of the matter. Banking establishments were perceived as being important and this was undisputed. Even advocates of monopoly of issue favored a plurality of non-issuing establishments, as exemplified by Torres Homem's decision to allow seventeen new deposit and discount banks to be incorporated, in 1859. In this particular point, he seemed to share Jequitinhonha's perception that banks could only go so far in creating investment opportunities. In other words, that money and credit were—and are—distinct things.[37] It was not enough to increase the money supply and expect viable investments to materialize instantly. In the specific case of agriculture, as argued, business opportunities were greatly constrained both by institutional arrangements protecting rural property from foreclosure, and informational asymmetries.

Be that as it may, given the belief shared by most contemporaries that money and credit were, essentially, the same thing and that the money supply (or, more specifically, the outstanding issue of notes and metallic coins) was the main determinant of the rate of exchange, issuing rights and convertibility turned out to be the main points of contention in the struggle over monetary and banking policy in nineteenth-century Brazil. To this the discussion now turns.

5.2 Issuing Rights in Imperial Brazil

The rules that regulated issuing rights in nineteenth-century Brazil can be broadly separated into two sets: the right to issue proper and what could be issued. The first one involved general legislation regulating the issue of liabilities of some form, *vales* and notes being the more prominent. Furthermore, and related to corporate law, the type of organization of the issuing establishments—for example, firms with limited liability or private partnerships—was a matter of concern for legislators. The second set of rules dealt with more technical aspects of the issuing process, such as denomination and extent of circulation. By themselves, matters pertaining to the first group were the object of often heated political disputes, while the finer, technical, aspects of legislation did not elicit as much controversy.

The question of issuing rights became central to the monetary debates in Brazil in 1829 when, following the de facto liquidation of the first Bank of Brazil, the Empire would be left without a single joint-stock banking establishment for seven years.[38] In 1836, with the creation of the Banco do Ceará, under the auspices of the provincial government and the authorization of its legislative assembly, this long interregnum was broken. Two years later, in December 1838, the Banco Commercial do Rio de Janeiro (BCRJ) was founded, with a capital of 5000 *contos* (£600,000). Yet, its statutes would only be approved by the imperial government in June 1842.

The successful experience of the BCRJ inspired a group of businessmen in Salvador to install the Banco Commercial da Bahia, in April 1845. This bank began its operations in May, although is charter was only provided in November. During the next four years, five other banks were authorized to issue *vales*, the largest of which was the second Bank of Brazil, set up by Mauá. This period, dominated by *vale*-issuing banks, was Brazil's first major experiment with government-supervised plurality of issue.

The lag between the start of operations of these banks and the granting of an official charter can be explained by the trauma caused by the failure of the first Bank of Brazil and the mismanagement that appears to have occasioned it. Crucially, though, it reflected the absence of specific legislation governing such an important matter as the establishment and operation of banks. In fact, the first pieces of banking legislation—but not a proper banking law—would only be passed on 10 January 1849 (Decree 575).[39] Still, the provisions of this decree did little to defuse uncertainty, and sheer confusion, regarding the rules applying to banks, which were just part of the broader category of corporations (*sociedades anônimas*), subsequently regulated by the 1850 Commercial Code.

In 1853, after more than a decade of plurality of *vale*-issuing banks, monopoly of note issue was introduced. An act of the Legislative created the third Bank of Brazil. As seen in Chap. 2, Itaboraí proposed the bill establishing the new, semi-official, bank as a way to replace the Holanda Cavalcanti proposal for provincial banks of issue. Itaboraí's main concern, as expressed in Articles 16, 18, and 19 of the statutes of the Bank, was with the potential over issue which plurality could entail. The earlier experience in Rio, where competition between the Banco Commercial and Mauá's Bank of Brazil was blamed for a monetary crisis, only served to strengthen the resolve of the advocates of monopoly. Underpinning this restrictive approach to banks was fear of the effects of excessive monetary expansion on prices and the rate of exchange.

No one better than Itaboraí represented the dominant view at the time that a monopoly of note issue was one of the main pillars on which sound finance stood (the other being convertibility).

> Competition among banks, gentlemen, has been the main cause of virtually every commercial crisis. It is the dispute in which everyone seeks to make more business, lure more customers, offer more dividends to their share-

> holders, that usually leads them to discount bills without the necessary guarantees; which forces interest rates down too much; that excites firms randomly; that makes real capital vanish from the market, and replaces it with fictional, imaginary, capital; it is the rivalry among banks that contributes greatly to produce failures, ruin, and despair in thousands of families, when the day comes in which this illusion dissipates.[40]

In short, monopoly of note issue was perceived by Itaboraí and his followers as the best way to ensure macroeconomic stability. Not everyone shared this opinion, however. There were those, like deputy Bandeira de Mello, who feared that with monopoly would come complacency and, ultimately, a deterioration in the quality of the paper being discounted.[41] Others preferred a monopoly in the hands of the government—and not a private bank—, who would be allowed to issue inconvertible notes.[42]

In Chap. 2, it was shown that the Bank of Brazil was unable to prevent the seasonal drain of currency from Rio to the provinces, a perennial problem at the time. The presence of Souza Franco at the Ministry of Finance in 1857 gave the supporters of plurality of issue the opportunity to promote the creation of six new note-issuing banks, thus breaking the short-lived monopoly enjoyed by the Bank of Brazil.

By chartering new banks of issue, it was hoped that the money supply would increase, and interest rates would be reduced. Fostering economic activity, therefore, was the main objective of those who supported plurality of issue. Yet, some contemporaries entertained mixed feelings about the impact on the economy of the banks created by Executive decree.

> If this over-issue were exclusively employed in opening roads and facilitating the transport of the immense national (sic) riches of such provinces as Bahia and Minas Geraes (...), there would be little fear but that an ample amount of products would always be available for the legitimate purpose of trade. As matters stand, these banks of issue can only give rise to reckless and improvident speculations.[43]

The apprehensions of the British Consul were never really put to the test. As discussed in Chap. 2, in late 1857, shortly after the first banks were chartered, the country was hit by the crisis that had originated in the United States and later spread to Europe and beyond. The financial panic that ensued delivered a fatal blow to the aspirations of supporters of plurality of note issue. Since it coincided with Souza Franco's decrees setting up the new banks, the crisis was said to have been so severe precisely because of the recently established plurality of issue.

Still, it was shown that the new banks had not even engaged in the issue of notes when the panic spread in Brazil. Additionally, news of the creation of the banks had no impact on the rate of exchange, which eliminates the possibility of agents' expectations having contributed to the crisis. Nevertheless, as discussed earlier, the operation needed to defend the rate of exchange proved very polemical, and attacks on it ultimately led to the fall of the *Conciliação* cabinet and would tarnish the idea of plurality of note issue for decades.

The incoming Conservatives went about reversing Souza Franco's policies. Yet, the attempt by Minister Torres Homem to modify radically banking and corporate legislation, in 1859, was initially rebuffed by Parliament. Moreover, it was noted that although a staunch opponent of plurality of issue, Torres Homem saw no problem in chartering seventeen new deposit and discount banks during his time in office. This revealed a crucial misconception in the monetary debates in Brazil, namely, the understanding that note issues were the sole means available to increase the money supply.

Torres Homem's convictions, of course, have no support in modern banking theory. With the development of deposit accounts, banks realized they could lend a percentage of their reserves in currency (coins and notes) without compromising their ability to honor claims on them. Through this mechanism, banks are capable of creating money regardless of their gaining the right to issue notes. Contemporaries either failed to perceive this or plainly considered notes and demand deposits as essentially distinct. The money supply (M2) reached 1.6 times the monetary base in the mid-1880s and, as such, deposit creation no doubt represented one form of monetary growth that the government was late in acknowledging.[44] As a result of this oversight, policymakers saw no contradiction in closely controlling the activities of the banks of issue, while leaving deposit and discount banks and *casas bancárias* to carry out their business at will.

This point was dramatically reflected in the discussion in Chap. 3 about the origins of the 1864 Souto crisis. It was then argued that the Peláez and Suzigan figures show, unmistakably—and contrary to most of the historiography—that the Law of Impediments did *not* cause a severe monetary contraction that, ultimately, resulted in a financial crisis. Moreover, it must be stressed that this conclusion is based on data that, as discussed earlier, underestimate the degree of liquidity in the economy in the early 1860s. This is because they omit other important forms of money at the time, namely, deposits held by the Mauá Bank (a deposit and discount bank organized as a partnership), liabilities of the *casas bancárias*, which include both deposits held by these establishments and their own issues of *vales*, and specie (see Table 5.1).

As already mentioned, the restrictive banking and corporate legislation enacted in 1860 left untouched an important, although difficult to gauge, part of the financial sector—*casas bancárias*. Private banks, it was shown, took demand deposits and issued their own, locally circulating, *vales*. In this regard, they operated in a similar fashion to joint-stock banks, with the difference that they went largely unsupervised by the authorities.[45] As a result, they took risky positions but, at the same time, provided the market with the liquidity that the government wanted to curtail through the Law of Impediments and Decree 2685.[46]

The unchecked operation of private banks was Brazil's neglected experiment with free banking. Indeed, few controls existed on the creation of *casas bancárias*, and their subsequent activities. In this respect, their development loosely resembled the laissez-faire system that characterized Scotland, except for the absence of a local clearing arrangement.[47] *Casas bancárias* were broadly unencumbered by government controls and seem to have ignored, for the most part, basic prudential rules. Still, the growth in their discounts does not appear to have helped lower the rate of interest, as hoped by pluralists. Abundant money need not result in cheaper credit, as already noted. More importantly, in all likelihood the unsupervised operation of private banks helped trigger the major financial panic in the history of the Empire—the 1864 Souto crisis.

Monopoly of note issue was restored in 1866, when the contract signed between the government and the Bank of Brazil was reviewed. At the time, the reason given for this decision was the Bank's incapacity, or unwillingness, to resume convertibility of its notes. In reality, as argued in Chap. 3, the needs of the Treasury in connection with war expenditures motivated the return of issuing rights to the hands of the government. Throughout the rest of the conflict, considerations of macroeconomic stability would have to be set aside. For the time being, monopoly of issue would be an instrument of national security, rather than a means to achieve a sound monetary system.

Apart from discussions about what establishments were allowed to put their notes in circulation, the question of issuing rights in Brazil was directly related to the broader legislation governing incorporation. Brazilian corporate law, as detailed in the 1850 Commercial Code, laid down in Article 298 the institution of limited liability. In other words, unlike the usual *sociedades*, governed by unlimited liability, shareholders in corporations (*sociedades anônimas*) would only be liable for the firm's debts up to the amount of shares they subscribed. A further set-up permitted by the Commercial Code, and which was modelled in its French counterpart, was the limited partnership (*sociedades em comanditas*). In this case, one or more controlling partners (*sócios solidários*) administered the firm, and were subjected to unlimited liability, while other, non-controlling (or "sleeping"), partners retained limited liability.

Choice of liability for shareholders in a bank involved a trade-off. If, on the one hand, limited liability could make depositors wary of their chances of recovering their money in case of liquidation, unlimited liability from the outset restricted the pool of potential investors. Joint-stock banks tended to be more stable than their private counterparts, given their ability to raise larger sums of capital. More capital meant more business volume, allowing greater economies of scale to be reaped, a feature that is deemed important in the commercial banking industry. Brazilian legislators seem to have sided with most nations of the time in deciding for limited liability for corporations.[48]

The 1850 Commercial Code also determined in Article 295 that *sociedades anônimas* could only be established 'for a fixed period of time, and by means of Government authorization, depending on legislative approval in case they benefit from any privilege'.[49] In practice, this reiterated earlier jurisprudence in Brazilian legislation, dating back to the beginning of the nineteenth century. As a result, in Brazilian law, incorporation was not a right, but a privilege.[50] Banks, if organized as corporations, had therefore to conform to the general provisions of Article 295 of the Commercial Code. As such, they had to seek government approval of their statutes before starting their operations. Nevertheless, as seen earlier, that determination was often not observed in practice. Furthermore—and this was the crucial point—should the issue of notes be interpreted as a privilege, granting of a charter was definitely dependent on legislative approval.[51] In spite of this interpretation, it was not until the 1860 Law of Impediments was enacted that the Legislative prerogative in authorizing banks of issue to operate was clearly established.[52]

Technical aspects concerning bank issues varied over the years. Banks that were established in the pre-1853 period engaged in the issue of *vales*. This contrasted with the first Bank of Brazil, which issued banknotes that circulated nationally and had legal tender status. *Vales* were not accepted as payment of debts and taxes to the government and could not be used

Table 5.3 Brazilian Banks: rules governing rights of issue, 1808/1851

Institution	*Date statutes approved*	*Denomination of notes or* Vales *and issuing limits*
First Bank of Brazil	12 October 1808	Notes with a denomination of 30$000 or above Unlimited issue with the sole proviso that it be done with 'the necessary caution so as to ensure redemption (for metallic coins) on demand'
Banco Commercial do Rio de Janeiro	10 December 1838	*Vales* with a denomination of 500$000 or above, redeemable in gold or Treasury notes Issues limited to 1/3 paid-in capital
Banco Commercial da Bahia	13 November 1845	*Vales* with a denomination of 100$000 or above, redeemable in gold or Treasury notes Issues limited to 1/2 paid-in capital
Caixa de Economia da Província de Pernambuco	27 April 1847	*Vales* with a denomination of 25$000 to 500$000, redeemable in gold or Treasury notes Issues limited to 1/2 paid-in capital
Banco Commercial do Pará	14 September 1847	*Vales* redeemable in gold or Treasury notes Issues limited to 1/2 paid-in capital
Banco Commercial do Maranhão	24 March 1849	*Vales* redeemable in gold or Treasury notes Issues limited to 1/2 paid-in capital
"Second" Bank of Brazil (Mauá)	2 July 1851	*Vales* of no less than 5 days and lowest denomination of 200$000, redeemable in gold or Treasury notes Issues limited to 1/3 paid-in capital[a]
Banco de Pernambuco	22 December 1851	*Vales* of no less than 5 days and lowest denomination of 100$000 Issues limited to 1/2½ paid-in capital

Sources: Franco (1984) and Cavalcanti (1893)

[a]The same ratio applied to the branches of the second Bank of Brazil in São Paulo and Rio Grande do Sul, while the lowest denomination of *vales* was 100$000

outside the provinces in which they had been issued. Furthermore, the decrees approving banks' statutes usually imposed a maximum limit on the issues of *vales*, which consisted of a multiple of paid-in capital (Table 5.3).

Notes of the third Bank of Brazil, created in 1853, unlike *vales*, were accepted in payment of taxes and debts to the government. In the case of paper issued by its branches, they could only circulate in the province where they had been issued. In time, this would come to include the markets formerly served by *vale*-issuing banks in the provinces of Pernambuco, Bahia, São Paulo, Minas Gerais and Rio Grande do Sul (Table 5.4).

Table 5.4 Third Bank of Brazil: rules governing rights of issue

Arts. 12, 13, and 16: the Bank is allowed to issue notes in denominations of 20$000 or more (head office) and 10$000 (branches), payable to bearer, redeemable in gold or Treasury notes (at the Bank's discretion) and accepted in payment of taxes and debts to the government.
Art. 16, para. 1: Issues limited to twice the Bank's *fundo disponível*, consisting of specie and 22-carat gold bars. Para 2: total issue cannot exceed the value of Bank's discount operations.
Art. 18: Additionally, Bank can increase the issue set in Art. 16 by a sum equivalent to the total amount of Treasury notes withdrawn from circulation, but never exceeding thrice the *fundo*.[a]
Art. 19: Finally, on top of the above limits, Bank can issue additional notes, so long as backed by gold at a 1:1 ratio, i.e., each extra unit of Bank of Brazil notes that is issued requires its equivalent in gold beyond the existing sum already in the *fundo*.

Source: Cavalcanti (1893, vol. 2, pp. 198–201)

[a]Art. 56, para. 1 of the statutes of the Bank of Brazil determined that it gradually withdraw Treasury notes then in circulation

At first, total issues of the Bank of Brazil were limited to an amount equivalent to twice its reserve fund (*fundo disponível*), comprised of both gold (bars and specie) and Treasury notes. Redemption could be made in either specie or government notes. As seen in Chaps. 2 and 3, limits on the issue of Bank of Brazil notes were frequently relaxed, in order to accommodate additional demand for its notes, a sudden loss of gold, or both.

Banks created by decree of the Executive in 1857–8 were all broadly governed by the same rules. They could only issue notes payable to bearer up to the value of paid-in capital (Table 5.5).

Issues of the banks created by government decree had to be partly guaranteed by an equal amount of *apólices* and railway shares, while the other half should correspond to a reserve fund made up of specie and Treasury notes. Their banknotes were not accepted in tax offices, a privilege which was held exclusively by the Bank of Brazil. They were not legal tender, either. In other words, private individuals were under no obligation to accept them in daily transactions.[53]

Finally, the imposition of minimum limits on the face value of notes and *vales* issued by banks was an additional feature that Brazil shared with other nations at the time. Two main reasons accounted for this practice. First, given that notes of small denomination tended to fall into the hands of poorer, less educated, individuals—who would present more difficulty in discriminating between issuers—, it was hoped counterfeiting would be

Table 5.5 Banks created by government decree: rules governing rights of issue

Institution	*Date statutes approved*	*Denomination of notes and issuing limits*
Banco Commercial & Agrícola	31 August 1857	Notes with a denomination of 20$000 or above (head office) and 10$000 (branches), payable to bearer, without legal tender status, and redeemable in gold or Treasury notes (at the bank's discretion). Total issue limited to an amount equivalent to bank's paid-in capital At least 50% of issues to be guaranteed by an equivalent sum in bonds of the consolidated government debt (*apólices*) and railway shares with profits guaranteed by the imperial government; remaining 50% of note issues to be backed by reserve fund made up of Treasury notes and specie[a]
Banco do Rio Grande do Sul	24 October 1857	Same as above, except for the railway shares. Given the absence of railways in the province of Rio Grande do Sul at the time, shares of any business enjoying a minimum rate of return of 7% guaranteed by either the imperial or provincial governments
Novo Banco de Pernambuco	11 November 1857	Same as Commercial & Agrícola
Banco do Maranhão	25 November 1857	Same as Commercial & Agrícola
Banco Rural & Hypothecario	27 February 1858[b]	Same as Commercial & Agrícola
Banco da Bahia	3 April 1858	Same as the Commercial & Agrícola

Source: Cavalcanti (1893)

[a]Profit guarantees referred to a minimum rate of return that the government ensured investors in railways and a few other infrastructure projects

[b]The Rural & Hypothecario had been operating as a deposit bank since 1854. After doubling its capital from 8000 to 16,000 *contos* it applied for, and obtained, permission to issue notes

discouraged.[54] Second, there was the fear that paper of small denomination would expel from circulation coins used in day-to-day transactions.[55] In the end, requiring that banks issue notes the individual value of which could well be in excess of the average worker's weekly wages, led to the widespread counterfeiting of copper coins (the so-called *xenxéns*). Moreover, it resulted in the issue of private notes of very small denominations, as a means to introduce crucial small change into circulation.[56]

5.3 Convertibility

As argued in section 5.1, exchange-rate stability precluded the shifts in income and wealth that accompanied currency fluctuations, and which lay at the root of the political economy of the exchange rate and, more broadly, of monetary management. In practical terms, this stability would be a direct result of the official commitment to the convertibility of domestic currency at a fixed weight of gold.

The importance of the exchange rate in an open economy like Brazil's in the second half of the nineteenth century cannot be exaggerated. This price had a bearing, to name only a few, on the amount of government revenue (which was highly dependent on import taxes)[57] and the cost (in milréis) of its foreign commitments. The exchange rate also had an influence on the price of urban wage goods (such as bread, which was made from imported wheat), and, more generally, the state of confidence in the economy as a whole.[58] Finally, the fortunes of exporters of commodities (*fazendeiros*) were heavily dependent on the behavior of the exchange rate (both its level and variability).

In the second half of the nineteenth century, for a country to enter a fixed exchange-rate regime implied the adoption of convertibility of note issues into gold. The first concrete step toward establishing a gold-backed currency in Brazil was taken on 11 September 1846, with Law 401. This very succinct piece of legislation comprised two main articles. The first one authorized tax offices to accept payments made with twenty-two-carat gold coins at the ratio of four milréis to the *oitava*.[59] The second article authorized the government to retire from circulation the amount of paper money deemed necessary to maintain the rate of exchange at the 27 pence to the milréis rate at which it stood in the occasion.[60]

Still, it must be emphasized that this exchange rate was of a notional nature, given that notes in circulation at the time, consisting for the most part of Treasury paper, were inconvertible. In practice, at that stage the country was under a fiduciary regime with flexible exchange rates, given that no part of its note circulation was backed by gold, nor was it redeemable into specie on demand. (Potential) convertibility, as seen in Chap. 2, would only come about after the creation of the third Bank of Brazil, in 1853.

Even though the spirit of the 1846 legislation would dominate most policy actions in the monetary and banking realm in the second half of the nineteenth century, the 27d/1$000 gold parity was only maintained through most of the 1850s, and during brief spells in the following decades (see Fig. 5.6).

From the mid-1850s to the early 1860s, the Bank of Brazil—and, for a while, the smaller banks of issue created by government decree—were required to redeem their notes into gold (or Treasury paper) on demand. Throughout this period, the exchange rate remained near par. Still, this was a peculiar type of convertibility. Unlike a traditional gold standard, or the gold exchange standard, note issues in this period were redeemable either in gold or in Treasury notes.[61] Yet, Treasury notes themselves were inconvertible, so that by giving them in return for its notes (as it usually did) the Bank was technically converting its own money into paper, not gold. Still, even with this peculiar system in place, exchange-rate stability was observed. As it turned out, the simple pledge by the Bank of Brazil and the issuing banks created by Executive decree in 1857–8 to redeem their notes into either gold or Treasury notes—in other words, potential convertibility—seems to have built credibility into the system, and helped maintain the milréis around its par value.

It should be noted that when a country is effectively under gold, its exchange rate can only vary within the narrow limits of the gold points. Outside this, specie will flow either into or out of its borders, thus redressing balance of payments surpluses or deficits. A look at the behavior of the exchange rate in the period when Brazil was potentially under gold reveals little deviation from the 27d/1$000 par value, when allowing for a cost for insurance and shipping of gold as high as 4% of its price (Table 5.6).

Apart from the periods displayed in Table 5.6 and the latter months of the Empire, following legislation enacted by the Ouro Preto cabinet (see Chap. 4), Brazil was under a purely fiduciary system. Therefore, it could not possibly benefit from the same degree of exchange-rate stability as when it was under this peculiar type of regime, where a handful of private

Table 5.6 Rate of exchange under convertibility of banknotes, 1857/64 (in pence per milréis)

Period	*Exchange rate*	
	High	*Low*
10 Apr 1854 to 11 Nov 1857	28 3/4	26 3/4
24 Aug 1858 to 17 Jan 1859	27	26
23 Oct 1862 to 14 Sep 1864	27 5/8	26 5/8

Note: As indicated in the text, issuing banks seldom offered gold in exchange for their notes, rendering convertibility at the time more of a potential nature

banks were allowed to issue notes redeemable either in gold or Treasury paper. Despite the, relatively, short duration of this period in which (potential) convertibility was in force, monetary orthodoxy prevailed throughout most of the second half of the nineteenth century and, accordingly, a majority of policymakers and contemporary commentators pushed for the adoption of a gold-backed monetary circulation.

In the Brazilian historiography, individuals who proclaimed the virtues associated with "hard money" have been labelled *metalistas*, whose ideas would be broadly akin to those of the Currency school in England (Saes 1986, p. 26).[62] The Visconde de Itaboraí and Torres Homem were the main exponents of this group in the mid-nineteenth century. *Papelistas*, on the other hand, would be the Brazilian equivalent of the Banking school.[63] Bernardo de Souza Franco was the undisputed leader of this current.[64]

The intellectual legitimacy for either camp was afforded by constant reference in contemporary debates to foreign authors. Gilbart, an English author identified with the Free Banking school, was a favorite, having had one of his works translated into Portuguese.[65] Hume, Ricardo, Mill, and other key participants in the English monetary controversies, were cited with varying degrees of familiarity. Additionally, some of the major tenets of the Currency school vs. Banking school controversy—such as the currency principle and the needs of trade doctrine—were repeated as undisputed truths. In this regard, two excerpts drawn from the reports published by the commissions set up to investigate the origins of the 1857 and 1864 crises will suffice.

> Apart from the guarantee arising from the prompt redemption of banknotes, the total sum of paper money in each country must vary in amount and value in a similar manner as it would vary (…) if replaced by a metallic currency. (*Relatorio da Commissão de Inquerito de 1859* undated, p. 53)

> (It is) an undeniable principle that the circulation of banknotes, redeemable in gold on demand, is always determined by the needs of the market, or of the circulation, and cannot go beyond (those needs). (*Relatorio da Commissão de Inquerito de 1864* 1865, p. 6)

As already noted, defense of convertibility tended to prevail in the monetary debates that spanned the 1850–89 period (and beyond). In this respect, a cursory look at the introductory section to most of the reports of the Minister of Finance in the second half of the nineteenth century provides as good a summary as any of the dominant credo on the topic, as exemplified by Torres Homem's opinion manifested in 1858:

> the essential condition which industry everywhere needs in order to grow and prosper is the stability of the value of the instrument used in the circulation of its products. This condition is met by a metallic currency, which, because of the precious material from which it is made, is the universal equivalent, the uniform and almost invariable unit of all other values, the basic product to which they are reduced, as into a common denominator. Bank paper – a mere promise to pay – cannot replace it in circulation unless under the condition of it being converted into this real object. (*RMF* 1858, p. 2)

Souza Franco's views on the subject of convertibility, as expounded in his 1848 book, were:

> Of itself (...) metallic circulation, or (circulation) under a metallic base and bank paper redeemable on demand, is preferable to non-redeemable Treasury notes (...). And the main reason for this is that precious metals are for general use and, being independent of the credit of public or private establishments, the circulating medium is not subject to repeated oscillations in value, which is totally lost as a result of fortuitous and unforeseen events. The same may be said of the notes of well-organized banks of issue, for they will always retain in reserve metal and bonds representing good debt in order to ensure convertibility (of their notes) into specie on request. (Franco 1984, p. 87)

Somewhat surprisingly, Souza Franco, the champion of the *papelistas*, was not so distant from his fierce opponent Torres Homem as far as support of a gold-backed currency was concerned.[66] In this respect, both men were in tune with the "sound" monetary principles of their time. Like Currency school and Banking school advocates, both *papelistas* and *metalistas* maintained that convertibility was paramount. This point is most important. It suggests the need for caution when interpreting the term *papelista*, which might convey the false impression of a supporter of a purely *paper* circulation, in clear opposition to the gold standard dogma of the day.

The broad *metalista* vs. *papelista* dichotomy found in the literature usually fails to grasp this crucial point in the debate, namely, the defense (or opposition to) the gold standard.[67] There is no doubt, for instance, that Souza Franco was in favor of imposing restraint on the six new banks of issue that he authorized to operate as Minister of Finance in 1857 and 1858. Proof of this, he established limits on their issue of (partly) *gold*-backed notes (see Table 5.5).[68]

It has been argued that the strength of the gold standard doctrine at the time was actually part of a broader defense of the monopoly of note issue by the Bank of Brazil, which was broken when Souza Franco extended this right to other banks.[69] Yet, as noted, the Minister, a *papelista* and pluralist, supported a gold-backed circulation as well. In this sense, his position was in fact similar to the Banking school's, which, like the Currency school, never questioned the idea of convertibility itself. This point is worth emphasizing, for the term *papelista* has often been used in a derogatory sense, as depicting irresponsible inflationists. Souza Franco's influential book, written in 1848, contains ample evidence of how mindful he was of the need to combine a banking system which would simultaneously meet two objectives: to foster economic activity while maintaining the stability of the currency. This combination would be attained, he argued, through convertible notes, not by means of a fiduciary circulation.

Contemporary references to the two schools of thought are very scarce, the terms *papelista* and *metalista* apparently having been disseminated by twentieth-century writers.[70] Yet, this research has unearthed a rare, and comprehensive, definition of *papelistas*, given in the Senate by Itaboraí, when asked by Souza Franco.

> They are those who proclaim that bank paper is capital, that it is desirable to create many banks, so as to have a larger circulating medium, for the greater the sum, the greater the number of transactions, and the greater the public wealth. They are those who create banks without imposing on them the indispensable conditions that will guarantee the redemption of their notes in gold (...), those who believe that banks, when under extraordinary circumstances, in which their gold reserves tend to fall and the portfolio to increase, should expand their operations (...). Those are the *papelistas*.[71]

In Itaboraí's definition, then, *papelistas* were advocates of plurality of issue, who paid little attention to prudential rules, and advocated counter-cyclical monetary policies in the event of panics. Yet, like *metalistas*, they were supporters of gold-backed issues.

Now, who were the "real" *papelistas*, in the sense of advocates of a purely fiduciary circulation? One needs to look no further than to Irineu

Evangelista de Souza, Barão (later Visconde) de Mauá. He was a close friend of Souza Franco's, whose thoughts and policies on money and banking he strongly supported.[72] Nevertheless, Mauá entertained ideas on the subject that were in essence much more radical. Throughout his prolific trajectory as the most important businessman in the Empire, he advocated the virtues of the "spirit of association". In terms of banking legislation, this translated into a much bolder approach to the question of plurality of issue than Souza Franco's. His stance against convertibility of banknotes into gold was heretical at the time, and clearly set him apart from his illustrious *papelista* friend.[73] An excerpt drawn from the chapter on the "Circulating Medium in Brazil", published in his 1878 autobiography, summarizes Mauá's view on the question of convertibility.

> If metallic currency, and banknotes convertible on demand, constitute the engine *par excellence* of the monetary transactions of most countries, on account of their not being just orders on the capital of the country but (of their) having the advantage of being accepted (…) by the value convened by their mint price (…), it does not follow that these superlative conditions of an *excellent circulating medium* (…) could not be replaced *at a gain, at a substantial gain even*, by temporary, non-convertible paper from banks (…) which may be led by special circumstances (…) to keep in their portfolios not gold, but private and State paper of good credit. (Mauá 1942, p. 316)

Mauá admitted that at times issuing banks had committed excesses. 'To the *use* of banknotes, followed *misuse*: the mission of the statesmen was to curtail the latter by means of restrictive legislation' (ibid., p. 319).[74] Nevertheless, as a rule, he opposed the straitjacket that a gold-backed circulation would impose on the banking system. Nor was he an irresponsible inflationist either, as the above remarks testify to. His hand is clearly seen in the text of the commission set up by the Bank of Brazil in reaction to the 1860 Law of Impediments.[75] On that occasion, the commissioners criticized both the currency principle and the real bills doctrine. They argued that there did not exist a "magic" relationship between the amount of currency in circulation and the number of transactions carried out in the economy. Instead, they suggested that the velocity of circulation depended on the state of confidence at a given point in time.[76] Finally, the report remarked on the adverse effects that the supposedly "natural" adjustment mechanisms of the gold standard had had in places like Great Britain, stressing that they would be even greater in a capital-importing nation like Brazil.[77]

Mauá was not alone in perceiving the potential damaging effects that the operation of the gold standard could have on Brazil. For Sebastião Ferreira Soares, a contemporary statistician,

> Everything that has been said in the chambers and outside about the metallic circulating medium are nice theories, which fail completely in practice, for no State will succeed in retaining gold and silver coins in circulation unless the value of production and exports is greater than imports and consumption (…). Brazil will not achieve a stable circulating medium in gold and silver, as desired, unless its exports exceed its imports, and the most advantageous medium will be the one that we had earlier, with very few changes. (Soares 1977, p. 312)[78]

These remarks were made at the same time as the government's determination to impose limits on the banks of issue was at its highest, namely, concurrently with the enactment of the 1860 Law of Impediments.[79] As part of its efforts to adapt to the new legislation, in October 1862 the Bank of Brazil announced convertibility of its notes, after almost four years in which they were redeemed in Treasury paper alone.

This new phase of convertibility would only last until the outbreak of the Souto Crisis, in September 1864, when the Bank sought (and received) government approval to suspend the obligation to redeem its notes into gold. Conceived as an exceptional measure to protect its metallic fund, this new episode in suspension of convertibility of the notes of the Bank of Brazil would prove to be the last. Two years later, in September 1866, financial needs arising from the Paraguayan War led the government to announce a radical review of its agreement with the Bank. Because of this innovation, the Bank lost its issuing powers, which were transferred back to the Treasury, and sold its gold reserves to the government.[80] The latter would once again be in charge of the printing press. Massive issues of fiat money followed and adoption of the gold standard would have to wait until much later.

As discussed in Chap. 4, over the course of the 1866–89 period, authorities keenly sought to promote convertibility of the currency. Barring the exceptional circumstances dictated by the war against Paraguay and expenses associated with drought relief in the 1870s and 1880s, monetary policy would be conducted with the aim of bringing the exchange rate back to the "mythical" 27d parity, perceived as a sine qua non for restoration of convertibility. This *desideratum* would be finally achieved just as the imperial period came to an end, in 1889. Along the way, "hard money" policies were the norm, helping to antagonize the regime to its traditional constituency—the coffee planters. Ouro Preto's attempt to woo the latter by means of the Auxílios à Lavoura initiative—combining generous amounts of credit to agriculture under a gold standard regime—proved to be insufficient to forestall the eventual overthrow of the Monarchy that would take place on 15 November 1889.

Notes

1. Friedman and Schwartz (1963).
2. Notable examples are Cavalcanti (1890, 1893), Wileman (1896), Calógeras (1910), Ortigão (1914), Neuhaus (1975) and, more recently, Franco (2017).
3. Peláez and Suzigan (1976).
4. This appears to have been the case in 1853, when the money supply (M1), measured by the sum of notes held by the public and demand deposits, was in the order of 47,000 *contos* and 'close to 30,000 *contos* in specie was to be found in the Brazilian market' (Calógeras 1910, p. 110). The second half of the 1850s witnessed the largest amount of specie struck by the Brazilian mint, with 21,000 *contos* in gold coins and 5800 *contos* in silver coins put into circulation between 1854 and 1859. This comprised approximately 30% of the average outstanding circulation of notes (issued by both the Treasury and private banks) at the time, and an equal share of the average money supply as measured by notes held by the public and demand deposits. Total coinage of gold pieces in the Brazilian mint between 1850 and 1888 amounted to 45.7 thousand *contos*, while another 20.9 thousand *contos* in silver coins were put into circulation in the same period. Copper and silver coins, used as small change and issued from 1868 and 1872 onward, respectively, totaled 7.6 thousand *contos*. Figures in Cavalcanti (1893, vol. 2, p. 327). Unfortunately, an annual series for the stock of specie *in circulation* (as opposed to specie coined at the mint) is not available. Throughout the period under study here, specie was often driven out of circulation, being either exported or hoarded. This precludes any attempt to arrive at a more precise estimate of the monetary base that would result from adding figures for specie in circulation (including British sovereigns and other foreign coins, which were legal tender) to the published series for notes issued by the government and issuing banks. For a discussion, Abreu and Lago (2001, pp. 363–71).
5. In connection to this, Schulz mentions yet another possible correction to the Peláez and Suzigan estimates of the money supply, but relating to the

final year of the Empire (1889). According to the author, the exchange-rate parity then achieved provided for the entry in circulation of the equivalent of £ 9 million in specie, or one-third of the money supply at the time. He goes on to cite page 336 in Cavalvanti (1890) as his source, although the latter does not provide this figure but, solely, estimates of gold coins *minted* in Brazil in different points in time—not specie in circulation. Schulz (2013, p. 164). Still, fragmentary evidence suggests that there was, indeed, an increase in the volume of metal coins in circulation (and, therefore, of the money supply) in Brazil in 1888 and 1889. Over these two years, there was a net inflow of £ 2.9 million in silver and gold coins from Britain, part of which was minted into Brazilian currency and put into circulation. The Brazilian mint produced just over 4.5 thousand *contos* in silver coins in 1888 and 1889, valued at £ 487,000. There are no detailed data on gold coins minted in Brazil in those two years, although Cavalcanti (1893, vol. 2, p. 315) provides a figure for 1.9 thousand *contos* (equivalent to £ 205,600) in gold pieces coined in 1888–9. Data on specie imported from Britain in Lago (1982). Coins minted in Brazil in Amato et al. (2008).
6. The Brazilian population roughly doubled between 1850 and 1889, from an estimated 7.3 million to 14.3 million according to the 1890 census. Brasil, IBGE (1990, pp. 33–4).
7. For the 1870–1913 period, Catão (1992b) provides a carefully constructed wholesale price index.
8. As discussed in the text, this is, admittedly, a restrictive definition of the monetary base, as it leaves out metallic currency in circulation and *vales* (promissory notes) issued by a number of agents at the time, including private banks, companies and, even, individuals.
9. At its peak, in December 1861, notes issued by the banks created by government decree in 1857–8 reached 13.5 thousand *contos*, or 16.5% of total notes in circulation. Thereafter—and because of their incapacity to comply with the rules set out by the 1860 Law of Impediments—, their combined issues declined significantly and would constitute but a marginal share of total notes in circulation (see Table A1 in the Appendix).
10. Chapters 2, 3 and 4 present this history in detail.
11. This includes the issue of 40.6 thousand *contos* in 1866, as its main objective was the acquisition of the Bank of Brazil's metallic reserves in order to help finance expenditures linked to the war against Paraguay.
12. For details, see Chap. 4 in this book and Summerhill (2015, ch. 4).
13. Figures on funded domestic debt outstanding in Levy (1995). Data originally published in milréis and converted to pounds sterling at the average monthly rate of exchange at each point in time over the whole series.

14. Average budget deficits between 1880–1 and 1885–6 exceeded 22,000 *contos* annually. See Table A6 in the Appendix.
15. Figures for *apólices* in circulation refer to March 1866 and March 1889. Levy (1995, pp. 243–9).
16. This figure does not include the 1889 conversion loan.
17. For Mauá's views on monetary matters, Fernandes (1974). Given the weight of receipts from coffee in total exports under the Empire (roughly 50%), much attention has been given to studying its influence in determining the exchange rate in the period. In this regard, Furtado's classic contribution, by pointing out the instability in the international demand for exports from primary-producing countries, highlights the serious consequences that sudden shifts in demand would have on export earnings from the periphery and, hence, the exchange rate of those countries. Furtado (1970, pp. 164 ff.). Furtado actually reinforces an argument made earlier by Wileman, relating oscillations in the value of the milréis and the price of coffee. Wileman (1896). Later, this relationship was challenged by Delfim Netto (1979, p. 26), who concluded that 'in the long run the exchange rate was relatively little affected by the price cycles (of coffee)'. Since the 1980s, there were renewed attempts to analyze the main determinants of the exchange rate in imperial Brazil. Most of these works sought to test the extent to which the foreign value of the milréis followed changes in coffee prices, monetary policy, capital flows, the terms of trade or a combination of these variables. The results are inconclusive, but most of the contributions tend to indicate that both domestic influences—linked to coffee output, money supply, and wage setting behavior—as well as international ones, via foreign lending and the international demand for Brazil's exports, had a bearing on the country's exchange rate. See Cardoso (1981), Franco (1986), Fishlow (1987), and Catão (1992a, chapter VI). On the difficulties in estimating the main determinants of the exchange rate in late nineteenth-century Brazil, Franco (1991, pp. 77–80).
18. For a similar discussion in connection with the political economy of the exchange rate during the First Republic (1889–1930), Triner (2000).
19. Topik (1994).
20. Session of 9 November 1864, in *ACE*, p. 404.
21. Foreign investors' concerns regarding the exchange rate were thus expressed: '(...) if the question be asked what is hum milréis, the integer of the Brazilian currency, no one can give a precise reply. It not only depends, like gold, on its scarcity or abundance in the domestic market, but on the clearness or obscurity of the foreign and domestic political horizons, and on the weather, and on the chance of getting in crops unaffected by blight and the numerous contingencies to which agriculture is exposed. A difficulty in the River Plate, or a succession of short coffee crops, would again reduce the value of the milréis to half or less of its value today. Nothing but

the unusual profits which are expected when unusual risks are concerned can tempt an investor to convert hard cash into the paper currency of Brazil'. Parliamentary Papers 1875, LXXV, *Report by Consul Lennon-Hunt on the Trade and Commerce of Rio de Janeiro for the Year 1873*, p. 309.

22. In the case of coffee, Brazilian exports constituted a significant share of the world total and, hence, exercised considerable influence on the world price of the commodity. For a discussion, Abreu and Tamega (2005).
23. The above discussion of the political economy of exchange rate and monetary policy is open to a few qualifications. The first point concerns the relative sensitivity of tradable producers to exchange-rate movements, which, in turn, depends on the price elasticity of demand for their products. In the Brazilian case, the coffee sector was characterized by quasi-monopoly power, coupled with a low price elasticity of demand for its product. This feature enabled coffee producers to weather phases of exchange-rate appreciation better than other exporters. Also, foreign investors, when bringing capital to Brazil, would initially benefit from a depreciated milréis. The income stream from those very investments, on the other hand, would be greater in foreign currency terms the more appreciated the rate of exchange. Finally, in a fixed-rate regime such as the gold standard, divisions might arise within a group of exporters if there is mounting pressure for a competitive devaluation of the currency. In this case, the policy decision will involve choosing between those with long-term contracts, that is, whose sale prices in foreign currency might have been set way beforehand—and who will tend to be against the instability that devaluation introduces—and other exporters who would gain immediate competitiveness as a result of a currency devaluation. Frieden (1994, pp. 85–6).
24. See, for example, the debates in the 1878 agricultural congress held in Rio, reprinted as *Anais do Congresso Agrícola* (1988).
25. This is what appears to be implied by Levy and Andrade, when they contend that financing of the agricultural sector via factors (*comissários*) 'reasserted the dominance of circulation over production, ensuring the control of the latter by mercantile capital'. Levy and Andrade (1993, p. 25).
26. Cf. Silva Netto (1865, Introduction).
27. Speech given by Minister of Finance Torres Homem in 1859, cited in Andrada (1923, p. 90).
28. Sweigart (1987).
29. See also Lago (2019) on the difficulty faced by creditors in foreclosing rural property in imperial Brazil.
30. This major obstacle in the way of the development of a long-term market for rural loans was clearly diagnosed by a contemporary. See the chapter "Do Crédito Rural e Sistema Hipotecário" ("On Rural Credit and the Mortgage System"), in Franco (1984, pp. 111–7).

31. On the falling prices for slaves in Brazil as contemporaries perceived the inevitability of abolition (without compensation), Mello (1978).
32. This "liquidity consciousness" was reinforced by the recurrent panics and crises that characterized the nineteenth century. Fears of a potential mismatch between the maturities of bank assets and liabilities has also been identified as a source of the short-termism of which nineteenth-century British banks have often been accused. Collins (1991, pp. 16–7).
33. It has been suggested that a further reason for the relatively high cost of credit in nineteenth-century Brazil was its underdeveloped banking system. The latter, in turn, stemmed in part from the strict control exercised by the government, including the Council of State, over the entry of new players in the market. Ultimately, political power concentrated in the hands of the Executive was used to shield from competition incumbent banks (including the Bank of Brazil), whose boards of directors often included national political officeholders. For an elaboration, Summerhill (2015, ch. 7).
34. The original argument is from Gerschenkron (1962, pp. 13 ff).
35. Session of 5 June, in *ASI* 1858, Tome II, p. 16.
36. Session of 21 May, in *ASI* 1858, Tome I, pp. 244–5.
37. Indeed, this was perfectly understood by some contemporaries. Commenting on the government's plans to allow the Banco Commercial do Rio de Janeiro and Mauá's Bank of Brazil to increase their issue of *vales*, in order to alleviate the monetary pressure felt in 1853, deputy Bandeira de Mello noted that the measure was fruitless: 'if the bills offered for discount do not have credit, if they are not sufficiently guaranteed, banks will not discount them, for banks cannot compensate for the lack of credit'. Session of 13 June, in *ACD* 1853, Tome II, p. 181.
38. The first Bank of Brazil was created in October 1808 and its operations started one year later. Throughout its twenty-year life, it was beset by demands from the State that, ultimately, led to its closure and a protracted process of liquidation, running from 1829 to 1835. For details, Franco (1984, ch. 1), Vieira (1962), Peláez (1975), and Gambi (2017).
39. Articles 9 and 10 of the said decree determined that 'the establishment of any corporation with the purpose of engaging in banking operations shall only be authorized once a quarter of its shares have been subscribed; however, if this total has not been realized within the time marked by its statutes, it shall be dissolved (…)'.
40. Speech delivered in the Chamber of Deputies on 20 June 1853, cited in Franco and Pacheco (1979, Vol. II, p. 106).
41. Speech delivered in the Chamber of Deputies on 18 June 1853, cited in Franco and Pacheco (1979, Vol. II, pp. 101–2).

42. This was the opinion expressed by a Mr. Robert Clinton Wright at the enquiry into the 1857 commercial crisis. See *Relatorio da Commissão de Inquerito de 1859* (undated, pp. 111–2).
43. Parliamentary Papers 1860, LXV, *Report by Mr. Morgan, British Consul in Bahia, on the Trade of that Port for the Year 1858*, p. 2.
44. In fact, official recognition of the role of deposits as part of the money supply would only come about when the government passed Decree 3339 (10 November 1864), which stipulated that deposits held in the Bank of Brazil in current account would henceforth count as part of its issues. The same rule would apply to three-fourths of total interest-bearing deposits. Cavalcanti (1893, Vol. 2, p. 279). In the United States, the procedure to include bank deposits with note issues when setting specie requirements was pioneered by the 1842 Louisiana banking act. Hammond (1957, p. 695).
45. 'In my opinion, receipts (...) issued by the bankers who failed represented an actual issue in disguise, one thousand times more dangerous and damaging to the public than those made by banks; because, although they acted as currency in commercial transactions, they had no limit whatsoever, except the individual credit of those who signed them; it was but an illicit means to circumvent the dispositions of the law of 22 August 1860'. Statement made by Sebastião Ferreira Soares for the inquiry into the 1864 crisis, in *Relatorio da Comissão de Inquerito de 1864* (1865, Annex C, Part I, p. 51).
46. This point serves to highlight the fact that to focus exclusively on traditional monetary aggregates to establish the degree of liquidity in the economy can be misleading, as argued by Kindleberger (1996, pp. 49–51). For example, Sweigart remarks that in 1865 'a Rio merchant had estimated that coffee factors had lent planters as much as 90,000 *contos*, a sum only slightly less than the total currency held by the public over the entire country. Not all of the planter drafts ended up in banks; drafts accepted by well-known planters and factors circulated as currency throughout the coffee provinces'. Sweigart (1987, p. 135). It is difficult to assess the extent to which planter drafts behaved as money, as well as the amount of outstanding obligations of this nature in other points in time. Still, their sheer volume in 1865 should add a measure of caution to any analysis of monetary trends based exclusively on aggregates such as M1 or M2. Goldsmith (1986) puts the total amount of deposits held at private banks in 1864 at somewhere between 25–50 thousand *contos* (see Table 5.1). When these other components are added to the estimates of the money supply provided by M1 and M2, it becomes clear that the Brazilian economy was not suffering from a monetary crunch in the early 1860s.
47. On the free banking experience of Scotland, White (1984, 1991).

48. It has been remarked that at that time 'only in England and Scotland were joint-stock companies generally subject to unlimited liability. In America, as well as on the Continent, the principle of limited liability became the general rule right from the beginning'. Cf. Smith (1936, p. 37, footnote 2).
49. *Coleção das Leis do Império do Brasil*, Tome 11, Part 1, 1850, p. 107.
50. Barman points out that Brazil was not alone at the time in making incorporation depend on official approval, as the same applied to France under its 1807 Commercial Code. See Barman (1981). Free incorporation was not introduced in the North German Confederation and Austria until 1870 and 1899, respectively. Cameron (1972, p. 17).
51. In a way, then, joint-stock issuing banks were invested with a double privilege, that of limited liability—which benefited shareholders—and that of issuing notes.
52. As seen in Chap. 3, the 1860 Law of Impediments imposed restrictions not only on the operation of joint-stock banks, but on corporations in general. Additionally, it strengthened the provisions of the Commercial Code, by laying down for the first time clear penalties (in the shape of fines) on those responsible for failing to obtain a charter before embarking on commercial ventures (Art. 2, para 1).
53. As expected, this provision could cause problems, as in the case of a respectable family from Rio, left stranded in a train station in the outskirts of the city, for want of legal tender currency to pay the fare. As it turned out, all they had in their pockets was a substantial amount of notes issued by the Banco Commercial & Agrícola, which the company refused to accept. This episode was mentioned during debates held in the Chamber of Deputies. See session of 29 May, in *ACD* 1858, Tome I, p. 149.
54. Minister of Finance Ferraz criticized the banks' issues of notes of small denomination on the grounds that they fell into the hands of the lower classes, who used them in daily transactions. This subjected the paper to wear and tear, when not total loss, something that would ultimately benefit the issuing bank, who would be free from redeeming them. *RMF* 1859, p. 69.
55. This prompted the adoption of Article 4 of Decree 2685 (10 November 1860), which imposed on the Bank of Brazil the requirement to withdraw from circulation notes of smaller denomination, should it fail to resume (gold) convertibility within six months.
56. Similar problems arose in the South of the United States, where states struggled to regulate the private issue of so-called shinplasters. Schweikart (1987, p. 115).
57. Throughout most of the period under discussion here, import duties were not collected on an *ad valorem* basis. Instead, they consisted of a fixed

amount (a lump sum) charged on "official values" of each merchandise as detailed in the tariff schedule. In the presence of exchange-rate swings, the market value of a given item could differ—at times, markedly—from "official values", causing importers to face tariff rates that were quite distinct from what they anticipated (and, sometimes, from the government's original intent). For a discussion, Villela (2005).

58. At the time, the degree of protection afforded to import-substituting industries by a depreciated milréis, as well as its influence on the imports of capital goods (and, hence, domestic investment), were not significant issues in the political economy of the exchange rate.
59. An *oitava* corresponded to 1/8 of an ounce, or 3.586 grams.
60. This was the third time the legal parity of the milréis was changed. Historically, the par rate of exchange had been 67.5d. The 27d/1$000 rate replaced the previous parity established in 1833 (at 43.5d/1$000) and would thereafter—and well into the republican period—constitute a veritable "Holy Grail", a mythical rate of exchange that would be doggedly pursued by the government.
61. In addition, as shown in Figure 5.5, in the case of the smaller issuing banks, note issues could be partly backed by shares of companies enjoying profit (dividend) guarantees from the government.
62. On the British monetary controversies, Viner (1937) and Glasner (1989, 1992).
63. Saes (1986) and Andrade (1987).
64. Major politicians identified with the *metalistas* were Angelo Muniz da Silva Ferraz (President of the Council of Ministers and Minister of Finance from August 1859 to March 1861), Paulino José Soares de Sousa (Visconde de Uruguai) and José Maria da Silva Paranhos (Visconde de Rio Branco). With Souza Franco's ideas sided Irineu Evangelista de Souza (Mauá), João Lustosa da Cunha Paranaguá and José Antonio Saraiva, to name the most important. Andrada (1923, p. 112).
65. The 1856 edition of Gilbart's 1827 book *A Practical Treatise on Banking* was translated by L. J. de Oliveira e Castro as *Tractado Practico de Bancos* (Rio de Janeiro: Garnier, 1859, 3 vols.). I am indebted to Carlos Gabriel Guimarães for drawing my attention to the Brazilian edition of the Gilbart book.
66. This similarity was not lost on a contemporary author (and professor at the Recife Law School), who remarked that 'every one of our Ministers of Finance (…), advocates of monopoly or plurality of banks, from Torres Homem to Souza Franco, all of them are blind admirers of gold'. Cf. Milet (1875, p. 25).
67. See, for example, Saes (1986, Part I), and Andrade (1987).

68. For a similar contemporary defense of plurality of issue with convertibility of (non-legal tender) banknotes, Hoyer (1880, pp. 38–40).
69. Andrade (1987).
70. An early example is Normano (1935, p. 190).
71. Debate held on 2 June, in *ASI* 1858, Tome II, p. 14.
72. His participation in the efforts to prop up the rate of exchange in the wake of the 1857 crisis bear witness to this. For details, see Chap. 2.
73. Still, this did not stop him from operating in Uruguay, where notes issued by the Mauá Bank were redeemable in specie.
74. Mauá's defense of inconvertible banknotes had already been made public much earlier, in his testimony to the enquiry into the 1857 commercial crisis. See *Relatorio da Commissão de Inquerito de 1859* (undated, Annex A, p. 96).
75. See Banco do Brasil, *Parecer Apresentado á Assembléa* (1861).
76. Ibid., pp. 14–5.
77. Ibid., pp. 16–7. As noted by many authors, the gold standard operated differently in the countries at the center and those in the periphery of the world economy, the latter being frequently hit by convertibility crises, devaluations, and internal dislocations. In effect, borrowing countries were not as capable as core ones to control the rate of their capital imports and exports. For the periphery, buoyant economic activity led to merchandise imports picking-up and, eventually, to a trade deficit. In the early stages of the cycle, this trade deficit would be financed by (foreign) capital inflows which, by their inherent volatility, were bound to return to their countries of origin at news of panics and the subsequent increases in Bank (of England) Rate. Given the lagged response of import demand to credit conditions, this capital flight could result in severe reserve losses that, under the gold standard, would bring about an equally strong monetary contraction. Depending on the magnitudes involved, that is, the size of the gold drain relative to the domestic monetary base, the ensuing deflation could be considerable. In short, capital flows tended to be pro-cyclical, that is, they would increase in boom times and as soon as the slump set in (but merchandise imports were still on the rise), they would return to the centers from where they had originated. This would aggravate the natural instability that derived from the periphery's frequent reliance on the exports of one or two primary products. For an elaboration of this argument, Ford (1962). For a discussion of these issues as applied to early twentieth-century Brazil, Fritsch (1988). Furtado had already made this point in his classic 1959 book, when describing the economy of nineteenth-century Brazil and its incapacity to adapt to the rules of the gold standard in the period. See Furtado (1970, ch. 27).

78. Soares' reference to "exports in excess of imports" (a trade surplus), as he himself elaborates in his book, would refer in modern parlance to the need for a balance of payments surplus if gold and silver coins were to be retained domestically.
79. Soares' *Notas Estatísticas* was originally published in 1860. Mauá's and Soares' advocacy of paper currency, as already noted, was highly atypical in a world convinced of the superiority of the gold standard. In this respect, they were close to the Birmingham economists of the nineteenth century, who backed inconvertible paper money as a means to enhance employment in times of distress in their city. In a debate in the Senate, Jequitinhonha stated that Souza Franco's opinions in favor of plurality of issue were akin to those of the Birmingham school, 'whose theories had been proven false'. See *ASI* 1858, Tome I, p. 244. On the opposition of the Birmingham economists to deflation and the gold standard, Fetter (1965, pp. 177–80).
80. These events are examined in detail in Chaps. 2 and 3.

References

Abreu, Marcelo de P., and Luiz A.C. do Lago. 2001. Property Rights and the Fiscal and Financial Systems in Brazil: Colonial Heritage and Imperial Period. In *Transferring Wealth and Power from the Old to the New World: Monetary and Fiscal Institutions in the 17th Through the 19th Centuries*, ed. Michael D. Bordo and Roberto Cortés-Conde, 327–377. Cambridge: Cambridge University Press.

Abreu, Marcelo de P. and Felipe Tamega (2005). Market Power and Commodity Prices: Brazil, Chile and the United States, 1820s–1930. *Texto para Discussão*, Departamento de Economia PUC-Rio, No. 511.

Amato, Claudio P., Irlei S. das Neves, and Arnaldo Russo. 2008. *Livro de Moedas do Brasil*. São Paulo: Artgraph.

Anais do Congresso Agrícola do Rio de Janeiro 1878 (1988). Rio de Janeiro, Fundação Casa de Rui Barbosa.

Banco do Brasil. 1861. *Parecer Apresentado á Assembléa Geral dos Accionistas do Banco do Brasil pela Commissão Especial Eleita em 2 de Maio de 1861*. Rio de Janeiro: Villeneuve.

Barman, Roderick J. 1981. Business and Government in Imperial Brazil: the experience of Viscount Mauá. *Journal of Latin American Studies* 13 (2): 239–264.

Brasil, Câmara dos Deputados, *Annaes da Camara dos Deputados*, 1850–89.

Brasil, Leis e Decretos, *Coleção de Leis e Decretos*, various volumes.

Brasil, IBGE. (1990). *Estatísticas Históricas do Brasil*. Vol. 3, 2nd ed. (séries econômicas, demográficas e sociais, 1550–1985). Rio de Janeiro: IBGE.

Brasil, Ministério da Fazenda, *Balanços da Receita e Despeza do Imperio*, various years.

———. *Proposta e Relatorio Apresentados á Assembléa-Geral Legislativa Pelo Ministro e Secretario d'Estado dos Negócios da Fazenda*, various years.

Brasil, Senado, *Annaes do Senado do Império do Brasil*, varios years.

Calógeras, João P. 1910. *La Politique Monetaire du Brésil*. Rio de Janeiro: Imprensa Nacional.

Cameron, Rondo, ed. 1972. *Banking and Economic Development: Some Lessons of History*. New York: Oxford University Press.

Cameron, Rondo, et al., eds. 1967. *Banking in the Early Stages of Industrialization*. New York: Oxford University Press.

Cardoso, Eliane A. 1981. Desvalorizações Cambiais, Indústria e Café: Brasil, 1862–1906. *Revista Brasileira de Economia* 35 (2): 85–106.

Catão, Luis A. V. 1992a. The Failure of Export-Led Growth in Brazil and Mexico, c. 1870–1930. *Research Papers*, No. 31, Institute of Latin American Studies, University of London.

———. 1992b. A New Wholesale Price Index for Brazil During the Period 1870–1913. *Revista Brasileira de Economia* 46 (4): 519–533.

Cavalcanti, Amaro. 1890. *Resenha Financeira do Ex-Império do Brasil em 1889*. Rio de Janeiro: Imprensa Nacional.

———. 1893. *O Meio Circulante Nacional*. Rio de Janeiro: Imprensa Nacional.

Collins, Michael. 1991. *Banks and Industrial Finance in Britain, 1800–1939*. Cambridge: Cambridge University Press.

da Silva Netto, A. 1865. *Formula Mais Effectiva para a Solução dos Nossos Bancos de Emissão*. Rio de Janeiro: Typographia Perseverança.

de Andrada, Antonio Carlos R. 1923. *Bancos de Emissão no Brasil*. Rio de Janeiro: Edições Leite Ribeiro.

de Andrade, Ana Maria R. 1987. 1864: conflito entre metalistas e pluralistas. Unpublished MSc. dissertation, Universidade Federal do Rio de Janeiro.

de Mauá, Barão. 1942. O Meio Circulante no Brasil. In *Visconde de Mauá, Autobiografia (Exposição aos Credores e ao Público) seguida de O Meio Circulante no Brasil*, ed. C. Ganns, 2nd ed., 93–309. Rio de Janeiro: Zélio Valverde. (originally published in 1878).

de Mello, Pedro C. 1978. Aspectos Econômicos da Organização do Trabalho da Economia Cafeeira do Rio de Janeiro, 1850–1888. *Revista Brasileira de Economia* 32 (1): 19–67.

de Saes, Flavio M. 1986. *Crédito e Bancos no Desenvolvimento da Economia Paulista, 1850–1930*. São Paulo: IPE/USP.

Delfim Netto, Antonio. 1979. *O Problema do Café no Brasil*. Rio de Janeiro: Editora da FGV.

do Lago, Luiz A.C. 1982. Balança Comercial, Balanço de Pagamentos e Meio Circulante no Brasil no Segundo Império: uma nota para uma revisão. *Revista Brasileira de Economia* 36 (4): 489–508.

______. 2019. Latifúndio e Pequena Propriedade: Estrutura Fundiária e Economia no Brasil da Colônia ao Império. *Texto para Discussão*, Departamento de Economia PUC-Rio, No. 667.

Fernandes, Santiago. 1974. Mauá, o Economista do Império: análise de sua crítica científica ao padrão-ouro. *Revista Brasileira de Economia* 28 (2): 3–28.

Fetter, Frank W. 1965. *Development of British Monetary Orthodoxy, 1797–1875.* Cambridge: Harvard University Press.

Fishlow, Albert 1987. Market Forces or Group Interests: Inconvertible Paper Currency in Pre-1914 Latin America. *Working Paper*, Department of Economics, University of California at Berkeley, No. 8753, September.

Ford, Alec G. 1962. *The Gold Standard: 1880–1914, Britain and Argentina.* Oxford: Clarendon Press.

Franco, Bernardo de S. 1984. *Os Bancos do Brasil.* Brasília: Editora da Universidade de Brasília. (originally published in 1848).

Franco, Gustavo Henrique B. 1986. Taxa de Câmbio e Oferta de Moeda, 1880–1897: uma análise econométrica. *Revista Brasileira de Economia* 40 (1): 63–88.

———. 1991. A Década Republicana: o Brasil e a economia internacional – 1880/1900. Rio de Janeiro: Ipea (Série PNPE, n. 27).

———. 2017. *A Moeda e a Lei: uma história monetária brasileira, 1933–2013.* Rio de Janeiro: Zahar.

Franco, Afonso A. de M., and Claudio Pacheco. 1979. *História do Banco do Brasil.* Brasília: Banco do Brasil.

Frieden, Jeffrey. 1994. Exchange Rate Politics: Contemporary Lessons from American History. *Review of International Political Economy* 1 (1): 81–103.

———. 2015. *Currency Politics: The Political Economy of Exchange-Rate Policy.* Princeton and Oxford: Princeton University Press.

Friedman, Milton, and Anna Schwartz. 1963. *A Monetary History of the United States, 1867–1960.* Princeton: Princeton University Press.

Fritsch, Winston. 1988. *External Constraints on Economic Policy in Brazil, 1889–1930.* London: Macmillan.

Furtado, Celso. 1970. *Formação Econômica do Brasil.* 10th ed. São Paulo: Companhia Editora Nacional.

Gambi, Thiago F.R. 2017. Bancos Nacionais do Brasil: os casos de 1808 e 1853. In *Historia Bancaria y Monetaria de América Latina (siglos XIX y XX): nuevas perspectivas*, ed. Carlos Marichal and Thiago Gambi, 63–99. Santander: Editorial de la Universidad de Cantabria.

Gerschenkron, Alexander. 1962. *Economic Backwardness in Historical Perspective.* Cambridge: Harvard University Press.

Gilbart, James W. 1859. *Tractado Practico de Bancos.* Rio de Janeiro: Garnier.

Glasner, David. 1989. On Some Classical Monetary Controversies. *History of Political Economy* 21 (2): 201–229.

———. 1992. The Real Bills Doctrine in the Light of the Law of Reflux. *History of Political Economy* 24 (4): 867–894.

Goldsmith, Raymond W. 1986. *Brasil, 1850–1984: desenvolvimento financeiro sob um século de inflação*. São Paulo: Harper & Row.

Great Britain, Foreign Office, *Diplomatic and Consular Reports* ("Blue Books"), various years.

Hammond, Bray. 1957. *Banks and Politics in America from the Revolution to the Civil War*. Princeton: Princeton University Press.

Hoyer, Martins. 1880. *Estudos Sobre a Reforma do Meio Circulante*. Maranhão: Typographia do Payz.

Junta dos Corretores de Fundos Públicos da Cidade do Rio de Janeiro. Livro Official de Cotações de Titulos e Valores, various volumes.

Kindleberger, Charles P. 1996. *Manias, Panics and Crashes: a history of financial crises*. London: MacMillan, 3rd edn.

Levy, Maria Barbara. 1995. The Brazilian Public Debt – Domestic and Foreign, 1824–1913. In *The Public Debt in Latin America in Historical Perspective*, ed. Reinhard Liehr, 201–228. Vervuert: Frankfurt am Mein.

Levy, Maria Barbara, and Ana Maria R. de Andrade. 1993. El Sector Financiero y El Desarollo Bancario en Río de Janeiro (1850–1888). In *La Economia Financiera y la Formación de la Banca Central en España y Latinoamerica*, ed. C. Marichal and P. Tedde, 209–254. Madrid: Banco de España.

Milet, Henrique Augusto. 1875. *O Meio Circulante e a Questão Bancária*. 2nd ed. Recife: Typographia do Jornal do Recife. (originally published in 1860).

Neuhaus, Paulo. 1975. *História Monetária do Brasil, 1900–45*. Rio de Janeiro: IBMEC.

Normano, João Frederico. 1935. *Brazil: a study of economic types*. Chapel Hill: The University of North Carolina Press.

Ortigão, Ramalho. 1914. *A Moeda Circulante no Brazil*. Rio de Janeiro: Typographia do Jornal do Commercio.

Peláez, Carlos Manuel. 1975. The Establishment of Banking Institutions in a Backward Economy: Brazil, 1800–1851. *Business History Review* XLIX (4): 446–472.

Peláez, Carlos Manuel, and Wilson Suzigan. 1976. *História Monetária do Brasil*. 2nd ed. Brasília: Editora da Universidade de Brasília.

Relatorio da Commissão de Inquerito Nomeada por Aviso do Ministério da Fazenda, de 10 de Outubro de 1859 (undated).

Relatorio da Commissão Encarregada pelo Governo Imperial por Aviso do Primeiro de Outubro e 28 de Dezembro de 1864, de Proceder a um Inquerito Sobre as Causas Principais e Accidentaes da Crise do Mez de Setembro de 1864. 1865. Rio de Janeiro, Typographia Nacional.

Rodrigues, José Honório, ed. 1978. *Atas do Conselho de Estado*. Brasília: Senado Federal.

Schulz, John. 2013. *A Crise Financeira da Abolição.* 2nd ed. São Paulo: Edusp.

Schweikart, Larry. 1987. *Banking in the American South from the Age of Jackson to Reconstruction.* Baton Rouge and London: Louisiana State University Press.

Smith, Vera. 1936. *The Rationale of Central Banking.* London: P. S. King & Son.

Soares, Sebastião F. 1977. *Notas Estatísticas Sobre a Produção Agrícola e Carestia dos Gêneros Alimentícios no Império do Brasil.* Rio de Janeiro: IPEA/INPES. (originally published in 1860).

Soares, Luis Carlos. 1984. A Manufatura na Sociedade Escravista: o surto manufatureiro no Rio de Janeiro e nas suas circunvizinhanças (1840–1870). In *La Préindustrialization du Brésil: essais sur une économie en transition*, ed. F. Mauro. Paris: CNRS.

Summerhill, William R. 2015. *Inglorious Revolution: Political Institutions, Sovereign Debt, and Financial Underdevelopment in Imperial Brazil.* New Haven: Yale University Press.

Suzigan, Wilson. 1990. Moeda e Sistema Bancário. In *Estatísticas Históricas do Brasil*, ed. IBGE, vol. 3, 2nd ed.. (séries econômicas, demográficas e sociais, 1550–1985). Rio de Janeiro: IBGE.

Sweigart, Joseph E. 1987. *Coffee Factorage and the Emergence of a Brazilian Capital Market, 1850–1888.* New York: Garland Publishing.

Topik, Steven. 1994. State Autonomy in Economic Policy: Brazil's Experience, 1822–1930. *Journal of Interamerican Studies and World Affairs* 26 (4): 449–476.

Triner, Gail. 2000. *Banking and Economic Development: Brazil, 1889–1930.* New York: Palgrave.

Vieira, Dorival T. 1962. *A Evolução do Sistema Monetário Brasileiro.* São Paulo: FCEA/USP.

Villela, André A. 2005. Política Tarifária no II Reinado: evolução e impactos, 1850–1889. *Nova Economia* 15 (1): 35–68.

Viner, Jacob. 1937. *Studies in the Theory of International Trade.* New York: Harper Bros.

White, Lawrence. 1984. *Free Banking in Britain: Theory, Experience and Debate, 1800–45.* Cambridge: Cambridge University Press.

———. 1991. Banking Without a Central Bank: Scotland Before 1844 as a Free Banking System. In *Unregulated Banking: Chaos or order?* ed. F. Capie and E. Wood. London: Macmillan.

Wileman, Joseph P. 1896. *Brazilian Exchange: The Study of an Inconvertible Currency.* Buenos Aires: Gali Brothers.

CHAPTER 6

Conclusions

Detailed examination of Brazil's monetary and banking history between 1850 and 1889 has allowed for a number of points of historical fact to be clarified. Additionally, it has shed light on the nature of State-society relations during the Second Reign.

Regarding monetary policy, the book has shown unequivocally that contemporary policymakers strove to confer on Brazil's currency the discipline associated with the gold standard. This objective, it was argued, stemmed not only from mimicry of Europe, as claimed by Furtado, but was a direct result of practical concerns.[1] Three of these concerns stand out. First, the desire to minimize the domestic cost of sterling-denominated liabilities of the imperial government. Second, the need to provide foreign investors with the necessary signal of financial rectitude—the "good housekeeping seal of approval", emphasized by Bordo and Rockoff.[2] Finally, the perception that the fixed exchange-rate regime that would accompany convertibility of the milréis into gold was the best insurance against income and wealth shifts that followed sudden changes in the foreign value of the currency.[3]

As for banks, the specialized literature agrees that Brazil's banking sector could be characterized as underdeveloped during the imperial period. High rates of interest and the resultant brake on economic activity have led authors and contemporaries alike to highlight an alleged failure of the banking sector to support agricultural production. Indeed, as factors (*comissários*) ultimately took over most of the direct lending to planters,

A. A. Villela, *The Political Economy of Money and Banking in Imperial Brazil, 1850–1889*, Palgrave Studies in the History of Finance, https://doi.org/10.1007/978-3-030-32774-3_6

banks limited themselves to discounting drafts previously endorsed by commercial capitalists. In this regard, some authors have emphasized what they consider were exploitative relations between factors and planters, with the latter having to face high rates of discount on their drafts.[4]

The book rejected this view, based on research carried out by Sweigart on the financing of the coffee industry in the imperial period.[5] It was remarked that the existence of several intermediaries in the financing chain of the coffee sector—a feature that certainly contributed to the high rates of discount faced by planters—was the direct result of imperfections in mortgage legislation. In particular, the excessive protection afforded planters during foreclosure procedures, combined with information asymmetries related to other types of collateral offered by farmers (such as slaves and crops), resulted in high transaction costs, keeping banks away from financing agriculture directly.

Research into the evolving nature of monetary arrangements in the Empire has also allowed two important points of historical fact to be redressed. First, the extent to which Brazil was bound by the rules of the gold standard after 1846. Second, whether conscious, counter-cyclical, policies were pursued during the second half of the nineteenth century.

For some authors, when Law 401 established the new official 27d/1$000 parity, it formally bound Brazil to the rules of the gold standard.[6] Yet, the book argues that this was hardly the case. Brazil was not under a proper gold standard when, from the mid-1850s to the mid-1860s, a few private banks obtained the right to issue notes convertible into gold. As redemption was left at the discretion of the issuing banks, more often than not note bearers would be given Treasury notes—not specie—in exchange for banknotes. As a result, convertibility during this brief period was more of a potential than de facto nature. In all, potential convertibility was in force for approximately six years, and it only covered notes issued by private banks. Treasury notes—which amounted to three-fourths of total circulation in 1854, falling to a low of one-third in 1864—remained inconvertible throughout.

The book has also established a second point of historical fact, involving earlier interpretations of the nature of the recourse to counter-cyclical monetary policies during the Second Reign. More specifically, it was shown that the Bank of Brazil's decision to abandon convertibility and increase its rediscounting operations in the midst of the 1857 financial crisis was taken at the initiative of the bank itself, and not at the behest of the government. In this regard, Peláez is wrong in seeing in that move a sign of a conscious governmental effort at counter-cyclical monetary policy.[7] In reality, the Bank was safeguarding its metallic fund, which had been suffering substantial losses since news of the international crisis first reached Rio de Janeiro. Yet, the research does corroborate Peláez's point about the adoption of similar counter-cyclical policies in the wake of the 1864 crisis.

Detailed analysis of monetary and banking policies in the period has also extended current knowledge about three major events—the 1860 banking and corporate law, and the 1864 (Souto) and the 1875 (Mauá) crises.[8]

As noted, the 1860 law went down in history as the Law of Impediments, owing to its perceived deleterious effects on the incorporation of new firms and on the operations of the banking sector. The book does not dispute the assertion that the 1860 legislation restricted the process of incorporation in Brazil, nor that it curtailed the activities of note issuing banks. Yet, it maintains that part of the claims found in the literature must be put in the correct historical perspective. First, it was argued that the Law did little more than reaffirm the provisions of the 1850 Commercial Code in respect to joint-stock companies. Indeed, its major innovation in relation to the Code concerned the imposition of fines on firms found operating without official approval. In addition, other authors have rightly pointed out that the Law of Impediments was no different from contemporary legislation elsewhere in respect to incorporation, which was considered a privilege, not a right.[9] Finally, it could be argued in favor of government supervision of the process of incorporation that it was salutary, since it protected the property rights of eventual investors against mismanagement, or outright fraud.

The other major part of the 1860 legislation, including Decree 2685, of 10 November, dealt with banks of issue. The received view has been that the ceiling imposed by the government on unbacked note issues led to a major reduction in outstanding note circulation and, hence, a monetary contraction that ultimately was at the root of the 1864 Souto crisis. The book challenges this assertion. It starts by noting that, essentially, the legislation enacted in 1860 capped total issue of banknotes at 53 thousand *contos*. In December of that year, those issues stood at 51.8 thousand *contos*, so that actually banks still had room to expand their operations and all the while remain within the limit imposed by the government.

There is no disputing that from the third quarter of 1860 to the third quarter of 1863, the volume of total outstanding issues, which included

Treasury paper, dropped by approximately 12%. However, it was demonstrated that as the Bank of Brazil resumed convertibility of its notes, it expanded its issues and partially compensated for the decline in the outstanding volume of paper issued by the Treasury and the smaller private banks.

The book has also emphasized how conclusions drawn from using the estimates of the money supply constructed by Peláez and Suzigan (1976) should be approached with caution, as the latter comprise solely liabilities of the joint-stock banks (including deposits) and Treasury notes. However, at the time there were other types of liabilities performing functions akin to money. Among these (partial) substitutes were promissory notes (*vales*) issued by private banks (*casas bancárias*), deposits held by these establishments, as well as metallic currency (including foreign coins) in circulation. The book drew attention to the fact that issues from private banks were barely touched by the Law of Impediments, except for the rule establishing legislative oversight in the case of the issue of *vales*. Instead, Law 1083 went into considerable detail into the operations of note issuing banks, both those created in 1857–8 by decree of the Executive and the Bank of Brazil. As such, it could well have been the case that in the early 1860s, in the wake of the Law of Impediments, *casas bancárias* stepped into the void left by the reduced supply of banknotes and Treasury paper, thus providing the economy with additional liquidity that is not captured by traditional estimates of the money supply.

In connection to this, the research has also provided new insights into the 1864 financial crisis. As indicated, previous analyses of the events—triggered by the failure of the Casa Souto—have often interpreted it as a direct result of the limit to note issues imposed by the Law of Impediments. Nevertheless, when deposits held in joint-stock banks are brought into the picture, it becomes clear that their expansion between 1860 and 1864 produced monetary growth *in spite of* the Law of Impediments. In fact, the book has demonstrated that the money supply (M1) in the first semester of 1864 was at a (nominal) level similar to that at the time of the Law—some 96,000 *contos*. If the other forms of money highlighted above are taken into account, the purported connection between the 1860 banking law and the 1864 crisis becomes even less tenable.

It is, therefore, unlikely that a monetary crunch sparked the problems at Souto. Instead, the research suggested that the crisis might have originated in the *casas bancárias* themselves. Based on anecdotal contemporary evidence, it was remarked how, free from official supervision, these establishments sometimes overlooked essential prudential rules, lending long- against short-term liabilities. Although hard evidence—particularly of a statistical type—is still lacking, this possibility must also be taken into account in future attempts to explain the origins of the Souto crisis.

As for the 1875 crisis, the book found little indication of a direct link between the panic in Rio, involving the closure of the Mauá Bank and several other establishments, and the 1873 crisis in Europe and the United States.[10] Not only do contemporary accounts of the general state of the Brazilian economy in 1873–4 indicate overall normalcy, but the chain of events leading up to the collapse of Mauá's business empire appear to confirm the domestic nature of the panic with, at most, a foreign ingredient in the form of Mauá's troubles in his banking ventures in Uruguay.

In addition to clarifying a number of episodes in the monetary and banking history of the Brazilian Empire, the book has provided a more informative taxonomy of the two major schools of monetary thought in nineteenth-century Brazil—*papelistas* and *metalistas*. To begin with, it has unearthed one of the few contemporary references to these schools.[11] More significantly, the book has argued that previous treatments of the debates between *metalistas* and *papelistas* have suffered from two major shortcomings: a tendency to exaggerate the degree of anti-bank sentiment among *metalistas*, and a failure to take proper heed of contemporaries' views on convertibility.

There is no doubt that *metalistas* generally opposed the creation of new banks of issue, as revealed by an examination of the records of the meetings of the Finance Standing Committee of the Council of State.[12] Yet, the research has demonstrated that opposition to deposit and discount banks among contemporaries was much weaker. Moreover, it was shown how previous treatments of monetary debates in nineteenth-century Brazil have often failed to make one crucial distinction between *metalistas* and *papelistas*, namely, their stance on the question of convertibility.[13] More specifically, a subtle, if crucial, difference between what may be called "ordinary" and "true" *papelistas* has often been neglected. Although both groups favored plurality of note issue and an expanding money supply—and, as such, stood opposed to the *metalista* dogma of monopoly of issue and monetary restraint—the book has shown that ordinary *papelistas* (such as Souza Franco) were in favor of convertibility. In this particular point, therefore, they were no different from their *metalista* opponents. On the other hand, "true" *papelistas*, like Mauá and Sebastião Ferreira Soares, preferred fiduciary, non-convertible, issues to gold-backed ones.

In practice, they opposed the gold standard itself, which they felt unsuitable for a small, capital-importing economy like Brazil.

In the Introduction, it was noted that the book would consist of a monetary and banking history with a political perspective. Although a political economy approach to the monetary question has never been fully attempted, earlier works on this period have sometimes claimed that the evolution of the banking framework roughly followed political events. More to the point, it has been argued that the conferring of a monopoly of note issue on the Bank of Brazil in 1853 constituted the economic facet of the political centralization obtained around 1850.[14] In other words, the primacy of the Rio-based political elite (the *saquaremas*) would be reflected in the dominance exercised by the Bank over commercial circuits across the Empire.

However plausible this interpretation of the political economy of banking in the Second Reign may be, it is not very compelling. Indeed, how was it possible that the interests of the city and province of Rio de Janeiro were so dominant while, at the same time, *fazendeiros* from that very region were constantly complaining about the cost of credit? Clearly, had Rio-based interests (embodied in the *saquarema* elite) been as powerful as these authors suggest, once in government they would have promoted policies allowing for cheaper credit for the agricultural sector. Repeated complaints and formal petitions issued by groups of *fazendeiros* in the province of Rio bear witness to the difficulties they were experiencing in obtaining cheaper credit throughout the Second Reign.

The political model implicit in the works of Levy and Guimarães suggests that the Bank of Brazil often prevailed over the government. Nothing could be more removed from the truth. Indeed, Souza Franco's authorization for the establishment of six new banks of issue in 1857–8 hardly squares with the view of an all-powerful Rio-based establishment. This measure represented an end to the Bank's monopoly of note issue, held since 1854. Likewise, when revising its contract with the Bank in 1866, the government cancelled its issuing powers, thereby removing a source of profits to the institution. Finally, refusal to increase the Bank's leverage on many occasions provides further evidence that the government was not held hostage by the Bank.

The opposite was also true, that is, the Bank was not freely manipulated by the government, as abandonment of efforts to defend the exchange rate in early 1858 clearly showed.[15] As seen in Chap. 2, on the occasion the Bank unilaterally suspended convertibility and, against official advice, lowered its rate of discount in order to assist firms seeking credit. The book also emphasized how the Bank would often clash with the government over its proper role in assisting economic activity, while also ensuring the stability of the milréis. The reactions to the Law of Impediments also attest to the conflicting relationship between Bank and government. Indeed, the commission set up by the Bank to look into the Law openly contested the convenience, and legality, of the new legislation.[16] In short, the rapport between Bank and government is more complex than it has sometimes been suggested.

It has also been claimed that Liberals were usually in favor of plurality of issue and soft money, whereas Conservatives tended to side with monopoly and hard money.[17] The question of the stance on monetary and banking matters maintained by the major political parties cannot be settled easily. It was not until the mid-1860s, when monetary debates had receded, that both Liberals and Conservatives first published an actual party program. Furthermore, anecdotal evidence about their views is inconclusive. Liberals, as shown by Jequitinhonha's opposition in the Senate, did not unanimously endorse Souza Franco's decision to charter new issuing banks in 1857–8. Subsequently, approval of the 1860 Law of Impediments counted on a solid Conservative majority in the Chamber of Deputies. Yet, this same majority had earlier rejected the Torres Homem proposal of corporate and banking reform, which essentially bore the same restrictive spirit. Lastly, a Progressive (i.e., dissident Conservative) cabinet and parliamentary majority saw through exceptional legislation dealing with the Souto crisis of 1864, which helped subdue the panic. Two years later, the same forces were responsible for stripping the Bank of Brazil of its issuing rights, and restoring monopoly of issue to the hands of the Treasury.

Ideas were also shown to have greatly influenced the direction of monetary and banking policy during the Second Reign. In particular, three misconceptions shared by most participants in the monetary debates at the time helped shape events in the area. The first one consisted in equating money and credit. Both were widely taken as being synonymous, leading to expectations that an expansion of the volume of notes in circulation would translate, necessarily, into lower rates of interest. The second fallacy stemmed from this and involved the notion that the money supply consisted of notes and metallic coins only. In other words, bank deposits were seldom perceived by contemporaries as part of the money supply, thus leading to an exclusive focus on banks' issuing rights in the debates.

The final obstacle to a proper understanding of the complex mechanisms at play in the monetary realm was the belief entertained by most that the money supply (approximated by the volume of notes and coins in circulation) was the main determinant of the rate of exchange. In conjunction, these three ideas go some way in explaining why banking activity was curtailed for most of the period under study here.[18]

Finally, concerning the question of the relative autonomy of the imperial State vis-à-vis the planter class, in the context of monetary and banking policy, the following schema was established:

SOFT MONEY (favored by planters): depreciated rate of exchange—monetary expansion—plurality of issue—cheap credit—*papelistas*
HARD MONEY (favored by the government): appreciated rate of exchange—monetary restraint—monopoly of issue—orthodoxy—*metalistas*

In Chap. 5, it was argued that, a priori, the planter class tended to favor soft money policies—consisting of monetary laxity and a slipping milréis. Contemporaries hoped that this would be achieved via the granting of issuing powers to the largest possible number of banks. This was consistent with a view of the role of banks as institutions primarily concerned with financing economic activity. Similarly, the research highlighted that, in principle, the imperial government entertained an opposite set of preferences as regards monetary and banking policies, encapsulated by the notion of hard money. Moreover, it was remarked that these policies were pursued with the aim of creating the conditions for the formal pegging of the milréis to gold and the adoption of the gold standard.

Careful analysis of the changing nature of the monetary regime in imperial Brazil revealed the importance of ideology in the conduct of policy. Ideology in this case was defined in a very loose way, as meaning particular views that people may entertain concerning what banks should do. The book drew attention to two conflicting views on the proper role of banks in the economy, which may be designated as "developmental" and "orthodox", respectively. Most of the scholarly research in the post-Second World War period implicitly embraced the former perspective, reflecting contemporary debates about the economic development of Brazil. While looking at historical events through developmental lenses, post-war scholarship projected into the past concerns that were at the top of the political debate in the second half of the twentieth century. In so doing, however, it overlooked a second major approach to the role of banks, embodied in the orthodox perspective. Apparently as a reaction to early-twentieth-century monetary historians—who emphatically advocated orthodoxy—many post-war authors failed to give due attention to the macroeconomic implications of banking policy. As a result, the concerns of mid-nineteenth-century policymakers with exchange-rate instability, depreciation, and inflation have been considered by part of the historiography as mere uncritical importation of foreign orthodoxy.

Contemporaries knew better. They were aware of how excessive monetary expansion might lead to frequent movements in the exchange rate and currency depreciation. As the book has shown, contemporaries also acknowledged the income and wealth shifts that large changes in the value of the milréis could bring about. Finally, policymakers knew perfectly well what would be the implications of a depreciating rate of exchange for the finances of the State.

True, like everybody else, they had their personal predilections as far as monetary and banking theory, and policy, were concerned. In addition, without question, the orthodoxy of the time praised the virtues of the gold standard. In practical terms, this meant pegging the domestic currency to gold, and relinquishing monetary policy autonomy. Yet, if convertibility could not always be maintained, at least it was thought that there should be controls over the process of monetary creation by the private sector. In the eyes of most nineteenth-century policymakers, this implied checking the expansion of banks of issue for, as already mentioned, most contemporaries wrongly assumed that only banks entrusted with issuing powers were capable of altering the money supply.

The book further argued that the orthodox approach to monetary policy that dominated debate and policy in the nineteenth century sometimes involved concerns with what would currently be seen as typical central bank functions. Even though central banking theory was still some decades away, policymakers who, in the mid-1850s, sought to invest the Bank of Brazil with the task of looking after the money supply and, indirectly, the rate of exchange, were ultimately concerned with defending the value of the national currency. This is what central banks are expected to do nowadays.

However, at the time, modern instruments were lacking. There was no requirement for commercial banks to deposit part of their reserves in the Bank of Brazil. Nor could the Bank influence overall liquidity via open market operations. In addition, the Bank had to face competition in the note issuing business. Its actions, then, could always be countered by the other banks of issue. Furthermore, as a private, profit maximizing, institution, the Bank had difficulty in performing typical central bank duties, such as acting as a lender of last resort, lest it overburden its own portfolio. In the end, therefore, the Bank could neither fully meet the demands of the productive classes for cheap credit, nor fulfill its "proto-central bank" functions, as expected by many contemporaries espousing an orthodox approach to banks.

The research has demonstrated that regardless of the specific difficulties faced by the Bank of Brazil, advocates of hard money triumphed through most of the period. This fact, in turn, was in no small part a result of the influence exerted by Joaquim Rodrigues Torres. It was shown how Itaboraí—in his capacity as Minister of Finance, president of the Bank of Brazil and, crucially, long-serving member of the Council of State—set the agenda for monetary management for the period. Additionally, his condition as *rapporteur* in most of the resolutions taken by the Finance Standing Committee of the Council of State ensured that hard money considerations usually prevailed over alternative views. To the extent that official policy stemmed from Council of State resolutions—and given that the Emperor himself appeared to sympathize with financial orthodoxy—, it is hardly surprising that hard money was generally followed. In addition, as the book argued, this approach held sway because it conformed to the dominant doctrine of the age and met the interests of a State that was politically capable of enforcing these policies.

To conclude, it should be said that the research would have certainly benefited from access to documents pertaining to preliminary stages of the discussions in Parliament and the Seção de Fazenda, even though there is no clear indication if these sources actually exist. In the end, the argument relied on close examination of the *result* of policies in the monetary and banking sphere, that is, those policies that were effectively implemented. In so doing, it emerged that monetary management between 1850 and 1889 was often—but not always—done in accordance with the hard money principles summarized above. Starting with the 1846 Law, which established the 27d/1$000 parity, hard money policies were promoted in 1853 (when the third Bank of Brazil was founded), culminated with the 1860 banking and corporate law, and would characterize most actions in the area after 1866, when a return to the mythical 27d parity was foremost on policymakers' minds.

However, it was also shown that departures from hard money were not so rare. Not only was the chartering of six new banks of issue in 1857–8 an exception to orthodoxy, but conscious counter-cyclical reaction to the 1864 crisis, and the monetary expansion throughout the Paraguayan War and in connection with drought relief were also unorthodox. In the end, then, it could be said that the imperial government displayed what could be termed "pragmatic conservatism" in its approach to monetary and banking questions. It was, therefore, willing to compromise on its hard money beliefs in cases of *force majeure*, such as the Souto crisis, the war against Paraguay or in providing much-needed assistance to victims of the Grande Sêca.

Still, the fact remains that under normal circumstances, monopoly of note issue, monetary restraint, convertibility, and an appreciated rate of exchange were pursued as an objective of policy. As argued throughout, this was diametrically contrary to the demands from the planter class for plurality of issue, monetary expansion, paper money and a depreciated milréis. It is, therefore, safe to conclude that, at least in regard to money and banking, the imperial government enjoyed a degree of autonomy from the economic elite. This lends further support to Holanda's claim that 'the empire of the *fazendeiros* in Brazil would only begin with the fall of the Empire' see de Holanda 1972, p. 283.

Notes

1. Furtado (1970, chapter 27).
2. Bordo and Rockoff (1996).
3. Thus, suggestions in the literature that adherence to the gold standard tended to advance British interests, however plausible, tend to miss these crucial points. See, for example, Granziera (1979) and Levy and Andrade (1993). These contributions appear to overlook the undisputed fact that exchange-rate stability is a public good and, as such, it can be enjoyed by both domestic and foreign agents.
4. See, for example, Soares (1984).
5. Sweigart (1987).
6. See for example, Levy and Andrade (1985) and, less emphatically, Peláez and Suzigan (1976).
7. Peláez (1976). The book has also shown that suspension of convertibility occurred on 27 November, not 11 November, as usually claimed.
8. A further clarification brought out by the research involves the nature of the remarkable recovery of the exchange rate in the aftermath of the war against Paraguay. It was noted that the milréis already appreciated mark-

edly prior to Rio Branco's appointment as President of the Council of Ministers (and Minister of Finance) in March 1871. In addition, the book argued that subsequent appreciation of the exchange rate—leading up, eventually, to the attainment of the 27d/1$000 parity in 1875—took place independently of the monetary and fiscal policies carried out by the Rio Branco administration.

9. Barman (1981).
10. Schulz (2013, p. 102), on the contrary, maintains that both the 1875 and the Souto crises originated in Europe and the United States. The author offers scant evidence to support either claim, however.
11. See Section 5.3.
12. For a detailed analysis of the debates and decisions on monetary and banking matters in the Seção de Fazenda of the Council of State, Villela (2000).
13. Saes (1986) and Andrade (1987).
14. See, for example, Levy and Andrade (1985), Mello (1984), Guimarães (1998, 2012), and Gambi (2013).
15. Its president, Dias de Carvalho, openly manifested the Bank's independence from the government in 1858. Speaking in the Senate on the operation to defend the exchange rate, Carvalho was emphatic: 'never had the Minister of Finance sent orders to the bank to draw, or not to draw (bills of exchange). The Minister agreed with the bank on this point (…), each part proceeded according to its sphere of action, and I can guarantee the Senate that if the bank's board of directors were convinced that it was not convenient to undertake the operation with drafts, it would not submit to orders from the Minister'. Session of 14 May, in *ASI* 1858, Tome I, p. 146.
16. 'The law of 22 August of last year (…) could not have been applied to our establishment without gravely offending our rights, without violating a bilateral contract that cannot be altered without the necessary mutual consent'. Cf. Banco do Brasil, *Parecer Apresentado á Assembléa* (1861, p. 5).
17. See, for example, Guimarães (1998, pp. 58–9).
18. As discussed along the text, the 1860 Law of Impediments would make things worse, as it mandated prior authorization for incorporation. It would not be until 1882 that legislation would be passed relaxing the rules for incorporation, which became a right.

References

de Andrade, Ana Maria R. 1987. *1864: conflito entre metalistas e pluralistas*. MSc. dissertation, Universidade Federal do Rio de Janeiro.

Banco do Brasil. 1861. *Parecer Apresentado á Assembléa Geral dos Accionistas do Banco do Brasil pela Commissão Especial Eleita em 2 de Maio de 1861*. Rio de Janeiro: Villeneuve.

Barman, Roderick J. 1981. Business and Government in Imperial Brazil: The Experience of Viscount Mauá. *Journal of Latin American Studies* 13 (2): 239–264.
Bordo, Michael, and Hugh Rockoff. 1996. The Gold Standard as a *Good Housekeeping Seal of Approval*. *Journal of Economic History* 56 (2): 389–428.
Brasil, Senado. *Annaes do Senado do Império do Brasil*, various years.
de Holanda, Sergio B. 1972. *História Geral da Civilização Brasileira*. Tome II, Vol 1. São Paulo: Difel.
Furtado, Celso. 1970. *Formação Econômica do Brasil*. 10th ed. São Paulo: Companhia Editora Nacional.
Gambi, Thiago F.R. 2013. *O Banco da Ordem: política e finanças no Império brasileiro (1853–1866)*. São Paulo: Alameda.
Granziera, Rui G. 1979. *A Guerra do Paraguai e o Capitalismo no Brasil: moeda e vida urbana na economia brasileira*. São Paulo: Hucitec/Unicamp.
Guimarães, Carlos Gabriel. 1998. *Bancos, Economia e Poder no Segundo Reinado: o caso da Sociedade Bancária Mauá, MacGregor & Companhia (1854–1866)*. Ph.D. dissertation, Universidade de São Paulo.
———. 2012. *A Presença Inglesa nas Finanças e no Comércio do Brasil Imperial: os casos da Sociedade Bancária Mauá, MacGregor & Cia. (1854–1866) e da firma inglesa Samuel Phillips & Cia. (1808–1840)*. São Paulo: Alameda.
Levy, Maria Barbara, and Ana Maria R. de Andrade. 1985. Fundamentos do Sistema Bancário no Brasil: 1834–1860. *Estudos Economicos* 15 (Special Issue): 17–48.
———. 1993. El Sector Financiero y El Desarollo Bancario en Río de Janeiro (1850–1888). In *La Economia Financiera y la Formación de la Banca Central en España y Latinoamerica*, ed. C. Marichal and P. Tedde, 209–254. Madrid: Banco de España.
de Mello, Evaldo C. 1984. *O Norte Agrário e o Império, 1871–1889*. Rio de Janeiro: Nova Fronteira.
Peláez, Carlos Manuel. 1976. The Theory and Reality of Imperialism in the Coffee Economy of Nineteenth-Century Brazil. *Economic History Review* 29 (2): 276–290.
Peláez, Carlos Manuel, and Wilson Suzigan. 1976. *História Monetária do Brasil*. 2nd ed. Brasília: Editora da Universidade de Brasília.
de Saes, Flavio M. 1986. *Crédito e Bancos no Desenvolvimento da Economia Paulista, 1850–1930*. São Paulo: IPE/USP.
Schulz, John. 2013. *A Crise Financeira da Abolição*. 2nd ed. São Paulo: Edusp.
Soares, Luis Carlos. 1984. A Manufatura na Sociedade Escravista: o surto manufatureiro no Rio de Janeiro e nas suas circunvizinhanças (1840–1870). In *La Préindustrialization du Brésil: essais sur une économie en transition*, ed. F. Mauro. Paris: CNRS.

Sweigart, Joseph E. 1987. *Coffee Factorage and the Emergence of a Brazilian Capital Market, 1850–1888*. New York: Garland Publishing.

Villela, André A. 2000. Brazil in Mid-Empire: The Council of State and the Banking Question, 1850–1870. *Estudos Economicos* 30 (4): 629–651.

Appendix

Table A1 Total notes outstanding, by issuer: 1854–6 (in *contos*)

Year	*Treasury*	*%*	*Bank of Brazil* Head office	%	Branches	%	*Other banks*	*%*	*Total*
1854	46,692.8	75.0	15,530.7	25.0	–	–	–	–	62,223.5
1855	46,692.8	68.9	21,062.9	31.1	–	–	–	–	67,755.7
1856	45,692.8	53.3	27,488.2	32.0	12,609.1	14.7	–	–	85,790.1
1857	43,676.7	44.7	33,175.0	34.0	20,860.9	2.3	–	–	97,712.6
1858	41,664.6	45.0	22,125.5	23.9	19,811.3	21.4	8967.7	9.7	92,569.1
1859	40,700.6	42.4	21,889.8	22.8	18,972.1	19.7	14,510.7	15.1	96,073.2
1860	37,599.9	42.0	22,626.3	25.3	16,189.9	18.1	13,038.7	14.6	89,454.8
1861	35,108.4	42.8	18,131.9	22.1	15,258.2	18.6	13,513.1	16.5	82,011.6
1862	33,323.6	43.3	20,152.4	26.2	18,556.0	24.1	4843.0	6.3	76,875.0
1863	30,594.4	37.5	27,297.3	33.4	19,654.6	24.1	4115.6	5.0	81,661.9
1864	29,094.4	29.2	43,168.0	43.4	23,270.5	23.4	4030.8	4.0	99,563.7
1865	28,090.9	25.8	43,767.6	40.2	34,154.4	31.4	2853.3	2.6	108,866.2
1866	28,900.9	25.5	42,902.4	37.8	39,197.6	34.5	2480.5	2.2	113,481.4

Sources: Treasury notes in *Legislação sobre Papel Moeda* (1923)
Bank notes in *RMF*, various issues

Note: Figures are for end of year

A. A. Villela, *The Political Economy of Money and Banking in Imperial Brazil, 1850–1889*, Palgrave Studies in the History of Finance, https://doi.org/10.1007/978-3-030-32774-3

Table A2 Brazilian banks of issue and their main accounts, 1850–9 (in *contos*)

Year/Bank	*Capital*	*Issues*	*Deposits*	*Loans*
1850				
Banco Commercial Rio	2500	5	7526	9839
Banco Commercial Bahia	2000	1000	1458	4236
Banco Commercial Maranhão	370	142	464	400
1851				
Banco Commercial Rio	5000	2	7395	10,243
Banco Commercial Bahia	2000	1000	1582	4205
Banco Commercial Maranhão	390	190	516	471
Bank of Brazil (Mauá)	2000	98	5138	4665
1852				
Banco Commercial Rio	5000	257	11,210	12,508
Banco Commercial Bahia	2000	1000	4822	552
Banco Commercial Maranhão	500	241	726	641
Bank of Brazil (Mauá)	4999	1594	6081	11,149
Banco Commercial Pernambuco	838	500	141	1371
1853				
Banco Commercial Rio	5000	1574	10,758	14,734
Banco Commercial Bahia	2000	1000	2565	4771
Banco Commercial Maranhão	524	298	801	688
Bank of Brazil (Mauá)	8000	1938	5763	14,028
Banco Commercial Pernambuco	1000	500	67	1500
1854				
Banco Commercial Bahia	2000	1000	2294	4848
Banco Commercial Maranhão	680	339	1010	908
Bank of Brazil (Mauá)	8000	1880	6464	14,150
Banco Commercial Pernambuco	1400	700	n.a.	n.a.
'Third' Bank of Brazil	11,000	16,125	3255	20,493
1855				
Banco Commercial Bahia	2000	1000	1457	4056
Banco Commercial Maranhão	680	325	924	65
Banco Commercial Pernambuco	1700	850	276	2046
Bank of Brazil (head office)	15,900	21,300	3605	25,598
1856				
Banco Commercial Bahia	2000	1000	817	2463
Banco Commercial Maranhão	800	81	44	n.a.
Bank of Brazil (head office)	19,752	27,829	1489	32,574
Bank of Brazil (branches)	4540	16,179	n.a.	7791
1857				
Bank of Brazil (head office)	22,560	34,007	9545	46,294
Bank of Brazil (branches)	6140	22,966	1760	14,295
Banco do Maranhão	800	41	n.a.	n.a.

(*continued*)

Table A2 (continued)

Year/Bank	*Capital*	*Issues*	*Deposits*	*Loans*
1858				
Bank of Brazil (head office)	22,560	35,209	15,263	32,470
Bank of Brazil (branches)	5932	29,460	462	18,493
Banco Com. & Agrícola	5822	5490	44	6509
Bco. Prov. Rio Grande	377	0	n.a.	n.a.
Banco do Maranhão	2	430	6	737
Banco da Bahia	2400	1255	940	5606
Novo Banco Pernambuco	1480	1460	271	2406
1859				
Banco Rural & Hypothecario	8000	1926	12,832	20,528
Bank of Brazil (head office)	22,560	36,334	9639	23,349
Bank of Brazil (branches)	5940	29,124	583	23,052
Banco Com. & Agrícola	7313	7238	358	9234
Bco. Prov. Rio Grande	580	1	300	824
Banco Maranhão	42	680	183	938
Banco da Bahia	4000	3200	2252	n.a.
Novo Banco de Pernambuco	2000	1466	304	2702

Sources: *RMF*, various years, and Levy and Andrade (1985, pp. 45–8)

Notes: Figures for end of year

Banking establishment for which data could not be found were omitted

n.a.: data not available

Table A3 Bank of Brazil, head office: portfolio balances, 1854–6 (in *contos*)

Date	*Discounts (a)*	*Payments (b)*	*Portfolio balances (c) = (a)–(b)*
30 June 1854	19,375	3075	16,300
30 June 1855	99,259	75,139	24,120
30 June 1856	120,443	91,008	29,435
30 June 1857	128,453	117,695	10,758
30 June 1858	208,251	162,471	45,780
30 June 1859	165,237	137,271	27,966
30 June 1860	110,068	83,467	26,601
36 June 1861	121,053	94,351	26,702
30 June 1862	130,329	99,900	30,429
30 June 1863	183,204	138,100	45,104
30 June 1864	178,601	141,261	37,339
30 June 1865	284,739	213,364	71,375
30 June 1866	346,516	265,389	81,127

Source: Banco do Brasil, *Relatório Apresentado à Assembléa Geral dos Accionistas*, various issues

Table A4 Average rates of discount at Rio Banks, 1850–60 (in %)

Period	*Rate*	*Period*	*Rate*
1850		1856	
1 Jan to 16 Jan	7	1 Jan to 27 Nov	8
17 Jan to 31 Jul	8	28 Nov to 31 Dec	8
1 Aug to 31 Dec	7		
1851		1857	
1 Jan to 16 Apr	7	1 Jan to 11 Jan	9
17 Apr to 22 Apr	6.5	12 Jan to 6 May	8
23 Apr to 2 Nov	6	7 May to 13 Aug	9
3 Nov to 31 Dec	5	14 Aug to 14 Dec	8
		15 Dec to 23 Dec	10
		24 Dec to 31 Dec	11
1852		1858	
1 Jan to 9 Jul	5	1 Jan to 27 Jan	11
10 Jul to 31 Dec	6	28 Jan to 10 Feb	10
		11 Feb to 24 Aug	9
1853		25 Aug to 11 Oct	11
1 Jan to 28 Apr	6	12 Oct to 3 Nov	10
29 Apr to 31 May	7	4 Nov to 20 Dec	9
1 Jun to 30 Jun	8	21 Dec to 31 Dec	8
1 Jul to 31 Aug	9		
1 Sep to 26 Sep	8	1859	
27 Sep to 29 Nov	7	1 Jan to 8 Jun	8
30 Nov to 31 Dec	7	9 Jun to 31 Dec	8
1854		1860	
1 Jan to 23 Apr	8	1 Jan to 31 Mar	9
24 Apr to 31 Dec	8		
1855			
1 Jan to 3 Apr	7		
4 Apr to 31 Dec	8		

Source: *Relatorio da Commissão de Inquerito Nomeada Por Aviso do Ministerio da Fazenda, de 10 de Outubro de 1859* (undated), Annex

Note: Rates refer to bills with two known signatures and, therefore, can be regarded as a minimum (prime) rate

Table A5 Rate of exchange in the Rio market, October 1857 to September 1858 (in pence per milréis)

1857				*1858*		
10/Oct	27 1/4	27 3/8		08/May	25 1/2	
12/Oct	27 1/4	27 3/8		10/May	25 1/2	
14/Oct	27 1/4	27 3/8	27 1/2	11/May	25 1/2	
				12/May	25 1/2	
05/Nov	27 1/4			14/May	25 1/2	
06/Nov	27 1/4					
07/Nov	27 1/4	27 3/8		04/Jun	25 1/2	
10/Nov	27	27 1/4		05/Jun	25 1/2	
11/Nov	27	27 1/4		07/Jun	25 1/2	
12/Nov	27 1/8			18/Jun	27	
13/Nov	27	27 1/8		22/Jun	26	
				23/Jun	25 1/2	
14/Dec	26 1/4			26/Jun	25 1/2	
15/Dec	26					
30/Dec	24			03/Jul	25 1/2	
31/Dec	23 1/2	24		05/Jul	25 1/2	
				06/Jul	25 1/2	26 1/8
31/Jan						
09/Jan	24			08/Jul	26	
11/Jan	24			09/Jul	26	
12/Jan	25			15/Jul	25 3/4	
13/Jan	25	25 1/4		26/Jul	27	
06/Feb	25			03/Aug	26	
08/Feb	24 1/2	24 3/4		04/Aug	25 7/8	26
09/Feb	24 1/2			05/Aug	25 3/4	26
10/Feb	24	24 1/4	24 1/2	06/Aug	25 3/4	26
11/Feb	24	24 1/4		24/Aug	26	
12/Feb	24			28/Aug	26 5/8	
13/Feb	24			30/Aug	26 5/8	
				31/Aug	26 5/8	
04/Mar	22 3/4					
10/Mar	23			01/Sep	26 3/8	26 3/4
13/Mar	25 1/2			02/Sep	26 5/8	
15/Mar	25 1/2			04/Sep	26 5/8	
16/Mar	25 1/2			06/Sep	26 5/8	
				18/Sep	26 3/4	
07/Apr	25 1/2			20/Sep	26 3/4	
08/Apr	25 1/4	25 1/2		21/Sep	26 3/4	
09/Apr	25 1/4	25 1/2		22/Sep	26 3/4	
10/Apr	25 1/4	25 1/2		23/Sep	26 3/4	26 7/8
12/Apr	25 1/2			24/Sep	26 3/4	
13/Apr	25 1/2			25/Sep	26 3/4	
				28/Sep	26 3/4	
				30/Sep	26 5/8	

Source: Junta de Corretores de Títulos e Valores da Cidade do Rio de Janeiro, 'Livro de Registro Official de Títulos e Valores', 1858 and 1859

Note: Rates refer to days in which there were transactions in the Rio stock exchange

Table A6 Revenues and expenditures of the imperial government, 1849–50 to 1889 (in *contos*)

	Estimated			*Realized*		
Fiscal year	*Revenue*	*Expenditure*	*Surplus (+) or deficit (−)*	*Revenue*	*Expenditure*	*Surplus (+) or deficit (−)*
1849–50	25,717.2	26,802.2	−1085.0	28,200.1	28,949.6	−749.5
1850–1	27,200.0	26,275.7	924.3	31,523.7	33,224.6	−1700.9
1851–2	27,200.0	26,275.7	924.3	35,786.8	42,754.8	−6968.0
1852–3	30,500.0	27,482.8	3017.2	36,391.0	31,653.5	4737.5
1853–4	32,353.0	29,633.7	2719.3	34,516.5	36,234.5	−1718.0
1854–5	34,000.0	31,153.3	2846.7	36,985.5	38,740.3	−1754.8
1855–6	34,000.0	32,441.2	1558.8	38,634.4	40,242.6	−1608.2
1856–7	34,000.0	33,785.4	214.6	49,156.4	40,374.0	8782.4
1857–8	35,500.5	35,500.5	0.0	49,747.0	51,755.7	−2008.7
1858–9	39,428.1	40,097.1	−669.0	46,920.0	52,718.6	−5798.6
1859–60	45,000.0	48,302.9	−3302.9	43,807.4	52,606.2	−8798.8
1860–1	45,000.0	48,302.9	−3302.9	50,051.7	52,358.4	−2306.7
1861–2	49,659.7	51,313.9	−1654.2	52,488.9	53,049.7	−560.8
1862–3	49,659.7	51,313.9	−1654.2	48,342.0	57,000.1	−8658.1
1863–4	51,500.0	53,878.7	−2378.7	54,801.4	56,494.4	−1693.0
1864–5	51,500.0	53,878.7	−2378.7	56,995.9	83,346.2	−26,350.3
1865–6	55,000.0	58,871.7	−3871.7	58,523.4	121,856.0	−63,332.6
1866–7	55,000.0	58,871.7	−3871.7	64,776.8	120,889.8	−56,113.0
1867–8	71,250.0	68,530.2	2719.8	71,200.9	165,984.8	−94,783.9
1868–9	71,250.0	68,530.2	2719.8	87,542.5	150,894.8	−63,352.3
1869–70	71,250.0	68,530.2	2719.8	94,847.3	141,594.1	−46,746.8
1870–1	94,100.0	83,326.7	10,773.3	95,885.0	100,074.3	−4189.3
1871–2	95,800.0	85,741.3	10,058.7	105,135.9	101,580.8	3555.1
1872–3	95,800.0	85,741.3	10,058.7	112,131.1	121,874.5	−9743.4
1873–4	103,000.0	98,250.2	4749.8	105,009.2	121,480.9	−16,471.7
1874–5	103,000.0	98,250.2	4749.8	106,490.5	125,855.3	−19,364.8
1875–6	106,000.0	105,001.3	998.7	103,499.6	126,780.0	−23,280.4
1876–7	106,000.0	106,911.0	−911.0	101,063.6	135,800.7	−34,737.1
1877–8	102,000.0	105,881.7	−3881.7	110,745.8	151,492.9	−40,747.1
1878–9	102,000.0	105,881.7	−3881.7	116,461.0	181,468.6	−65,007.6
1879–80	116,958.0	115,458.2	1499.8	120,762.0	150,133.6	−29,371.6
1880–1	116,958.0	115,458.2	1499.8	131,275.0	138,583.1	−7308.1
1881–2	116,592.0	114,280.7	2311.3	131,987.0	139,470.6	−7483.6
1882–3	128,960.7	129,823.7	−863.0	129,697.7	153,058.0	−23,360.3
1883–4	128,960.7	129,823.7	−863.0	134,568.7	154,257.1	−19,688.4
1884–5	133,049.1	138,796.7	−5747.6	124,155.6	158,495.8	−34,340.2
1885–6	133,049.1	138,796.7	−5747.6	130,309.4	153,623.1	−23,313.7
1886–7	132,881.6	137,606.7	−4725.1	221,658.6	227,044.8	−5386.2
1888	138,395.0	141,230.1	−2835.1	145,896.1	147,450.5	−1554.4
1889	147,200.0	153,148.4	−5948.4	160,840.3	186,165.9	−25,325.6

Sources: Carreira (1980), Brasil, IBGE (1990), and Diniz (2002)

Note: Estimated revenues and expenditures refer to amounts approved by Parliament for the given fiscal year Data for the 1886–7 fiscal year refer to three semesters

Table A7 Outstanding notes and bills issued by the imperial treasury, 1850–89 (in *contos*)

Year	*Notes* (notas)	%	*Bills* (letras)	%	*Total*
1850	46,770	91.0	4631	9.0	51,401
1851	46,684	87.9	6448	12.1	53,133
1852	46,684	98.5	723	1.5	47,407
1853	46,684	98.5	723	1.5	47,407
1854	46,693	99.5	246	0.5	46,939
1855	46,693	96.8	1566	3.2	48,259
1856	45,693	92.7	3596	7.3	49,289
1857	43,677	99.2	367	0.8	44,043
1858	41,665	99.9	34	0.1	41,698
1859	40,701	99.9	27	0.1	40,728
1860	37,599	99.9	32	0.1	37,631
1861	35,109	88.4	4600	11.6	39,708
1862	33,324	88.5	4337	11.5	37,660
1863	30,594	84.5	5592	15.5	36,186
1864	29,094	78.7	7852	21.3	36,946
1865	28,091	69.4	12,400	30.6	40,491
1866	28,901	47.9	31,481	52.1	60,381
1867	42,560	48.5	45,162	51.5	87,722
1868	81,749	55.0	66,819	45.0	148,568
1869	127,230	66.7	63,481	33.3	190,710
1870	149,398	72.5	56,687	27.5	206,085
1871	151,078	79.0	40,132	21.0	191,210
1872	150,807	91.9	13,255	8.1	164,062
1873	149,579	91.9	13,109	8.1	162,688
1874	149,547	90.2	16,256	9.8	165,802
1875	149,501	88.1	20,179	11.9	169,681
1876	149,380	88.0	20,339	12.0	169,719
1877	149,318	87.1	22,156	12.9	171,474
1878	181,279	80.0	45,393	20.0	226,672
1879	189,258	85.7	31,465	14.3	220,724
1880	189,200	93.2	13,767	6.8	202,966
1881	188,155	89.1	22,991	10.9	211,146
1882	188,012	86.6	28,985	13.4	216,997
1883	188,011	80.1	46,652	19.9	234,663
1884	187,937	80.1	46,549	19.9	234,485
1885	187,344	78.9	50,076	21.1	237,419
1886	194,283	72.2	74,796	27.8	269,078
1887	184,335	85.6	31,009	14.4	215,344
1888	188,869	85.8	31,351	14.2	220,220
1889	179,971	100.0	78	0.0	180,049

Source: *RMF*, various issues

Notes: Notes refer to legal tender notes. Bills are short-term (less than one year) interest-bearing liabilities issued in anticipation of government revenues

Data for notes refer to March or April. Bills outstanding as of March

Table A8 Issues of bonds of the consolidated imperial debt (*apólices*), 1851/89 (in *contos*)

Year	*Purpose of Issue*	*Amount*
6%		
1851–3	Deficit financing	5213.8
1858	Payment of Portuguese claims	5.4
1860–2	Share swaps of the Pernambuco Railway Co.	2466.4
1860–3	Share swaps of the Bahia Railway Co.	186.6
1860–72	Share swaps of the D. Pedro II Railway Co.	11,328.6
1861–2	Payment to Bank of Brazil for Treasury notes retired from circulation	2150.0
1863	Compensation for goods captured from the Spanish in the wars of Independence and in the River Plate; withdrawal of Treasury notes and bills from circulation	5890.4
1864	Nationalization of the União e Indústria Co.	3161.0
1865	Withdrawal of Treasury notes from circulation; wedding expenses of Princesses Izabel and Leopoldina	1228.0
1865–72	Expenses incurred in the Paraguayan War	143,894.7
1869	Purchase of property at the Lagoa	50.0
1870	Purchase of the Enxadas Island	1705.8
1870	Retirement of Treasury bills	25,000.0
1871	?	0.6
1873–6	Payment to the Rio Dock Co.	2734.0
1876	Deficit financing	8600.0
1877	Sundry services	30,000.0
1877	Dowry for Princess Januaria	1200.0
1879	Consolidation of the floating debt	40,000.0
1880–2	Share swaps of the Baturité Railway Co.	606.0
	Total 6% Issued, 1850–89	285,421.3
5%		
1886	Consolidation of the floating debt	50,000.0
Total		335,421.3

Source: *RMF* 1889/90, Table N.6

Table A9 Foreign loans contracted by the imperial government, 1850/89

Date	*Purpose*	*Nominal value*	*Issue price*	*Net value*	*Rate of interest*
		(£)	(%)	(£)	(%)
1852	Payment of remaining part of loan contracted by Portugal in 1823, and taken up by Brazil	1,040,000	95	954,250	4.5
1858	Nationalization and extension of the D. Pedro II Railway	1,526,500	94.5	1,425,000	4.5
1859	Rescheduling of 1829 loan	508,000	100	508,000	5.0
1860	Loan for Cia. União e Indústria, Cia. Mucury, and Pernambuco Railway Co.	1,373,000	90	1,210,000	4.5
1863	Liquidation of outstanding part of the 1824 and 1843 loans; consolidation of part of the floating Treasury debt	3,855,300	88	3,300,000	4.5
1865	Financing of extraordinary expenses of the Treasury with the Paraguayan War	6,963,600	74	5,000,000	5.0
1871	Consolidation of the floating debt; extension of the Pedro II Railway; deficit financing	3,459,000	89	3,000,000	5.0
1875	Railroad construction and dividend guarantees	5,301,200	96.5	5,000,000	5.0
1883	Investments in assorted public works	4,599,600	89	4,000,000	4.5
1886	Deficit financing; consolidation of the floating debt	6,431,000	95	6,000,000	4.5
1888	Anticipation of difficulties arising from abolition of slavery	6,279,300	97	6,000,000	4.5
1889	Consolidation of the foreign debt (conversion loan)	19,837,000	90	17,440,300	4.0

Sources: Bouças (1955), Carreira (1980), and Summerhill (2015)

References

Bouças, Valentim F. 1955. *Finanças do Brasil*, vol. XIX ("Dívida Externa, 1824–1945"). Rio de Janeiro: Ministério da Fazenda.

Brasil, IBGE. 1990. *Estatísticas Históricas do Brasil*, vol. 3 (séries econômicas, demográficas e sociais, 1550–1985). 2nd ed. Rio de Janeiro: IBGE.

Carreira, Liberato de C. 1980. *História Financeira e Orçamentária do Império do Brasil*, 2 vols. Brasília: Senado Federal/Casa de Rui Barbosa.

Diniz, Adalton F. 2002. Centralização Política e Apropriação de Riqueza: análise das finanças do Império brasileiro (1821–1889). Ph.D. Dissertation, Universidade de São Paulo.

Levy, Maria Barbara, and Ana Maria R. de Andrade. 1985. Fundamentos do Sistema Bancário no Brasil: 1834–1860. *Estudos Econômicos* 15 (Special Issue): 17–48.

Summerhill, William R. 2015. *Inglorious Revolution: Political Institutions, Sovereign Debt, and Financial Underdevelopment in Imperial Brazil.* New Haven: Yale University Press.

Index[1]

[1] Note: Page numbers followed by 'n' refer to notes.

A. A. Villela, *The Political Economy of Money and Banking in Imperial Brazil, 1850–1889*, Palgrave Studies in the History of Finance, https://doi.org/10.1007/978-3-030-32774-3

FSC
www.fsc.org
MIX
Papier | Fördert
gute Waldnutzung
FSC® C083411

Kolibri 360 GmbH
Ferdinand-Jühlke-Straße 7
99095 Erfurt, Deutschland
produktsicherheit@kolibri360.de